Checkering

A Book of Checkering for the Beginner

Copyright 2009 by
Sherman L. Mays

All rights reserved. No part of this book may be reproduced or transmitted in any form or by any means, electronic or mechanical, including photocopying, recording or by any information storage and retrieval system, without written permission of the Author(s).

ISBN: 978-00615246444

Second Printing

Published by 4D Reamer Rentals LTD
432 E. Idaho St., Suite C420, Kalispell, MT 59901

www.4drentals.com

Introduction

To preface all you are about to see and read, let me state that the primary reason I make and refinish gunstocks is so I can checker them. With that said, you can assume that I love to checker wood.

Over the years, I have checkered pistol grips, rifle and shotgun stocks, a watch fob and several duck calls. Once, I replaced the handles on an antique all steel screw driver with wooden slabs for handles and then checkered the handles. The metal was polished to a mirror finish and blued, and the wooden handles would grade out as something well above exhibition grade and carried thirty-two lines per inch checkering.

While at the World Skeet Shooting Championships several years ago, I was asked about the wood on the guns used by myself and my son Paul. I later heard one of the shooters tell another that he couldn't say much about my shooting, but I sure could checker. To me, hearing that was far better than winning the shoot off I had just lost.

Years ago, when my two youngest sons wanted to take Karate lessons, I asked them what their goals were. Both responded their goal was to achieve Black Belt status. I committed to supporting those goals, and through all of the driving to and from the lessons before the older son obtained a driver's license, or taking them to competitions and watching them give and take punches and kicks, and their mother always asking "Why", I was there.

When the ceremony was held several years later and I had watched both boys receive their black belts, I cannot describe the pride I felt in my sons. No, it was not so much the achievement of Black Belt Status, as it was the setting of goals and the subsequent achievement of those goals through very hard work over a prolonged period of time that I was most proud.

To my two youngest sons, Jonathan and Paul, goes my everlasting gratitude for providing an example in setting a goal and achieving it. Without the reminder of your achievements, I would never have been able to complete this book.

From a father to his sons, Thank You.

Love,

Dad

CHECKERING

TABLE OF CONTENTS

Introduction 4

Section 1 6
    TOOLS 6
    FIXTURES FOR CHECKERING FOREARMS 6
    FIXTURES FOR BUTT STOCKS
    CUTTING TOOLS 18

Section 2 24
    STARTING OUT

Section 3 54
    RECUTTING OLD/FACTORY CHECKERING 54

Section 4 64
    COPYING PATTERNS 64

Section 5 80
    DEVELOPING PATTERNS 80

Section 6 97
    CUTTING IMPRESSED PATTERNS 97

Section 7 110
    REPAIR AND SALVAGE 110

Section 8 118
    RIBBON/PANEL CHECKERING 118
    STOCKS AND BUTTSOCKS 129
    FOREARMS 136

Section 9
    Glossary of Terms 138

Section 10
    Completed Jobs 157

    About the Author 175

Section 1

TOOLS

Two basic rules apply to checkering; the first is that the object to be checkered must be secured held in place and any movement eliminated. The second rule is simpler, your tools must be in a condition to do the required work – they must be sharp.

So let's take rule number one first. Commercial checkering vises are not inexpensive, a broad price range is available, and sometimes you get what you pay for. Sometimes you pay more, and sometimes less. I have used a variety of checkering vises over the years, everything from an elaborate specially built bench with rotating work position, to a small electricians vise with a screw on clamp. Over the last ten years I have developed several very basic means of holding work to be checkered. They are simple, inexpensive, and accomplish all of the tasks I ask of them. I will divide the fixtures into two groups, those intended for use with forearms, and those intended for use with buttstocks. A third group could be identified, but it would basically be an extension of the other two. So let's just settle with two types of fixtures.

FIXTURES FOR CHECKERING FOREARMS

In the following picture an eighteen-inch length of three-quarter inch outside diameter black pipe provides the basis of a checkering cradle for a variety of forearms to be checkered. The one requirement the forearm must have is threaded bushings into which the forearm iron screws attach. Examples of forearms in this category are the Krieghoff K-80 and Model 32 as well as the 680 through 687 Beretta.

Other forearms without threaded bushings, but with an aperture in the bottom of the forearm for a release mechanism, such as the KOLAR, Perazzi and some side by sides, can be held on the same pipe fixture by modifying the attachment means somewhat. But the basis is the length of pipe.

To prepare the cradle first create a line down the length of the pipe. I do this by placing the pipe in a vise, and using a file to "draw" down the length of the pipe, effectively providing a readily discernable line. Yes, there are other ways, but I have found this way to be quick, and effective.

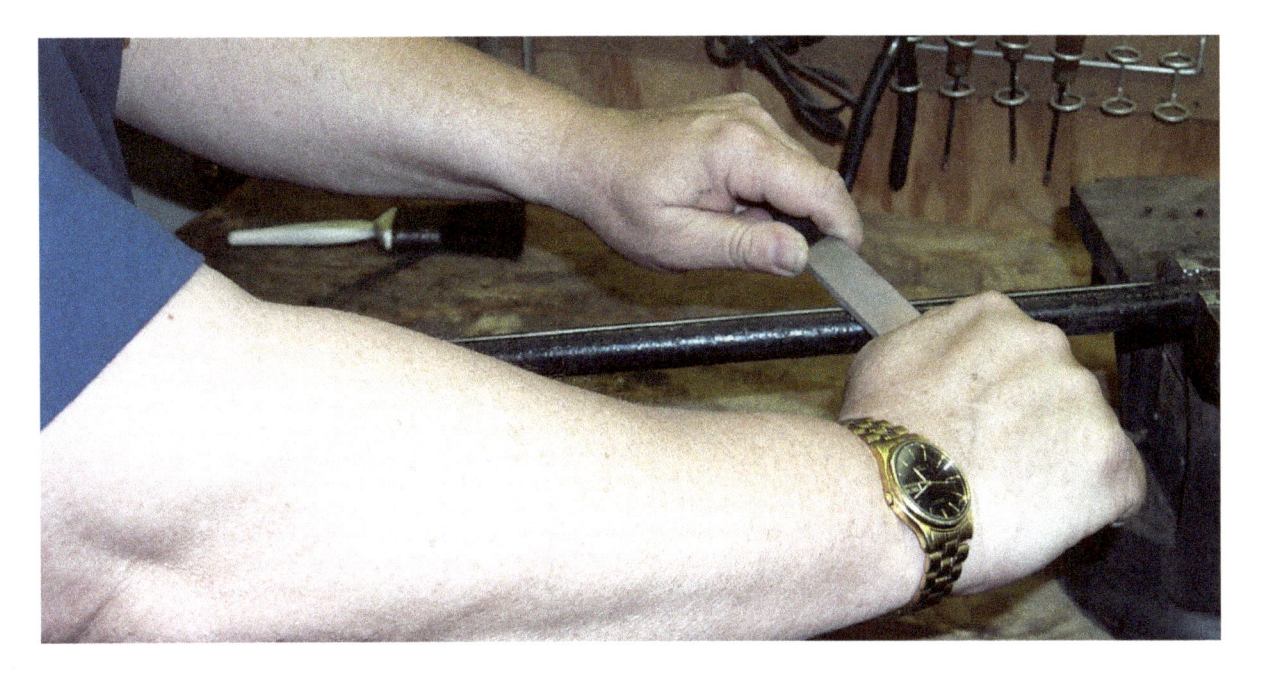

Centering the forearm laterally along the length of the pipe, I first mark the approximate location of one of the forearm bushing screw holes on the pipe. No, this mark is not critical a miss of a quarter inch is not a biggie. Center punch this location on the line provided by the file.

Determine the distance between the two forearm screw bushings on the forearm. I use a pair of dividers to obtain this measurement. I find that their exact measurement is easy to "read" and easier to transcribe onto the pipe. You can use a steel tape or even a yard stock if you are comfortable with the measurement you obtain. But remember, if the screws coming through the pipe are off very much, you may have to re-drill your holes.

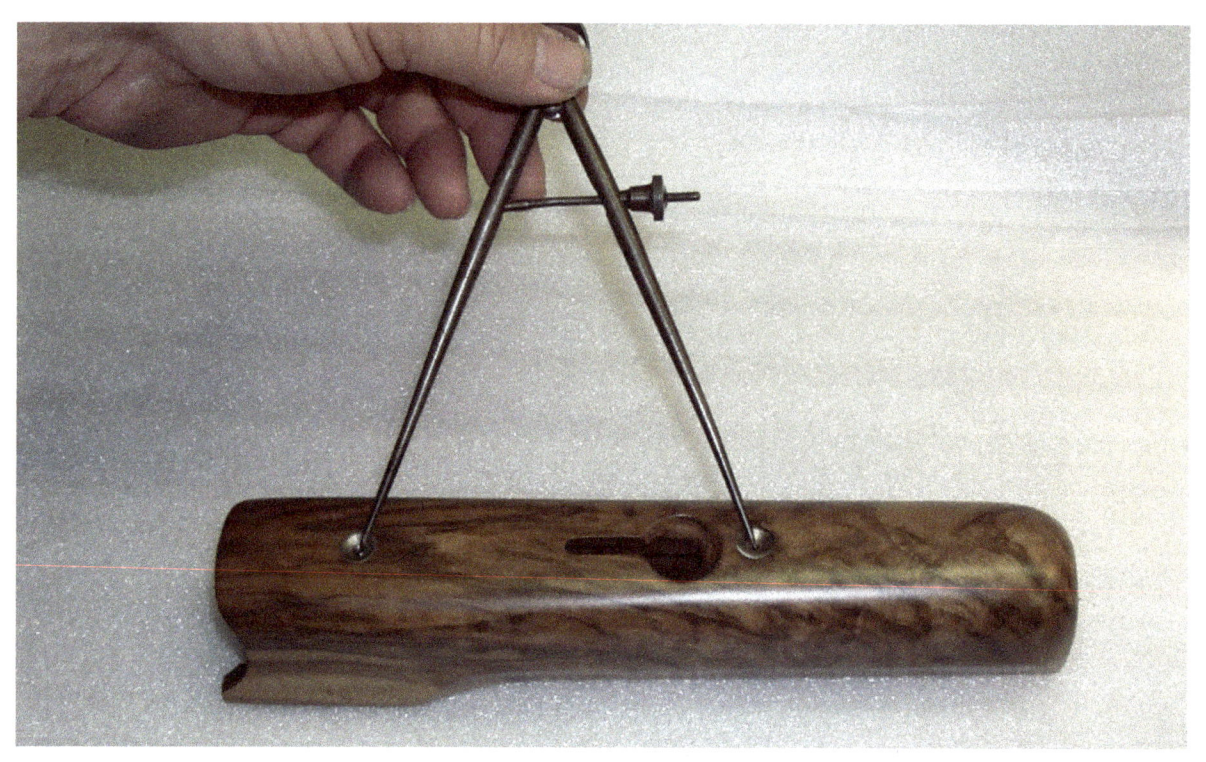

Place one leg of the adjusted dividers in the center punched hole on the line on the pipe, and use the other leg to scribe a mark across the line on the pipe. Center punching this second mark prepares the pipe for a trip to the drill press. A poor center punch mark can lead to a poorly positioned hole requiring the re-drilling of the holes. Use a center punch with a point you can identify and one which will "hold" the drill bit. Be sure to take a moment and double check your measurement with a second laying on of the points.

The Japanese have a system used in their quality control in which the quality is built into the product, not checked for after the product is built. The process is called PDCA, Plan, Do, Check, Act. I have found this a very useful tool, and have saved myself from serious errors in following it. Checking for accuracy and compliance is far less time consuming than correcting the error or scrapping the work.

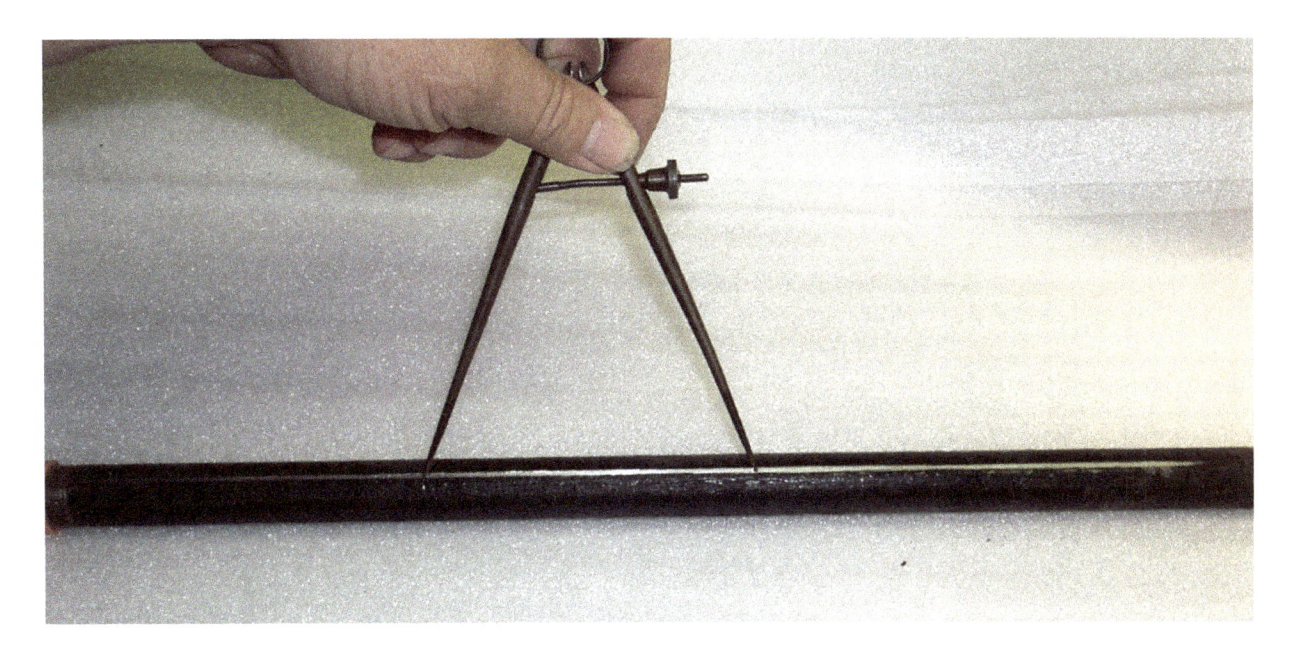

Select a drill which will provide a clearance hole through which a screw of the same diameter and threads as the forearm screws can pass. When the appropriate drill has been selected, drill straight through both sides of the pipe. Without enlarging the holes on one side of the pipe, any screw used to secure the forearm to the pipe would have to be very long. So, we need a second drill, which will allow a screw to drop down into the pipe and the shank of the screw to continue on through the other side of the pipe. I use a 7/16 drill for this.

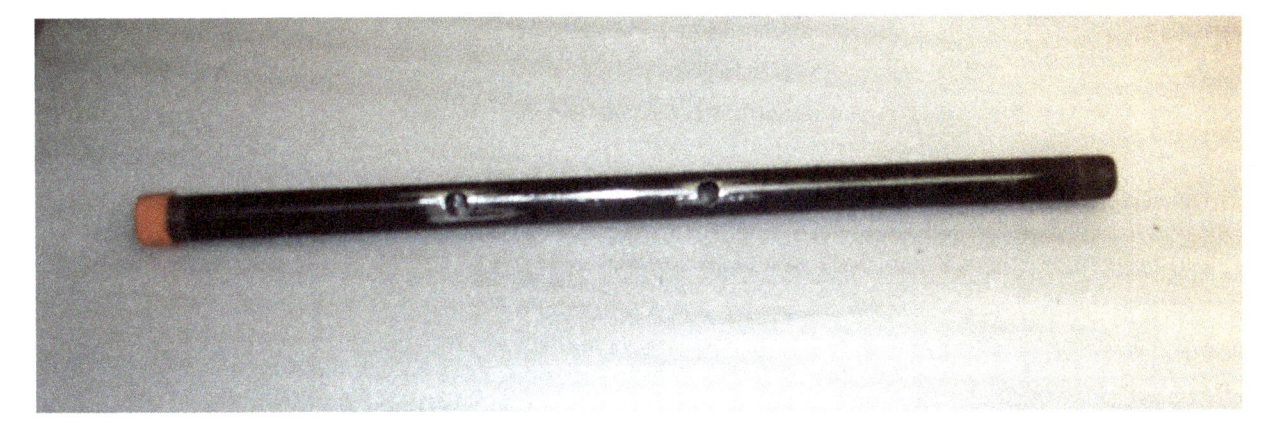

Do not make the mistake of thinking the cradle is completed; it isn't. A spacer must be attached to the pipe, which will set cleanly down into the recess made for the forearm iron. To use the pipe without this spacer allows the pipe to contact the forearm and act as a wedge when the screws are tightened. This may result in a cracked forearm. I learned this lesson well ? several times. It may not seem important, but imagine working on a forearm matching a very nice stock, and cracking the wood. The first thing that comes to mind is where you will find another piece of wood that matches the buttstock? It ain't fun, and it is definitely not cheap.

Put the spacer in place on the bar. It is an act you will come to appreciate over time.

I have used several types of spacers; on one of my pipes I have a small piece of walnut acra glassed in place, this arrangement works very well for the specific make forearm it was created for. On another, I have several small washers taped to the pipe, and this also works well. The object of the spacer is to occupy the area between the bottom of the forearm iron channel and the pipe. The thickness of the spacer is the thickness of the forearm iron at that point, and just a little more to keep it from bearing on the sides of the inlet and becoming a wedge.

I am very fond of allen headed screws, and keep a selection of standard and metric of varying sizes on hand. I use this type of screw for the forearm fixture. As the screws will differ between forearms, I label the pipes identifying the type of gun the screws holes are spaced and the correct screws taped to the pipe when not in use.

There will be times when the diameter of the pipe is slightly larger than the inletting in the forearm to allow for the barrels. Although I have used a smaller diameter pipe for the smaller gauges, an infrequent event, I usually modify the diameter of the pipe by "flattening it" just a little by compressing it in the vise or draw filing the sides a little. If this does not flatten the pipe sufficiently, I bring out the large hammer and head for the anvil. Just a few blows usually achieves the desired result, and I am back in business. Make sure the flattening is symmetrical with the screw holes, or your fun will just start.

With the forearm mounted on the pipe fixture, I can secure the end of the pipe in my large bench vise, and tilt and rotate the work to almost any position I want and lock it in place. The rotary table of the vise is very positive, and allows me to remain almost stationary and elevate and rotate the work to my satisfaction. I have been forced to accommodate other means of holding work to be checkered, and my current arrangement is superior to anything I have had in the past, plus it is simple and inexpensive.

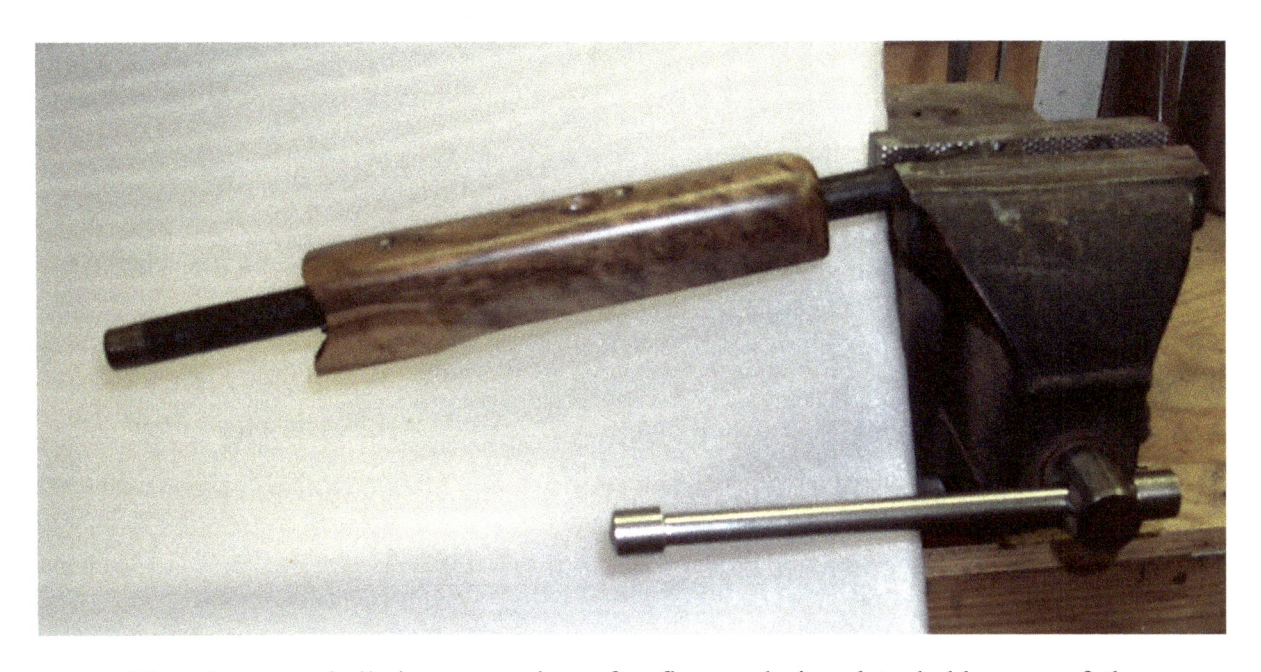

That, in a nutshell, is my version of a fixture designed to hold some of the forearms I work on and checker. It meets my requirement of securing it, and still allows me to checker in a comfortable position. Just a side note: I find that when I am comfortable – to include a little 60's music – the work progresses quicker, and seemingly with less difficulty.

A second way I use a length of black pipe to hold a forearm while checkering it is when there is a pronounced shoulder in the inletting for a forearm latch assembly and a single forearm attachment screw is used. Such as forearms on the Perazzi and KOLAR shotguns.

Use the same procedure to establish a line from one end of the pipe to the other, and as I have stated, a couple of passes draw filing the length of the pipe will do it. An eighteen inch long piece of black pipe has been my choice for these fixtures, but I do have several twenty-four inch lengths I make use of when checkering a "special project," such as a forearm on a single shot varmint rifle. Center the forearm along the length of the pipe, and make a mark on the pipe at the point of the forearm inletting which provides a shoulder. This mark does not have to be precise, again, a quarter inch error is not a biggi here. A white pencil inserted down through the inletting will make a good reference mark on the pipe.

In selecting a screw to use for this purpose, I use an allen head screw in 10 x 32 threads, because I have a supply of nuts of that thread selection, as well as several special made plugs. Anyway, select a clearance drill for the screw you select, and drill through both sides of the pipe at the marked location. Basically, the same procedure is used as when drilling holes in the pipe as previously covered.

Select a larger drill of a diameter which will allow the head of the screw to pass through it, I use a seven-sixteenths inch drill for this purpose, and enlarge the hole on one side of the pipe to this diameter.

The pipe must have a spacer inserted between the pipe and the channel inletted for the forearm. You can use wood epoxied or acra glassed to the pipe, or a small stack of washers of the appropriate size taped to the pipe. Regardless, the pipe should not come in contact with the top edge of the channel inletted in the forearm for the forearm iron. This requirement is discussed earlier in this section, and holds very valid for this application.

I install the forearm to be checkered on the pipe fixture by first placing several inches of the end of the pipe in my vise and securing it in position. I can then position the forearm so that the area of the forearm inletting having the shoulder, is directly over the drilled hole in the pipe.

Selecting a washer that fits down into the inletting, and rests on the shoulder should not be a problem. It doesn't have to be the exact same diameter, just close. A second smaller washer, just large enough for the threaded portion of the selected screw to pass through, is placed on top of the first larger washer.

The screw is positioned on an allen wrench – I prefer the plastic "T" handle type - then inserted up into the larger hole of the pipe and up through the smaller hole. The screw should then protrude through the center of the two washers, and a nut can be affixed securing the forearm to the pipe, and making it ready for checkering.

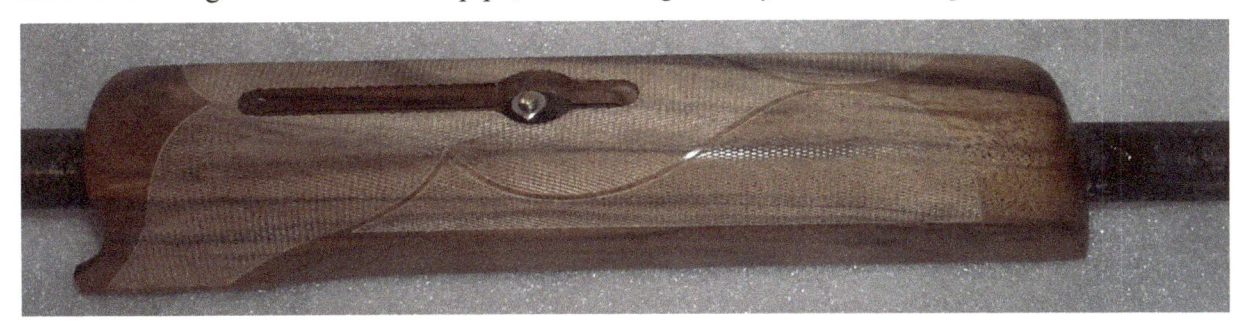

As I checker quite a few KOLAR and Perazzi forearms, I have had several plugs turned to the diameter of the forearm latch inletting hole and threaded for a 10 x 32 screw. This arrangement is quickly set up and holds the forearm securely without any indication they were ever in place.

Forearms without forearm irons or attachment screws, such as pumps and automatics, as well as a lot of side by sides, require another type of fixture to secure them firmly for checkering. To achieve this requirement, I again went to the black pipe, but this time I used a set of pipe clamps on it between which the forearm is fastened. After a lot of time spent in shaping, sanding and finishing forearms, I have no intention of scratching the ends with the pipe clamp, or having insufficient area on the pipe clamp to securely hold the forearm so modifications are in order. Obtaining two pieces of bar stock a quarter inch thick and one and a half inches wide and three inches long, I position them on the pipe clamps, and weld them. Bear in mind, the clamps are cast and the bar stock used is of mild steel.

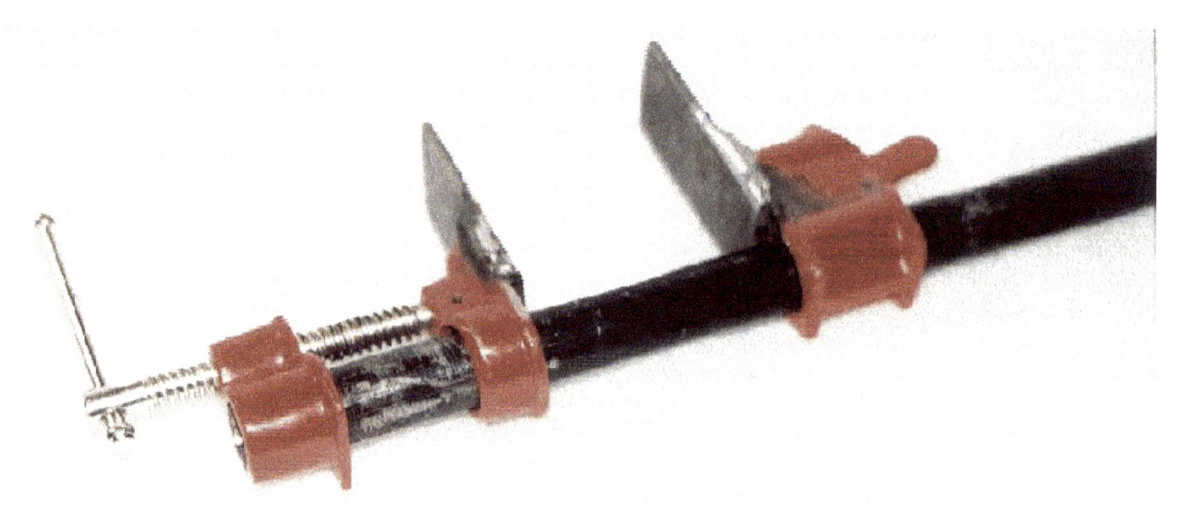

With the surface area of the clamp increased, there was still room for improvement. I first tried quarter inch thick leather strapping to pad the clamp surface, but with a small supply of take off rifle pads I soon had the clamp area covered with pieces of rifle pads such as the Ruger rifle pad acra glassed to the clamp surface

This left only one area of concern the pipe itself. A scratch on a finished buttstock or forearm is just more work that needs repair, and I didn't need the "no pay" additional work. So, out came the box knife and a trip to the garage. I recalled several pieces of lawn hose with holes that I had removed from a hose before joining the "good" pieces. The neighbor's dog had an affinity for my hose, he just loved to lie there and chew until the water came out. Of course, after the water began coming out, he lost interest in my hose until I repaired it.

Creating several six inch lengths or hose without too many tooth marks in it, I made a spiral cuts resulting in a cork screw piece of hose. I then wound the cut pieces around the pipe, allowing some space between the wraps. The pieces of hose could move along the pipe as different lengths of work was used on the clamp, and provided a soft barrier between the pipe and the wood being checkered. I later found that the same design worked even better when I located a piece of rubber garden hose, rather than the plastic hose the dog had chewed up.

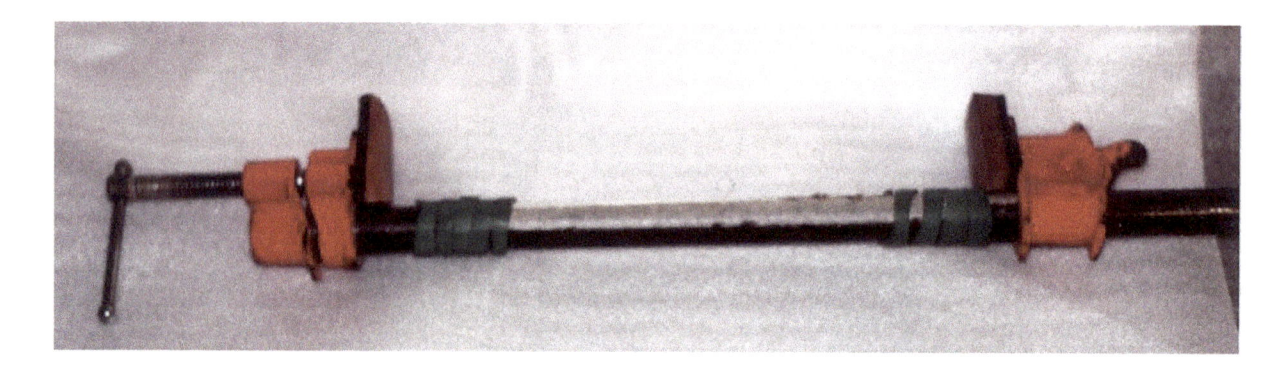

Later, and quite by accident, I discovered a second manner of installing a barrier between the stock or forearm and the pipe fixture. "Pipe insulation". That foam stuff with a slit in it enabling a conscientious home owner to insulate his water pipes. Just cut off a couple of two inch pieces, slip them over the pipe near the clamp ends, and there you are.

The trouble with the recoil pad rubber was that it allowed the piece being held to "squiggle around" unless tightened very tight, which I didn't want to do. So several layers of "mole skin" were applied. After several projects have worn the mole skin a little, it is very easy to replace.

With the mole skin and the foam insulation on the pipe clamp, and the extensions welded in place, I have an excellent fixture for holding the type of forearm to be checkered. And it didn't cost a lot of money. All materials were available from several of the local home improvement stores. I am sure others have come up with fixtures as simple and easy to use, but as I stated at the start of this book, what I am writing about is what I do and use. My way of doing things may not be the way you want to do them, but they work for me.

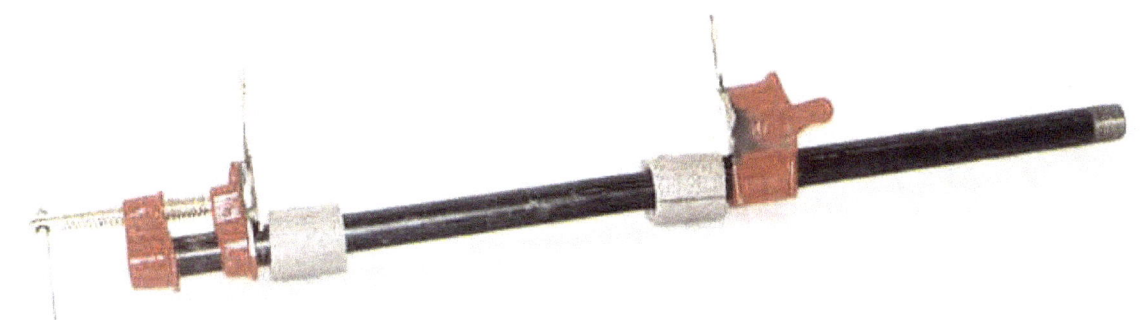

With this fixture I can easily secure forearms such as the Model 12 and 21 Winchester, the Remington Model 1100, and even some of the smaller splinter forearms.

FIXTURE FOR BUTTSTOCKS

The fixture I use when checkering most buttstocks is similar to the clamp fixture I use for checkering forearms, except it is a little longer, being made from 24 inch pipe rather than 18 inch lengths. The fixture is very versatile and has thus far accommodated many a buttstock.

There are some buttstocks which cannot be held securely in a clamp because the wood at the breech end of the buttstock is thin or for whatever reason will not stand the pressure required to secure it. The buttstocks for a many sidelock shotguns fall into this category. For this type of buttstock, there are several choices. The easiest way is to checker the stock in a clamp type fixture with the receiver firmly attached to the buttstock. Thus one is able to tighten the clamp without fear of damaging the buttstock. I have checkered many in this manner.

When attaching the buttstock to the receiver is not an option, I have two different fixtures to choose from. The first is an electronics repair vise I have had for many years and have modified and rebuilt several times. The jaws have been extended and padded and exert sufficient pressure to hold the work securely. I secure it to my bench with a bolt up through the bench into the base of the vise. It does however have a clamp type arrangement which can be secured to a table or bench top.

I set the jaws just behind the grip cap area with the comb opposite and forming a parallel, the padding on the jaws allows sufficient compression to hold the work securely without damaging the wood. If the stock does not lend itself to being held in this manner, I have a small chamois skin bag, about the size of a Bull Durham tobacco bag, filled with fine sand. I use the bag as an insert behind the grip area to fill in the space and allow a little more compression with the jaws of the clamp.

I also carry several strips of heavy rubber which I used to protect the comb.

While in the service, this small vise left its "mark" on many a motel table, bench and desk, and was usually *accompanied by dust from the checkered wood.*

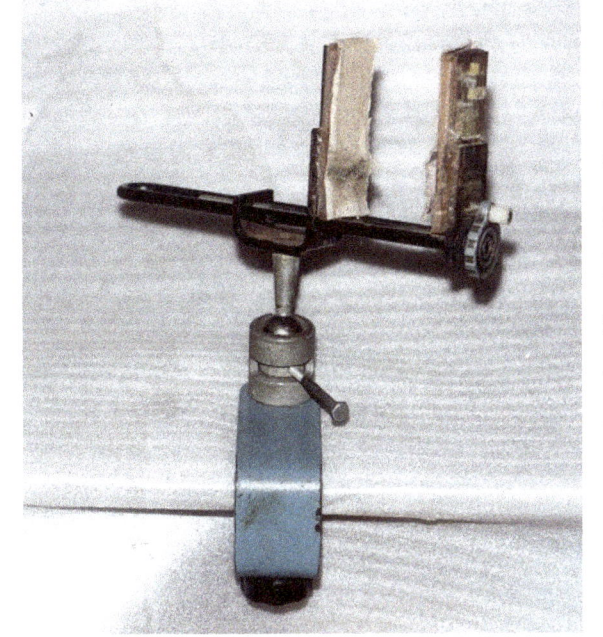

An alternative fixture is a modification of the first, and provides for the attachment of a plate to the butt of the buttstock. This plate in turn, attaches to a ball swivel which can be locked into position. If the buttstock has a flat, rather than curved butt, I attach the plate to it using the recoil pad or buttplate screws for the buttstock.

Because the place to be anchored to the buttstock should use the original buttplate or recoil pad holes, I elongated one of the holes to provide the necessary latitude to accommodate a variety of hole spacings. When I encounter a buttstock with a curved surface, I use several small flat washers as spacers. The wood does not contact the plate.

With the plate attached to the buttstock, I then secure the plate to the fixture base and when I say secure, I mean it. That's why there is a half inch connector bolt with a set screw and a lock nut. I do not want that buttstock to move at all once I have set it in position. The remaining opportunity for movement is the ball swivel permitting the positioning of the work.

While the buttstock can be worked on with only this support, I have an additional means of support on my bench, a large bag, a little larger than a bag containing lead shot, made of heavy thirty-two ounce naugahyde, and filled with cat litter – unused cat litter. I can move it around and shape the surface to conform to the buttstock with little trouble. It doesn't scratch the finish, it is easy to clean, and it works nicely. What more could you ask for? Please remember one thing if none other, whatever means you choose to use in securing the work to be checkered, will reflect in the finished product.

CUTTING TOOLS

And now we come down to the tools that actually cut the lines for checkering. Personal preference! I started out with GunLine tools more years ago than I want to remember, and I still use them. Yes, I have tried others, some were good, some were not as good, but I found none that were better. So, I have stayed with a brand in which I have developed a lot of trust over the years.

Only twice in the last twenty years have I found cause to contact the manufacturer and question something about a cutter purchased from a vendor. In both cases resolution was quick and favorable.

When you receive your checkering tools, especially the spacers, use a thread gauge to insure the spacing listed on the package is correct and then return them to the package for identity and future use. Unless you have a very secure means of storage, which will absolutely preclude mixing the cutters if the container is dropped, keep them in the envelope.

However, I have made, and continue to make "modifications" to some of the Gunline tools. I prefer a short pointer when getting into the corners, and have had to correct too many overruns over the years caused by dragging the tail of the pointer over the line. For that reason, I mount the pointer on a shank, and then remove a little over half of it on the belt sander. In this manner I get the stability of the long attachment to the shank with a short cutting area.

While this solution may be an accommodation to one of my mannerisms, I have found it works for me and encourage others to put aside their fear of non-conformability and modify the tools to suit their individual style.

If the modification works, tell the world, if it doesn't, you don't have to tell anyone and can trash the piece in the scrap bin.

I have found that the angle of the cutter when installed on the shank is very good for most use, but on some cuts, such as terminating a line at the border, I like a little shorter shank and a little less angle on the shank. So, I set the shank in the vise and drive the handle a little deeper onto the shank. This lessens the shank length by about an inch. I like more of the point of the cutter in the wood, and use a pair of heavy pliers to bend the shank slightly. The following picture is a comparison of a "factory" tool on top, and one I have modified on the bottom.

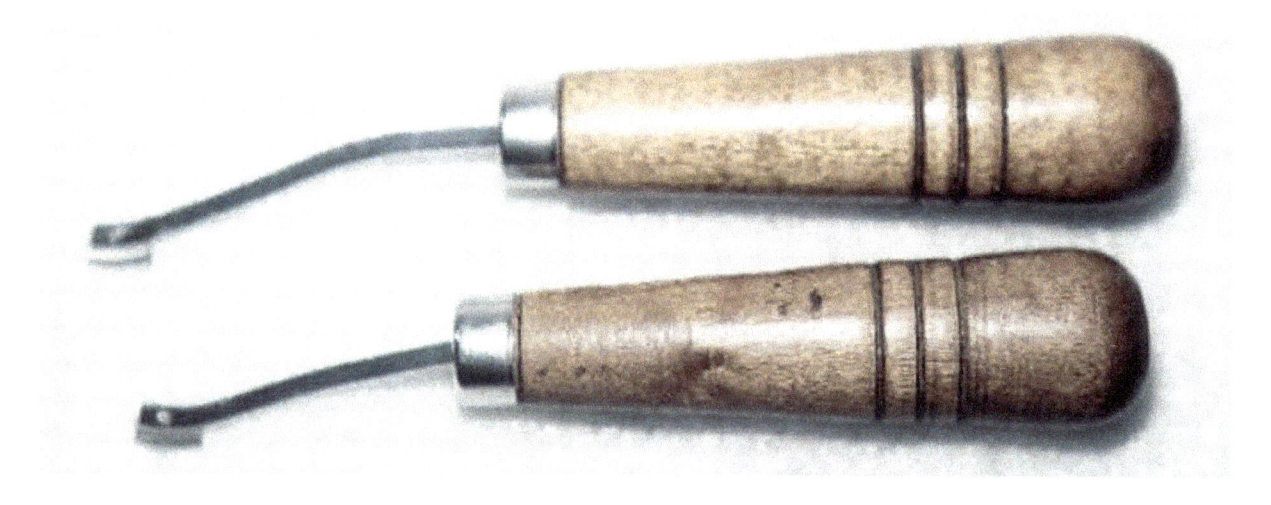

Yes, there is a "knack" to installing the checkering cutters to the handles. I have tried a variety of means of accomplishing this task, but the one tool that is absolutely essential is a hardened surface upon which to place the handle with the cutter in place. For the novice in this task, holding the pin with a pair of needle nose pliers worked for me. In time I have become adept at balancing the small roll pin on the hole and tapping it into place.

I quickly adapted the Gunsmith's Block – metal – to the task as well as the one-thirty-second punch. With the aid of a six ounce ball-peen hammer, changing the cutters is no longer the task it was when I started.

As the punch size needed has a tendency to bend or break, I have become accustomed to using "short" punches for the cutter replacement, and will use one on this demonstrated cutter replacement. The first task is to remove the small roll pin holding the cutter in place. Depending upon how well the roll pin had been braded over, it may be necessary to file the roll pin flat with the shank in order to determine the center of the roll pin or achieve a stable place upon which to place the punch to drive the roll pin out.

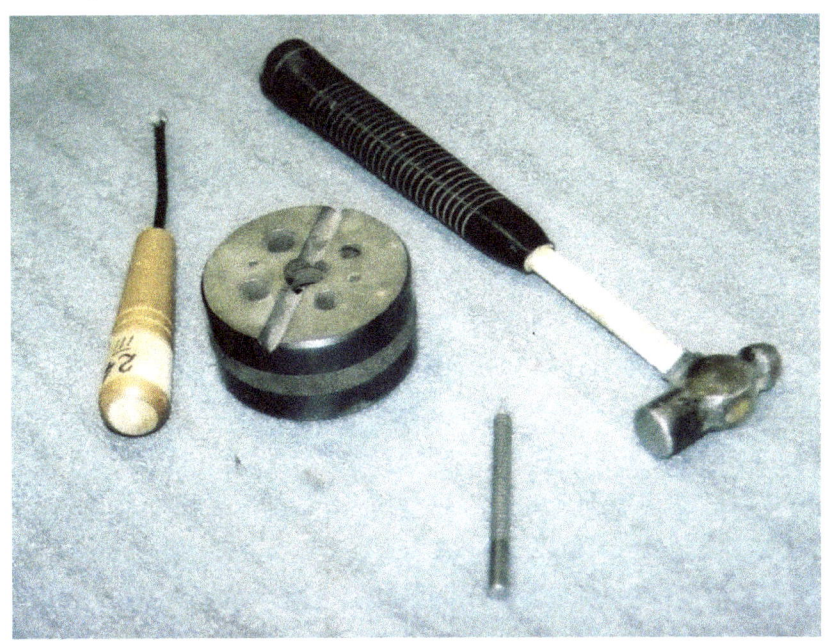

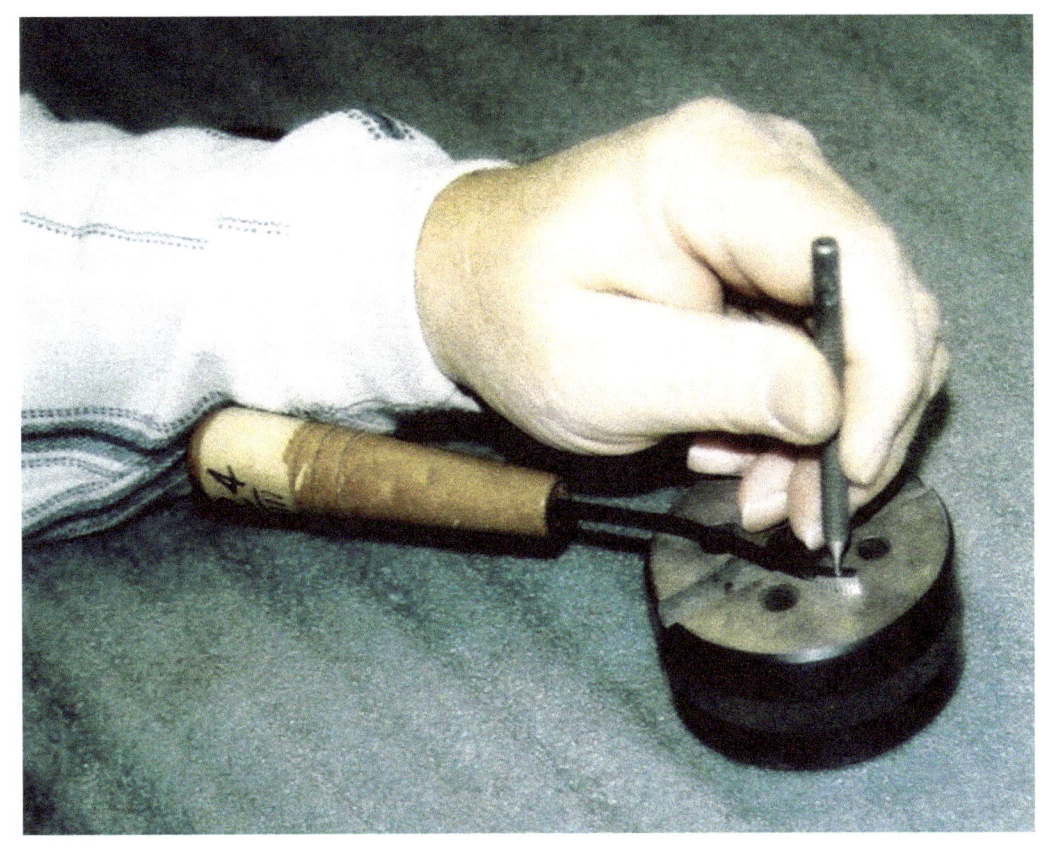

With the braded over roll pin removed down to the shank level, placement of the punch is critical. Get it off to one side and you will be pounding on the shank, not the roll pin. For this task, as well as many others requiring careful alignment, I wear a visor with a magnification plate, and have found this works well.

Being careful to insure the roll pin is placed over one of the smaller holes in the Gunsmith's block, once you have the roll pin movement started, drive it through the shank, and remove the cutter from the shank. Do not drive the shoulder of the punch into the hole, thus enlarging it.

Just a note, if the cutter slips easily into the shank, narrow the shank gap in which the cutter is to be inserted. When you insert the cutter you will want the shank to hold the cutter securely while the roll pin is being hammered into place. Closing the shank gap is easily accomplished by placing the shank flat on the metal gunsmith's block and taping it lightly. Remember, you just want to tighten the gap, not eliminate it.

Assuming that the gap of the shank has been corrected, before you slip in the cutter, please be aware that the pointers are uni-directional, while spacers and edgers have some tolerance for being inserted backwards. For pointers, look at the small teeth at the bottom of the cutter, then run your finger lightly along the teeth one direction, and then the other. The pointer should be rough to the skin coming away from the point, as in a pushing motion used when using the tool. If this is not the case reverse the pointer on the shank.

With the cutter inserted in the shank, use the punch to insure the hole in the shank and the hole in the cutter are aligned. Once they are aligned the "fun" starts. The fun being the insertion of the small roll pin into the shank and through the cutter.

I use a pair of needle nose pliers to hold the roll pin over the hole in the shank while the shank is laying flat on the Gunsmith's block. This is not as easy as it sounds, and this simple process will take some time to master, and involves aligning the cutter in the shank several times. It is times such as these, that a third hand is a definite plus.

I have used several "special punches" designed for the purpose of inserting roll pins, and found several do indeed work. But I have my way of doing it, as you will develop yours, and I am happy with the results.

Again, I am writing on how I perform certain tasks. The way I do things is not the only way the task can be accomplished, just the way I do them. You can develop your own technique, your own take usage pattern and disregard what and how I do it entirely.

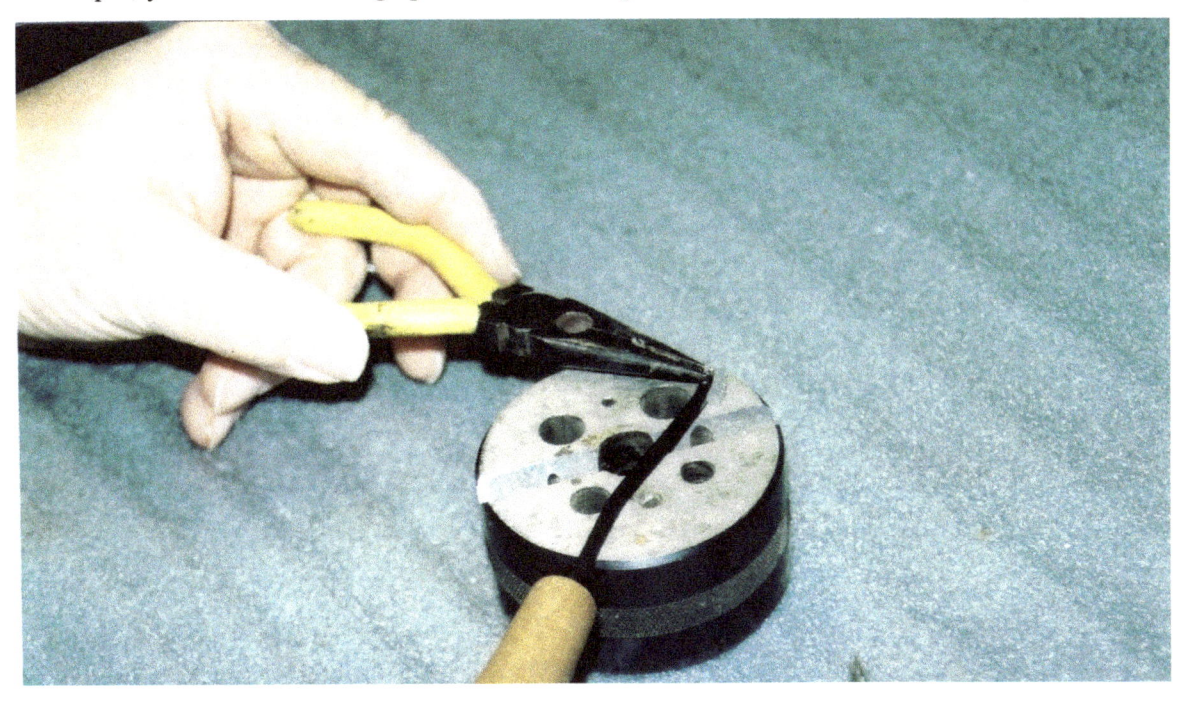

With the roll pin started into the shank, lightly, drive the roll pin through the cutter. If you encounter resistance or see that the roll pin beginning to brad over, STOP. The alignment of the holes in the shank and cutter may have been knocked out of alignment. If this is the case, align the pieces and continue. If the roll pin has become bent or braded over to the extent it will not be driven in place start another roll pin from the opposite side and drive it out with the installation of the new roll pin. Would this be a good place to recommend the purchase of a small lot of roll pins?

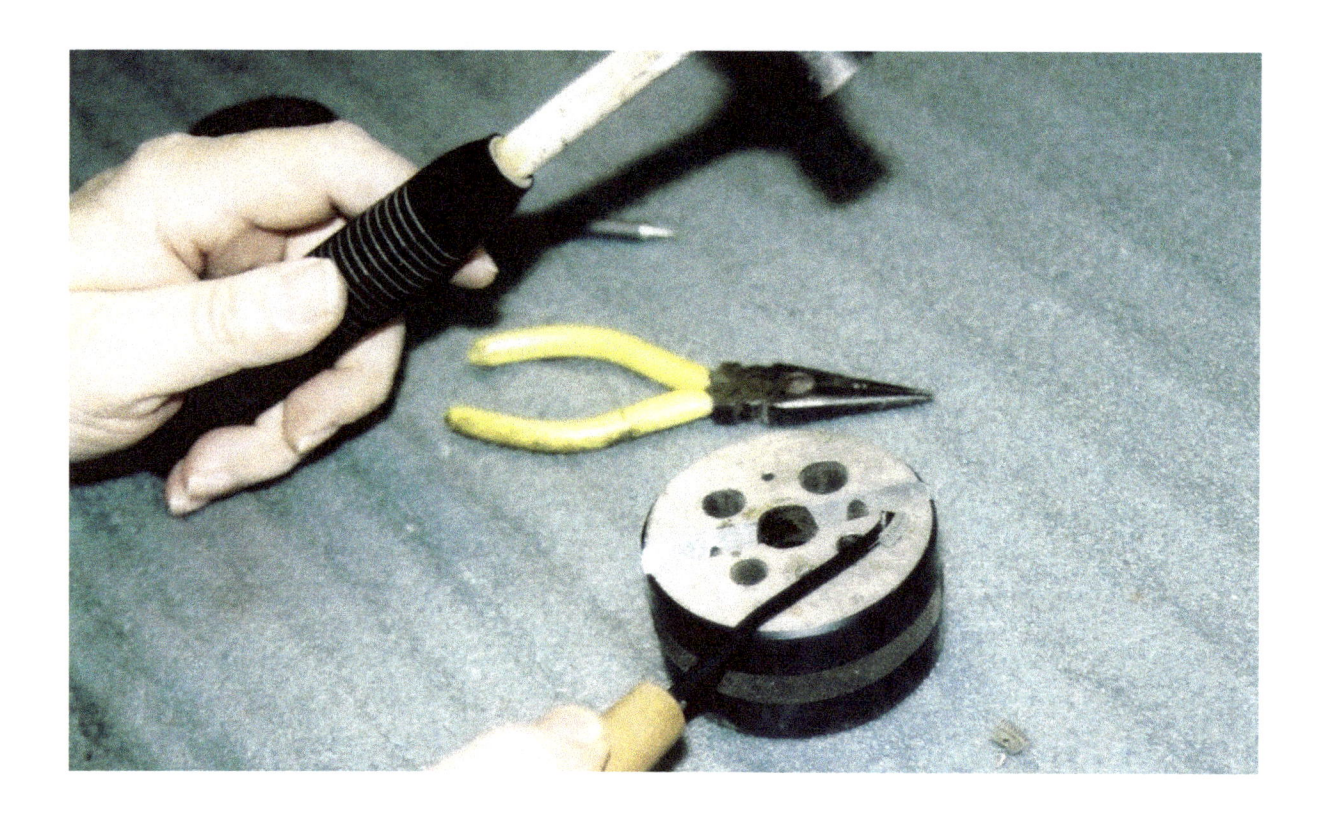

With the roll pin evenly spaced in the shank, lightly brad over the tips of the roll pin using the Gunsmith's block as your anvil. Thus, you should have a fresh cutter installed on your tool handle.

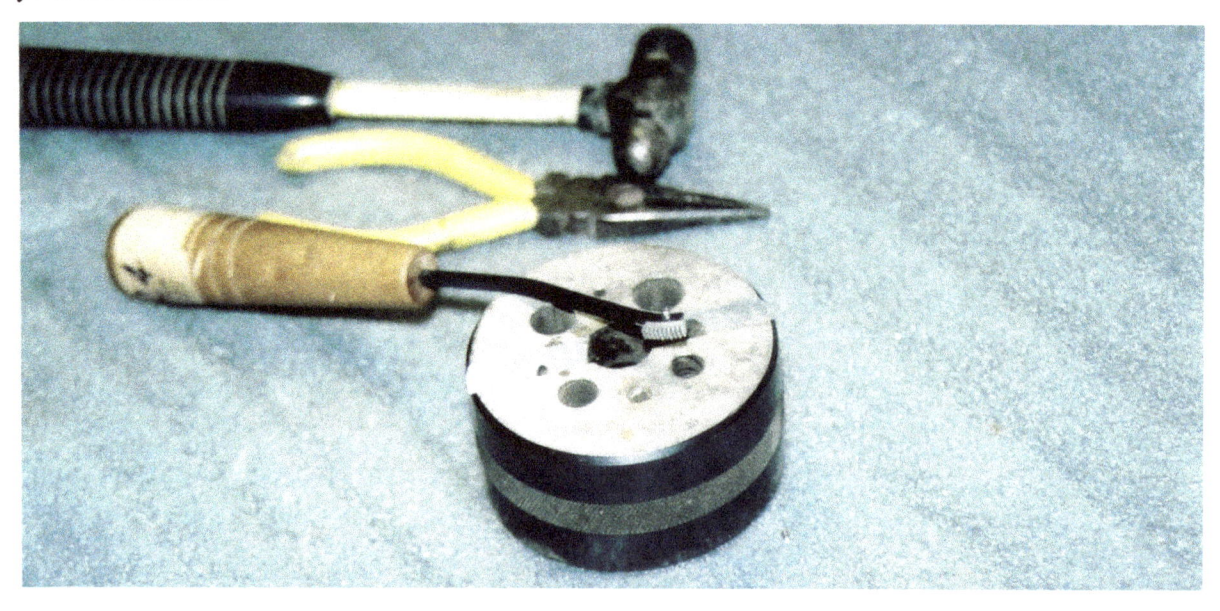

Just a few notes: The cutter should be held in the shank with NO movement. If there is movement, it must be removed before using the tool. In most cases I have found that the gap in the rear of the shank has become too wide. To correct this condition I use a one / eighth inch drift punch to "slightly narrow" the gap. It doesn't take much to tighten it up. If the cutter moves because of enlargement of the hole in the shank, remove the shank from the handle by placing it in a vise, and carefully driving the handle from the shank and then, discard the shank and be happy that you have an excellent tool handle.

Yes, there are ways of salvaging the shank but none of them are worth making an error on a checkering job caused by a loose cutter and spending precious time in correcting it.

Another note, many times I will drop a tool or one will roll off of the bench. When this happens to you, inspect the tip of the tool carefully for damage. If there is the slightest hint of damage replace the cutter.

Section 2

Starting Out

Very little checkering is done on a flat surface, but like running track, one must start out with the basics, and than means learning to cut parallel lines, and doing so on flat surface is easier than on a non-flat surface. So, with small pieces of finished wood, which I call "proofs," we will start out with the basics of checkering. However, if you really feel your talent is surpressed and need to skip the learning process and proceed directly to the high grade wood recently purchased and laboriously fitted and finished, then you may later be in need of some expensive "assistance" which I can also offer. But, believe me, working on the "proofs" is much less expensive.

Assuming you have the basic checkering tools and have modified a pipe vise to use as a checkering vise, and most importantly, a very securely mounted heavy bench vise, the learning process is ready to begin.

I make the small pieces of wood I call proofs from pieces of wood sawn from the stock blank as it is being prepared for the duplicator. As I deal primarily with the higher grades of wood in my work, some of the proofs I create are breath taking. You can create your own proof from straight grained hardwood – I much prefer walnut – and finish it as you would a gun stock. Worse case, contact me, I sell the finished uncheckered proofs. The checkered proofs do have one very strange characteristic – the darned things either turn invisible when the checkering is really great, and I can never locate them to show anyone, or – in the case the project did not turn out too well – they seem to appear on the bench for the customer's viewing. Something strange about them little pieces of wood.

Some of my proofs are finished in a gloss epoxy finish, some in a satin epoxy finish, some in TruOil, some in Tong Oil, and some in a satin gloss cabinet finish, and a very few are finished in a hand rubbed oil. I prefer to finish my proofs with the epoxy finish, either gloss or satin, as the vast majority of my finishing is with one of these two finishes.

Regardless of the type of finish the wood should be finished. The finish fills the pores of the wood making it stronger and it lessens the number of "chipped out" diamonds. One of the primary means of determining when the checkering lines are deep enough is when the little bits of shiny / reflective finished wood are no longer on the tops of the diamonds. At that point the diamonds are fully pointed and the lines are deep enough. And in a nut shell, that is how one determines the correct depth of a checkering line.

I have seen some very expensive guns carrying some great looking wood, and the diamonds of the checkering are flat topped – the checkering lines were not cut deep enough. This kinda takes the pride out of the ten thousand dollar purchase in a hurry!

The above pictured proof was from a stock blank that eventually found a home on a Krieghoff K-80 Super Scroll. It is finished in a satin epoxy and is about the size I like to keep my proofs. Others, some over fifteen inches long, lend themselves to several types of finishes. With the division created by a band of tape, I can apply several different types of finishes on the same piece of wood. This did not start out as an idea especially for proofs, but resulted in a piece of wood from the stock blank being finished in several finishes to allow the customer to determine which was "right" for his gun, how the color of the grain would show.

The first step in laying out a proof – getting ready to checker - is to determine the ratio of the diamond created by the checkering lines. The ratio is the length of the diamond divided by the width of the diamond. I am very fond of the three and one-half to one as well as the four to one ratios when working in highly figured wood.

For the proof pictured, I will lay out a four to one (4 to 1) diamond. The first step is to determine the centers of the surface, both vertical and horizontal. A steel rule and a white *Marks Everything* pencil will suffice for this chore. While the measurements do not have to be
"exact" they must be close. Once these lines are drawn measurements and "tic" marks can be made on the vertical and horizontal lines indicating the size of the diamond. As illustrated

in the following picture, the diamond size is one and a half inches by six inches – a 4 to 1 ratio.

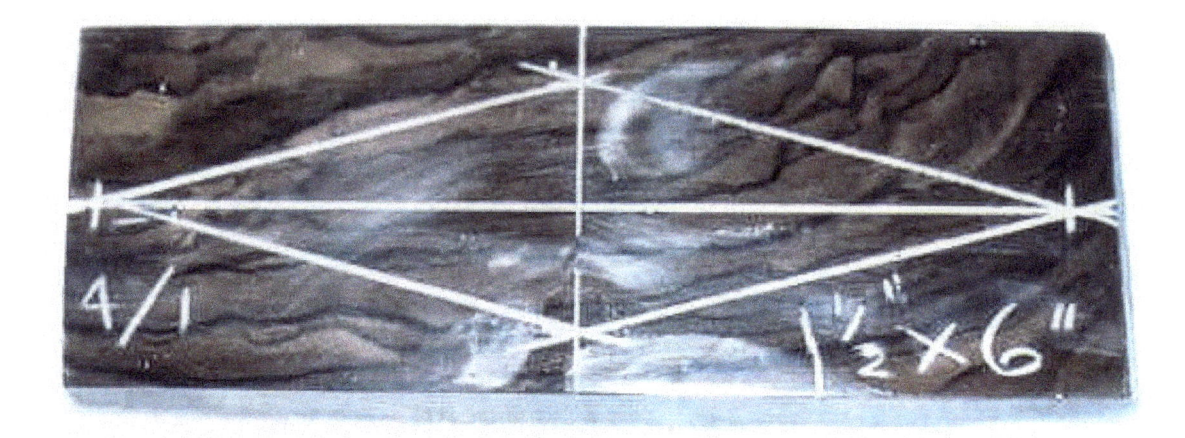

I use the *Marks Everything* pencils in my work because they are not hard enough to indent the wood, they leave a distinctive line, and they wipe off easily leaving no trace of a line on any kind on the wood. I have found that an electric pencil sharpener works great in keeping a point on them, but if the white material forming the lead of the pencil gets hot, it will break off and gum up the sharpener. Of course, a file or belt sander would probably work as well. Anyway, they are a fine tool, and one should consider buying a package of them and keep several sharpened and handy.

With the ratio and size of the diamond established, the master lines should be laid out. Now some will argue that the pair of opposing lines – the two top lines on the preceding picture for example – could be used as the master lines, and they would be correct. However, in my experience I have found that by starting out in the middle of the proposed diamond, the results are less carry over of error. This is caused by the start being in the middle with only half the distance to the border to checker. Doesn't really matter one way or the other, just sharing a few years experience.

So, I divide the four lines forming the diamond in half, placing a small tic mark at the division point, and then draw in the resulting lines. These two lines are my **master lines**.

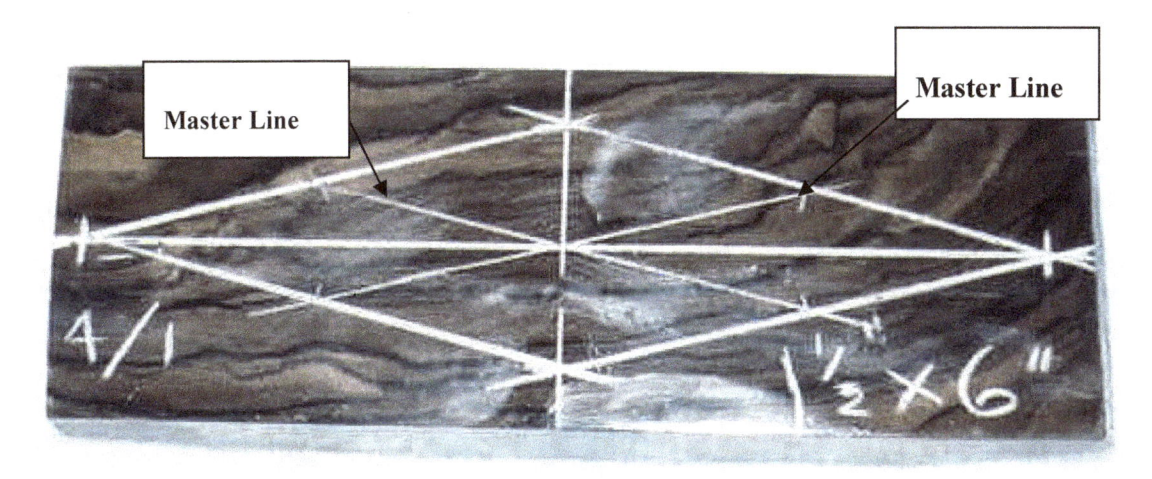

With all of the lines serving as reference points that we need now established, it is time to start cutting. First of all, the decision has been made to create a *point pattern*, and thus let the lines forming the checkering to extend out and form the borders of the diamond to be checkered. Therefore, we are NOT GOING TO CUT THE BORDER LINES.

On a *fill-in pattern*, we would cut the border lines first and then fill in the area with checkering and let the lines come out where they will, as is the case on the forearm illustrated.

Before we start cutting lines, the work must be placed SECURELY in the checkering vise, and then positioned so the cuts being made are an extension of the straight line formed by the forearm, the wrist and the shaft of the checkering tool. Yes, they should form a straight line. Too often I have said that checkering is like playing pool, obtaining a smooth straight stroke takes time and experience. Save some time by positioning the work correctly. Yes, I know that there will be times when the work cannot be positioned exactly as you would like it, but when you can, doesn't it make sense to position it correctly and eliminate a little possibility of error?

From experience I have found that the lighter I cut the master lines the easier making subsequent lines with a spacer becomes. Cut too deeply, and the line is difficult to follow with the spacer. For that reason I use a sixty degree pointer to lightly cut the master lines.

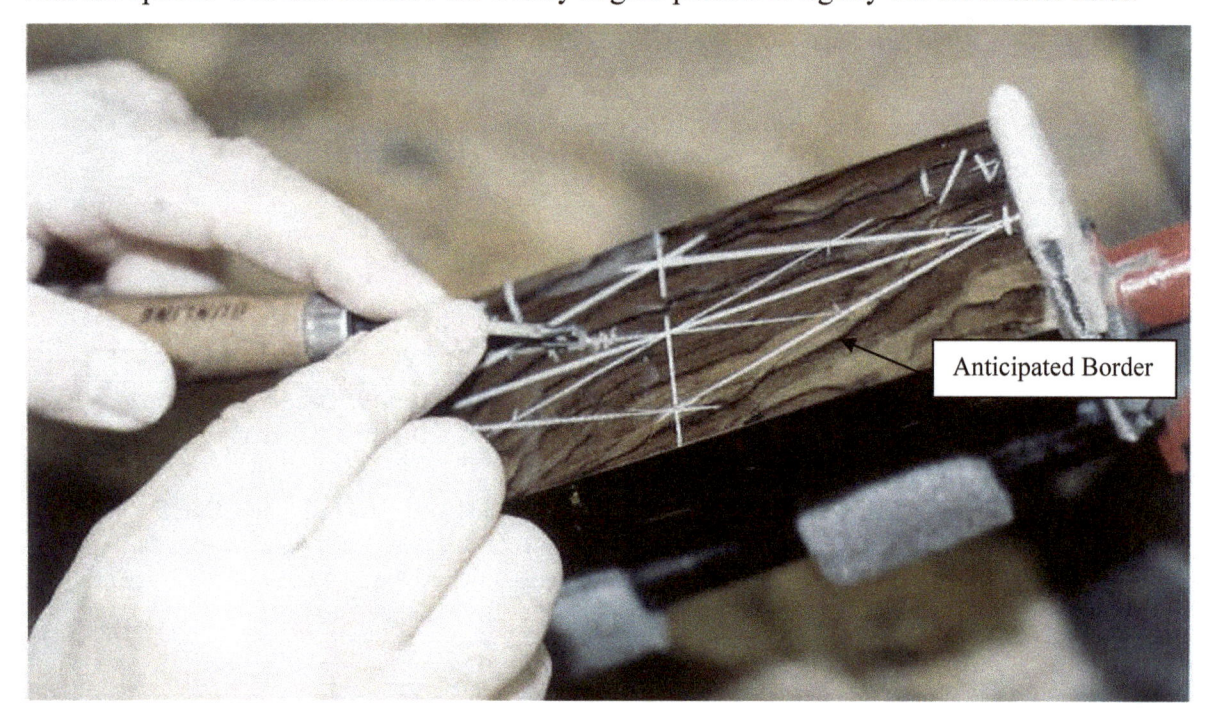

I start cutting the line slightly before center of the diamond and carry the line out to within an eighth of an inch of the anticipated border. I do not cut all of the way to the anticipated border, as the border line may "shift" as the diamond expands. The line is not cut deeply. It is difficult to judge how deep but no more than a sixty-fourth of an inch. Experience is a great instructor in this case, just don't make it costly experience! Remember, lines can be continued, but lines which are cut into the wood CANNOT be erased! Cut a little, save a lot of time, it will pay in the long run, believe me.

The large vise I use has a single large lever to secure the rotary motion, I keep it just tight enough to prevent accidental movement, but loose enough that I can swing the vise around with a little effort. This makes repositioning the work very quick, and it eliminates mistakes made when one tries to save time by not repositioning the work correctly.

Once the first master line is cut almost to the anticipated border, reposition the piece to cut the second master line. This is where the pipe checkering vise mounted in a heavy duty bench vise with rotary capability really proves its advantage. Just rotate the pipe in the vise jaws a little, loosen the bench vise base, swing the vise around, tighten it up, and you are ready to go again.

Cut the second master line just as you did the first: Start towards the middle of the line, and cut to a point approximately an eighth inch from the anticipated border. Notice the positioning of both hands - and no, the negative has not been reversed, I am left handed – I hold the tool in my left hand which provides the stroke, but the right hand grasping the shank of the tool provides the downward pressure and acts as a brake. Checkering is a two handed job. I left the dust from cutting the first master line on the work for illustration purposes only, I normally either blow it from the surface of the work or use a fine bristle tooth brush to remove it.

With both master lines extended in one direction almost to the anticipated border, reverse the proof in the vise and continue each line form your starting point out to the anticipated border. Cut the second line to the same depth as the first, if you are satisfied with the depth of the first. If not, adjust the depth to your liking. There, your master lines are in as shown in the photo below, and you are ready to begin using the spacer to lay out your checkering lines.

I like to checker as fine as the wood will allow. The more dense the wood, the finer the checkering it will accept. But trying to cut fine line checkering in straight grain standard grade American Walnut for example will result in the diamonds chipping off, and the lines appearing "fuzzy" instead of finely cut. Later on I will share a technique I use when I have overestimated the density of the wood or run into a soft spot, and the checkering gets "fuzzy."

The proof being shown is a fancy grade of English Walnut, and would accept checkering as fine as is functional – thirty-two lines per inch in my opinion – but for this exercise, twenty-four lines per inch will be used.

I use a three-line spacer – contains three rows of cutting teeth - for laying out most of the checkering lines on my work. Why a three row spacer? Because once I get started I will cut only one new line with each pass. The remaining two rows of cutting teeth will be tracking lines already cut. In this manner I have less errors, and my lines are more parallel.

Using the row of teeth on one side of the tool, I tilt the head of the tool slightly to the side, insuring the row of cutters is firmly into the master line, and then slowly – using short strokes – track the master line. This will result in the master line becoming deeper, and as it does so, the middle row of cutting teeth on the spacer will come in contact with the wood and begin tracking a line. As the second line appears, I slowly – after several passes over the same line – tilt the head of the tool back to a flat position which allows all three rows of teeth to cut the wood. The picture below illustrates the master line and one other line having been tracked, and with the head of the tool back to almost vertical, the third line would be tracked onto the wood.

Do not try to start the line too close to the near border. It is best to begin your lines away from the border and conclude them just short of the anticipated border. As one line is tracked near the anticipated border, move the spacer head over, allowing two rows of cutting teeth to reside in previously tracked lines, and cut only one new line at a time.

Yes, it is slow going. And yes, the three line spacer could track two lines at a time. I have found when only one row of cutting teeth is in a previously tracked line, and two rows of teeth are cutting new lines, I have more errors. Those errors being lines which come together, or lines which stray apart, and not only take time to correct, but in some cases will be noticeable after being corrected because of missing wood.

As you progress across the proof, tracking in lines, each time you start a line it will be shorter than the one previous. Experience will guide you on when to stop tracking in lines, and reverse the work and complete the lines you have started. My experience has been a half dozen lines will still be straight and parallel a dozen could lead to disaster.

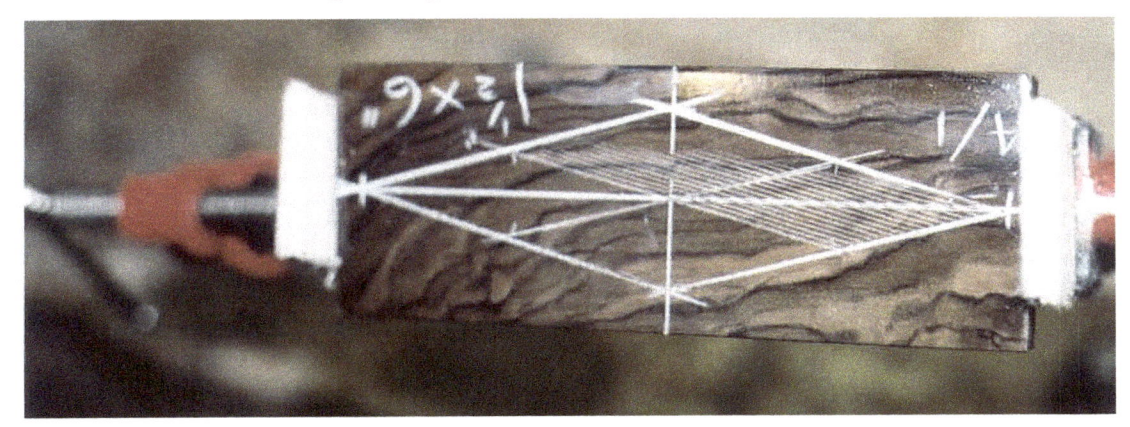

Reversing the proof in the checkering vise will allow the partial lines cut thus far to be completed. When bringing the lines up to the anticipated border, notice that you are cutting at an angle to the anticipated border, and in the picture below the right side of the spacer head will be cutting a line reaching <u>nearer the anticipated border than the other two rows</u> of cutting teeth. Watch where all three of the rows of cutting teeth on the tool are tracking, not just the row you are cutting.

Lesson to be learned, in this case, watch the track of the right most row of cutting teeth. If you were to judge by the left most row of cutting teeth, the right row would extend onto or beyond the anticipated border line. This is a common mistake that can be prevented by focusing on each line you are cutting and being aware of what the cutter is doing. Loose focus by letting your mind drift off to visions of the completed work, and you will be turning to the Section on Correcting Errors and Salvaging Work.

No, this opportunity for error does not go away, I have been making this same error for over forty years, although less frequently in recent years. Several times a month I find a line or two that needs "adjusting" because of my lack of focus. It happens.

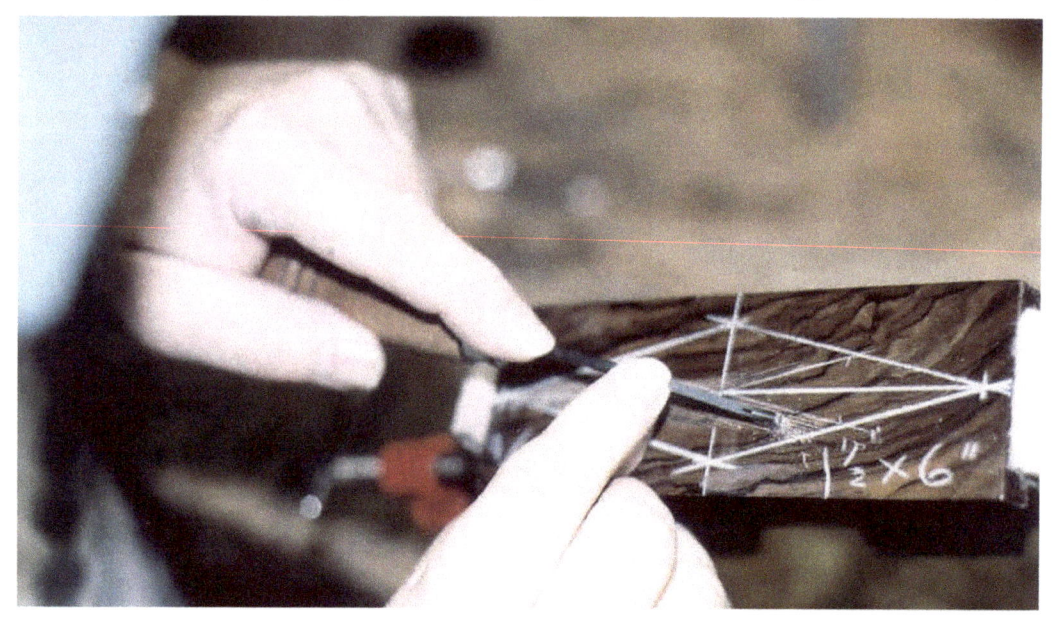

At this point you can make a decision to cut all of the lines going one way, or do spaced lines off of both master lines at once. I do it both ways depending upon the work involved, my mood, and sometimes influenced by the phase of the moon. So much for scientific reasoning.

Whichever way you choose you can change back and forth as you like. After all, all of the lines will need to be cut before you are through. On some pieces, if the grain of one series from a master line is more difficult than the other, I will cut the most difficult lines first. My reasoning is that if I make an error I will have to correct the error on lines running one direction.

With the lines complete for one direction, I begin laying lines from the opposing master lines in the same manner. As you cut across the lines previously tracked into the wood, you will notice laying the new lines is much easier. It also affords the greatest opportunity for error, and these errors are very difficult to correct – take your time.

As with the first series of lines, as the lines become shorter and shorter with each line, you will soon need to reverse the proof, and continue the lines to the approximate border.

As you carry these lines out to completion, the results of your work will become more and more apparent. In the picture below half of the required lines have been tracked in. Don't get over confident, take your time with each line. Just a little note, if the spacer does not feel or appear to be cutting readily, clean the finish clogging the space between the teeth. In most instances I use the same toothbrush used to clean the dust from the work to clean the space between the teeth. In some cases, I clean the finish from between the cutter teeth with the tip of the blade from a box cutter. Regardless of what you use monitor the spacer and keep it free of clogging finish.

As your lines are being tracked in parallel to the anticipated border, insure the lines continue to be straight and on the ends, carried not quite to the anticipated borders. As your lines approach the parallel border line, be aware that only with the greatest stroke of luck will the line you are tracking in land exactly on the white anticipated border line. If it does, great! If it doesn't, I would prefer the last line cut, which will become the ACTUAL BORDER LINE of the pattern, be on the white line, <u>or ever so slightly beyond it</u>.

Continue tracking in all of the lines until you establish the ACTUAL BORDER LINES, and then use the sixty degree pointer to deepen these line approximately twice as deep as the lines you have been tracking in. This deep and narrow line will shortly serve as a stopping point when bringing all of the lines to the actual border line. But, please, be very careful when bringing the lines out to the border line. Use both hands, one with the push, and the other determining the amount of downward pressure AND serving as a brake to the cutter. Having done all of the preceding, the proof should look something like the one below.

Because a three line spacer has been used to track the lines onto the wood, and because of its width, the ends of the pattern are not fully complete – the actual border lines do not meet/join and complete the outline of the diamond desired. At this point, I remove the white lines from the proof – a damp cloth over the surface – leaving only the lines which have been tracked in.

Using the sixty-degree pointer to complete the border lines, continue each line to a point just short of where it will join the opposing border line is all that is needed. Then, I continue the opposing border line and repeat this process until I have joined the two border lines. I can then bring those few other lines to completion and complete the pattern.

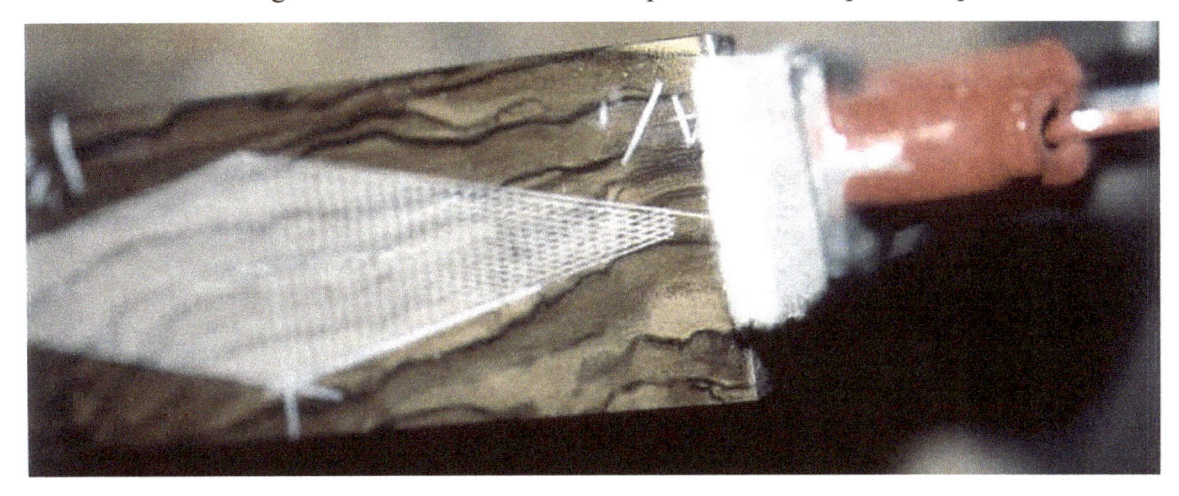

With the border lines tracked in you can now breathe a little, and prepare to deepen the tracked in lines. I do this with a ninety degree pointer, and prefer to start each job with a new pointer, but do not deepen the border lines, only the lines inside the border.

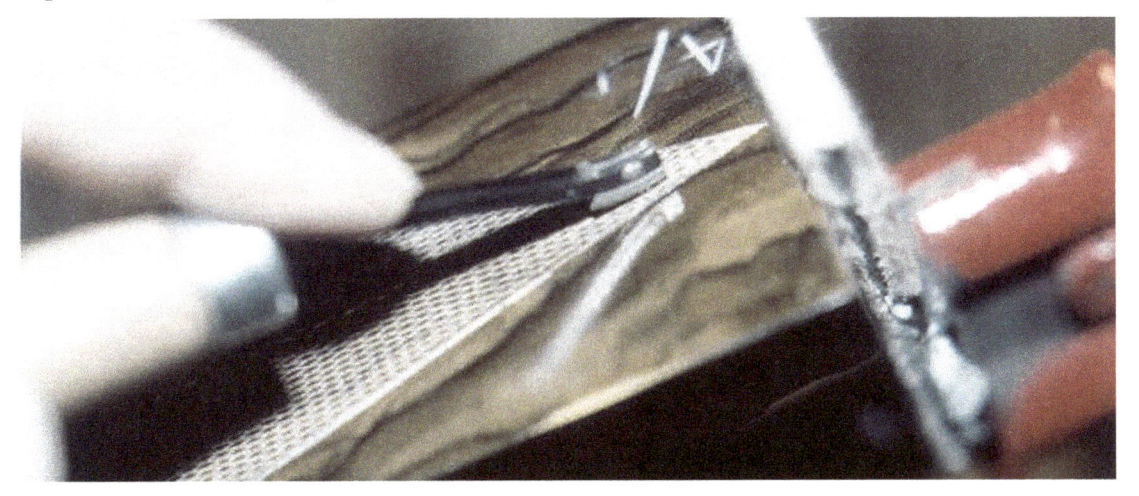

Notice the angle of the cutter on the preceding picture. Notice that the tip of the cutter in making the first contact with the wood and when the line is cut to completion, completion being the termination at the border line. This is achieved by bending the shank down slightly using channel lock pliers. There is a point at which the angle will cut smoothly. Too much angle will force the pointer tip to plow too heavily and chip the wood, and too little angle will allow the pointer tip to ride up over the anticipated border. Only experience will provide the answer as to what angle is correct for you. The manner in which you hold the tool, the angle and elevation, are the determining factors.

In addition, I have shortened the shank by placing the shank in a vise and driving the handle down over it until the shank bottoms out in the predrilled hole. This reduces the length almost an inch and make the tool much easier to control when cutting lines out to the border.

I have several shanks bent in this manner and have them identified as being a different style handle than on other unbent shanks. I have found that with this slight modification, the number of run overs and the severity of the run overs are significantly decreased.

I use both hands when checkering, but at no time is careful control of the cutter more important than when bringing lines out to the border. I prefer to position my right hand – guiding the cutting action and determining the amount of downward pressure – resting on the work. In this manner I have found it makes an effective brake. I would caution you to use very short strokes when bring a line to culmination at the border.

. I deepen the outside lines running parallel to the border lines, and then deepen the lines terminating at the border line. The interior of the pattern, regardless of its size, I deepen last. With the outside lines deepened the proof should look something like the one pictured below.

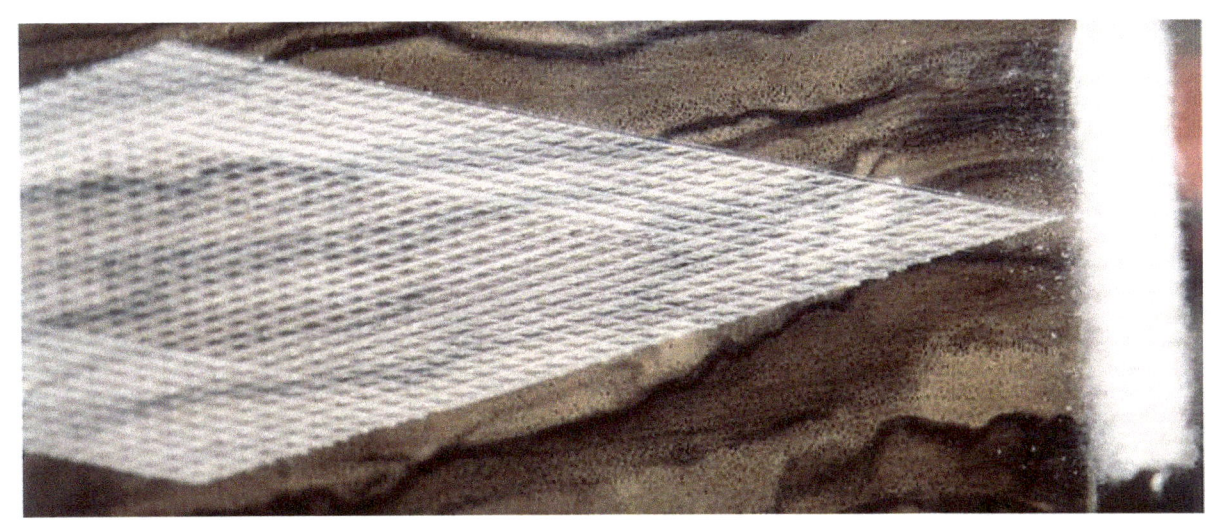

Yes, the border lines have been "nicked" with the pointer as the lines were terminated at the border line. That is expected. Why? The angle of the cut – remember we are cutting a diamond that is four times as long as it is wide – allows the near side of the pointer to come into contact with the border line <u>before</u> the line is completed, resulting in the nick. The reasoning behind cutting the border lines with a sixty degree cutter will become apparent soon.

Before we "clean up" the border lines, all of the lines must be taken to full depth. To do this, we want a pointer which makes contact with the wood being cut at the middle of the radius of the pointer. The following picture illustrates the correct angle between the pointer and the wood to achieve the best cutting action.

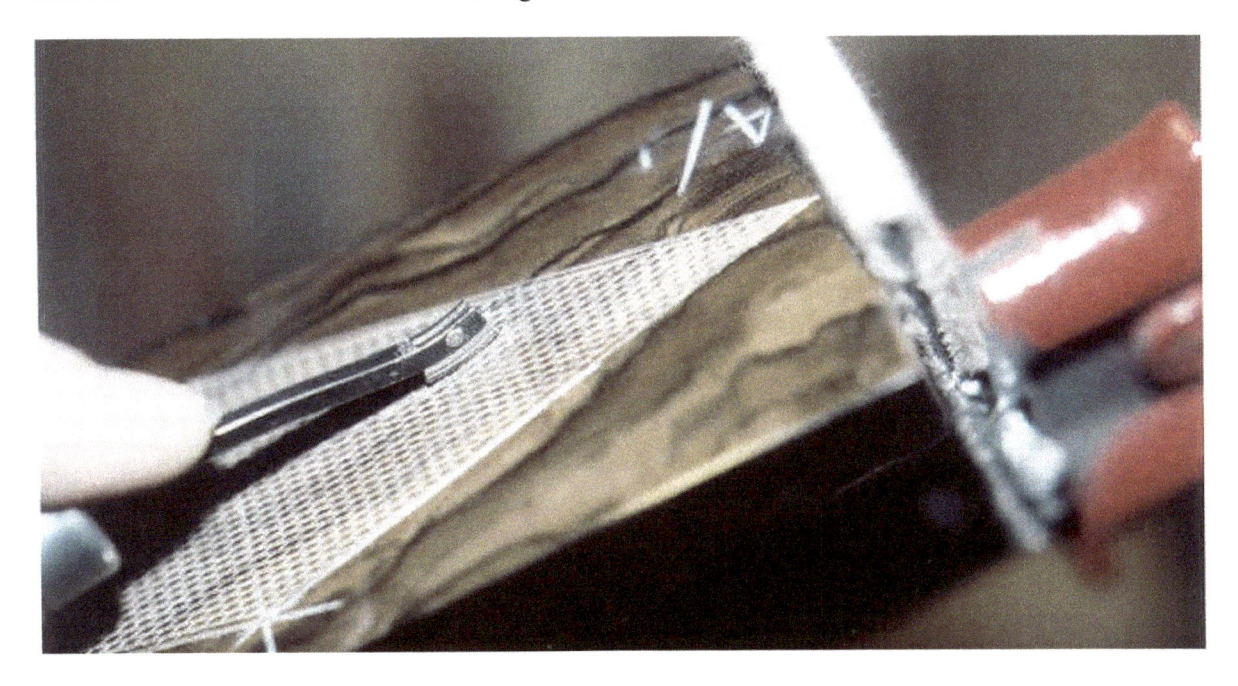

With all of the lines, except the border lines, taken to full depth the proof should display clean straight lines from border to border. Remember, by reflecting a light across the surface of the proof, any finish on the tops of the diamonds will reflect and provide guidance on where the lines must be deepened. Only when there is no finish showing from the tops of the diamonds are the lines considered to have been taken to full depth as illustrated below.

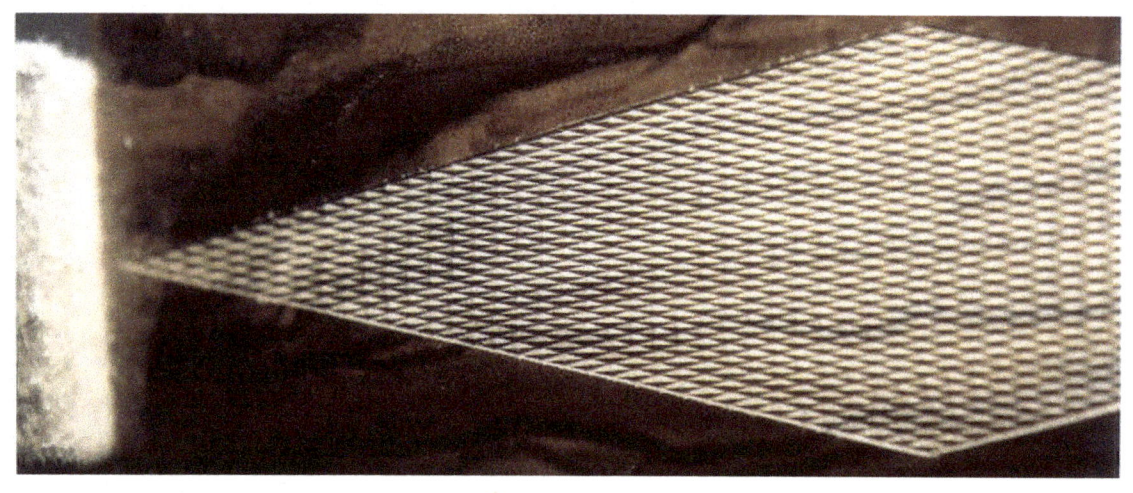

With all of the lines culminating at the borders, and with "some" nicks in the border lines showing, it is time to clean up the borders. For this task, we use the ninety-degree pointer we have used to deepen the lines. The difference between the sixty-degree pointer and the ninety- degree pointer is more than thirty degrees, it can be the salvation of a piece of work. These nicks in the border lines are what we are going to clean up.

Please use extreme care when deepening the borders with the ninety-degree pointer. I use the short shanked pointer to deepen the lines coming into the points of the pattern, and the longer shanked pointer to deepen the long line. I use very short strokes, no more than a quarter inch, and control the downward pressure exerted on the pointer carefully. One double line on the border or one lapse of focus can create an error that would require excessive time to clean up. But yes, just in case you really screw up there are ways to correct the problem.

And there you have it, a completed checkered proof. But one not quite completed. The checkering is exposed wood, and with a little time moisture will come into the exposed wood and under the finished wood, ruining it. So, a sealer must be applied to the checkered areas. In this case a liberal coating of thinned TruOil is applied with a toothbrush.

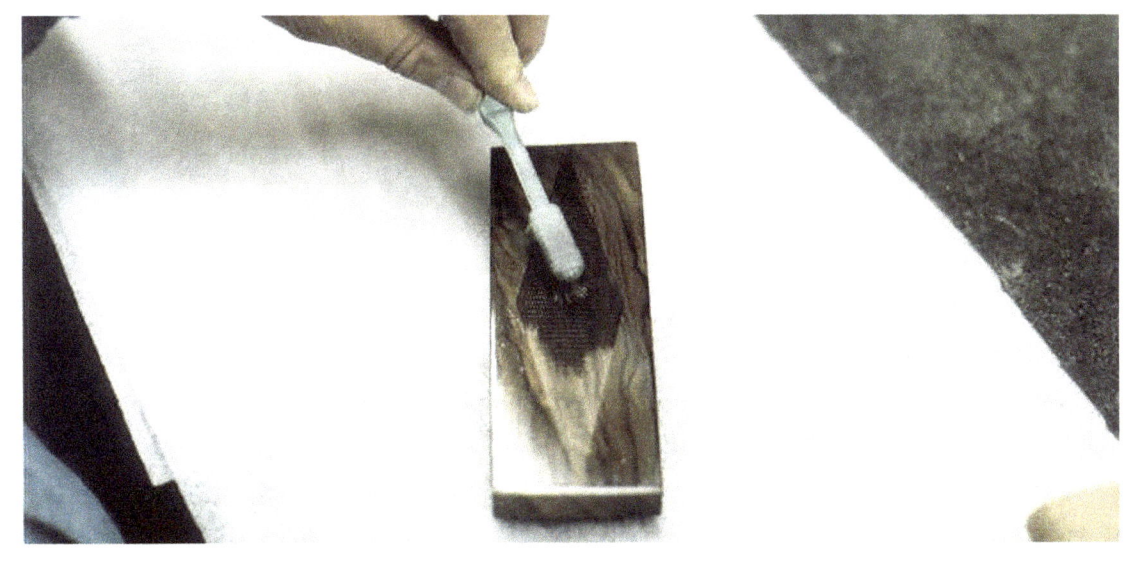

For all intents and purposes, the proof is complete other than possibly signing and dating it on the back. No, really. Do it. And in the future review the proofs you have completed and judge the progress of your work.

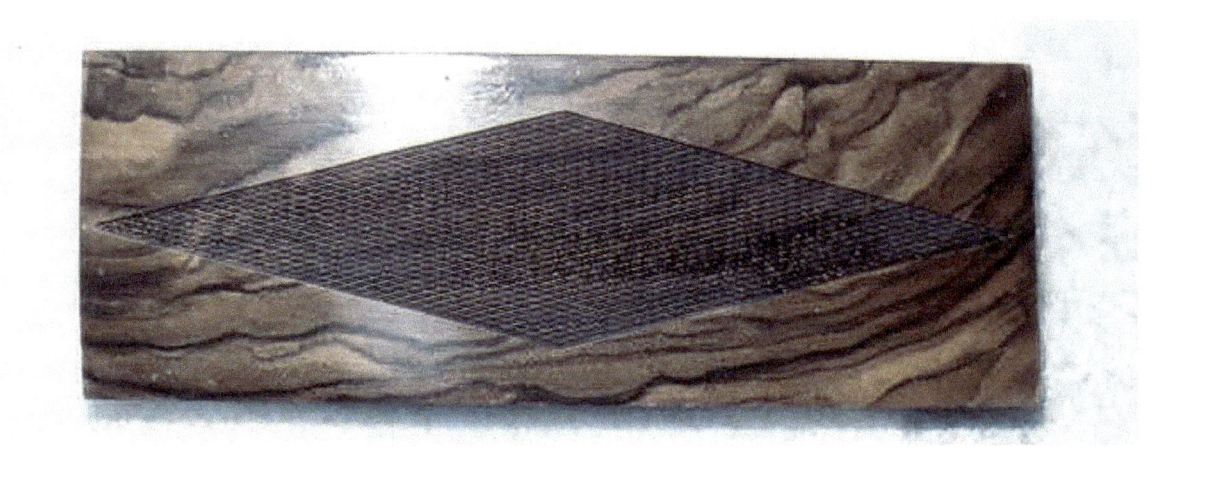

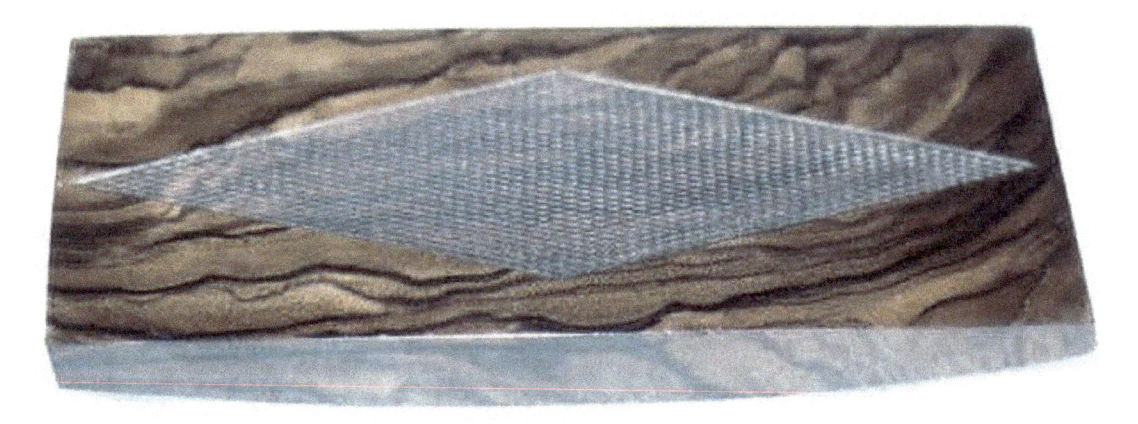

Now lets progress on to a proof that will simulate the checkering on a rifle forearm. Instead of a wrap around pattern, we will do a pattern similar to that found on a Winchester Model 70 rifle as illustrated in the photograph below. Note, the finish has been removed from the stock in preparation for refinishing and re-cutting the factory checkering.

One item you should notice is how the checkered lines form the ends of the checkering pattern. This is not a fill in pattern, although I have seen some Model 70's which were.

We are going to use a Proof of English Walnut approximately twelve inches long for this project. The proof is finished in a satin epoxy finish, and the wood, while not exceptionally figured, is dense and should accept checkering in excess of 24 lines per inch.

The upper and lower border lines of the pattern on the forearm in picture 04-24 are not parallel, the distance between the lines at the rear – near the receiver – of the pattern are further apart than those same lines near the forend. So, on the proof one of the border lines will be parallel to the edge of the wood – as is the pattern on the rifle stock – and the other line will be place to reflect the rear of the pattern being wider than the front of the pattern.

The front of the pattern on the proof will come to a natural point through extension of the master lines, as will the rear of the pattern come to a natural split "V" through extension of the master lines.

First, we want to draw in the top line of the checkering pattern and we can accomplish this task in several ways. I acquired a tool many years ago, and it has served me well in a variety of applications.

An alternative to this is to use a flexible straight edge such as a piece of stiff plastic found around the collars of new shirts. When I use a straight edge, I do not depend on my ability to hold it in position as I draw the line in with a white pencil. I use a small piece of tape to secure one end of the plastic, then position the remaining end to match the distance, and holding one end, draw in the line.

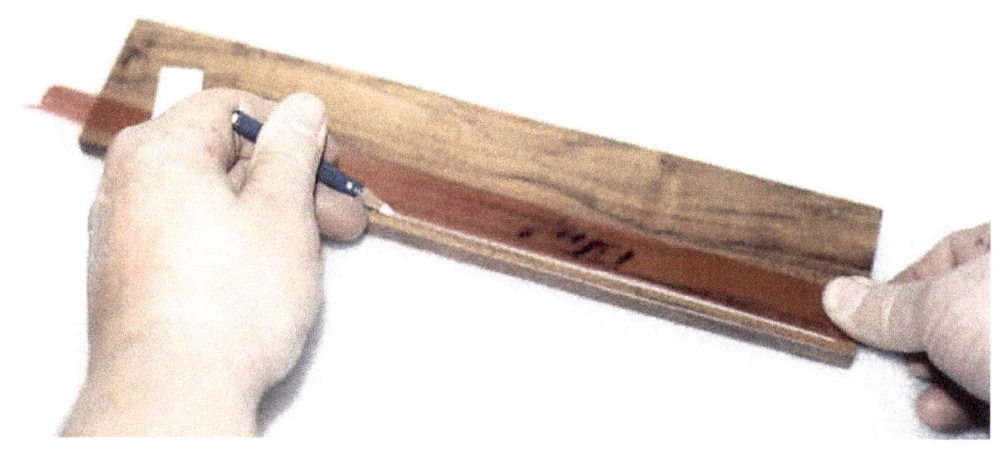

Where the lines of a forearm pattern are not parallel, it is advisable to establish the center line between the two border lines. So, after determining the approximate length of the pattern to be checkered on the proof, the first task at hand is to determine the centerline of the pattern. The simplest way of accomplishing this task is to place a small piece of paper with a straight edge at the anticipated end of the pattern, and place tic marks on the edge of the paper where it intersects the upper and lower anticipated borders.

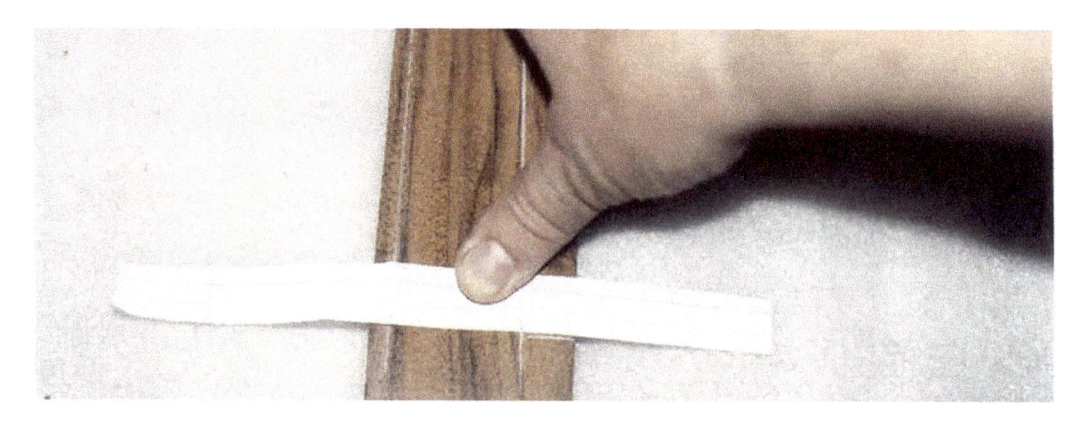

A group of men were discussing local politics at a small coffee shop near the Interstate when one made a statement loud enough for all to hear, "I say we shoot the whole bunch, all six lawyers and the Stockmaker."

There was silence , and then an elderly man, obviously a tourist spoke up, "Why the Lawyers?"

Turning to the other in the group, the originator of the comment offered, "I told you no one cares about Stock makers."

Fold the paper over until the tic marks overlap and crease the paper. The center of the distance between the two lines is accomplished and the crease is the center. Place the paper back on the same position and place a tic mark on the stock at the location of the crease in the paper.

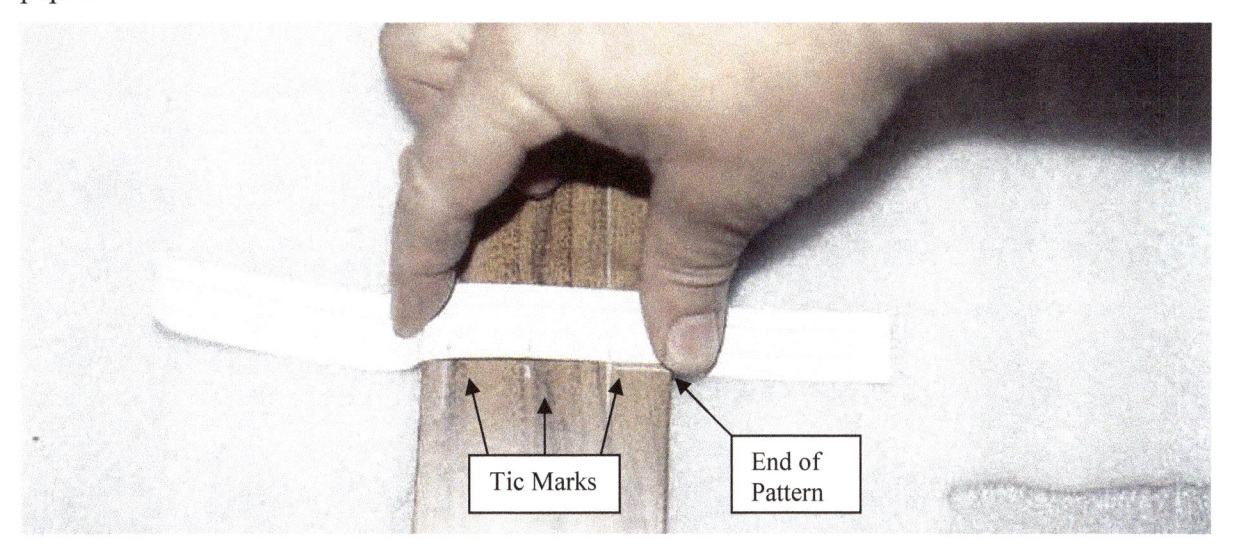

Tic Marks

End of Pattern

With the center established on each end of the pattern, use the plastic straight edge to create a centerline running the length of the pattern. This line is important in that from it the master lines are laid out, and these will affect the angles of the split "V" on the rear of the pattern and the "V" on the front of the pattern.

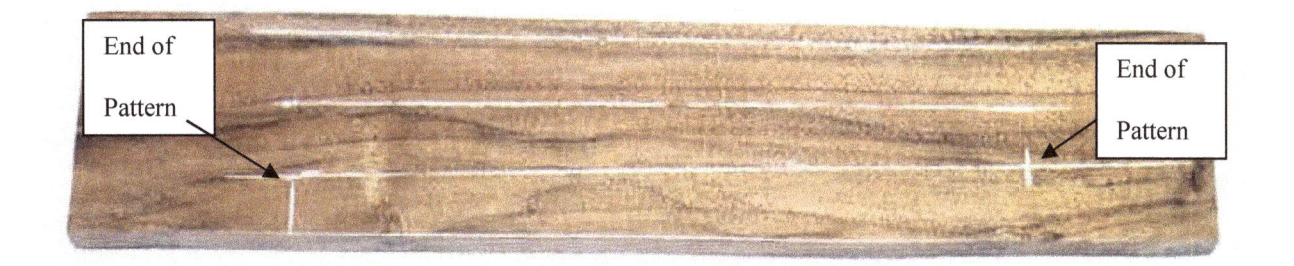

End of Pattern

End of Pattern

At this point the proof is ready. Draw in the master lines and for the ends of the pattern to be identified and "anticipated" border lines drawn in. A three and a half to one ration for the diamonds will be used, although a three to one would also be good. Using the plastic template for the three and a half to one ratio, lay the line for the forward point of the pattern by aligning the centerline of the template with the centerline of the pattern and placing the tip of the template at the anticipated end of the pattern, and white pencil in the line.

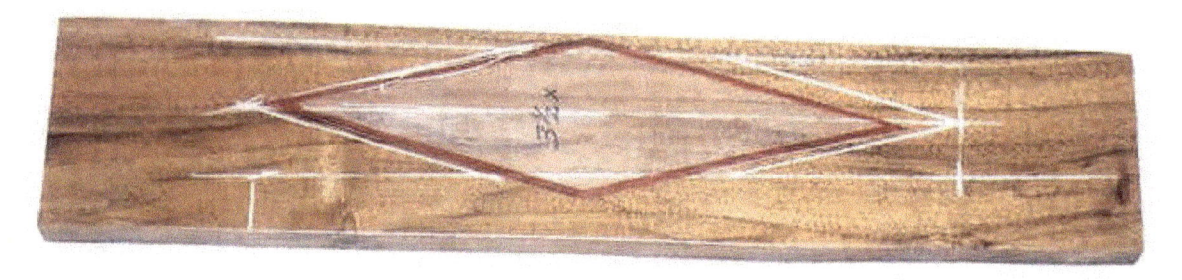

Position the tip of the template at the anticipated end of the rear of the pattern, aligning the centerline of the template with the centerline of the proof. Although the pattern will be a split "V" at the rear, we must first white pencil in "V" lines as illustrated in the picture above.

With what appears to be a "V" at each end of the pattern, we transform the "V at the rear of the pattern by creating a parallel line from the lines of the "V". The easiest way of doing this is to use a plastic strip of constant width. Insuring the line to be drawn is parallel with the "V", it must terminate at the upper and lower border lines of the pattern.

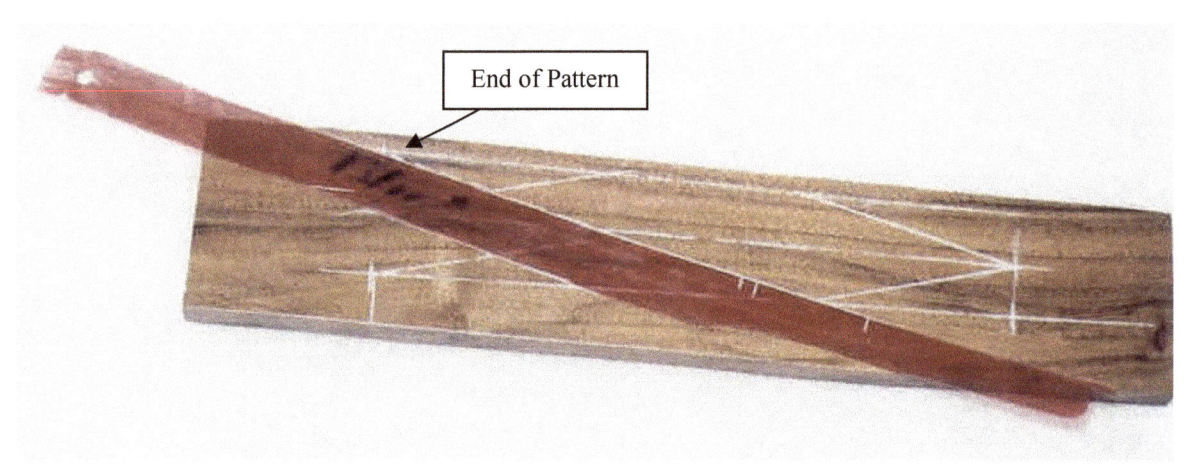

The preceding picture is a good illustration on the proper use on one of the heavy plastic strips I use a lot. To create contrast in order for the photo to pick up the edges, I "colored" the strip with a red marker pen. Even with the coloring on the strip I am able to identify tic marks and wood grain below it.

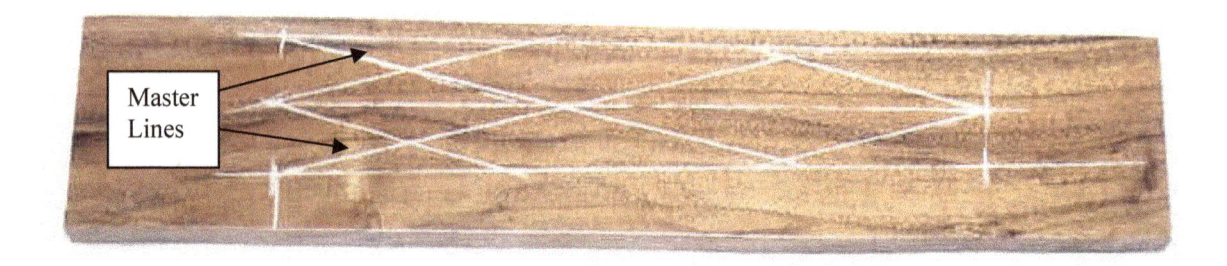

The proof is now ready to start cutting lines. Notice that the rear of the pattern has both a split "V" and a point. This occupies the wood well and would provide a good grip area as well as looking nice. The two lines which will be used as master lines are those coming from the top and bottom of the split "V".

To repeat instructions from the four to one proof previously cited, use a sixty-degree pointer to cut the upper and lower border lines, and then the master lines, but cut the master lines very shallow as the three line spacer must be able to track from them. If the master lines are too deep, the spacer will not have a narrow path to follow and the lines tracked from them may not be straight or parallel. Remember, you can always make a line deeper, but you can't make it less deep. Take your time as this is a learning process.

One thing, if you make an error, such as running lines over one another, or over a border, do not throw your tool in anger or disgust, you'll just have to go get it… Take a break, I do!

Another great way to start out on something new and add to your growing collection of proofs is an exercise combining developing a pattern, transferring a pattern, cutting a fill in pattern, and cutting a pattern with irregular borders. It sounds more difficult than it is.

First, as we want to work on a small scale, I am selecting a relatively small proof of Claro Walnut with excellent fiddleback and finished with five coats of sprayed TruOil over already filled grain. The Claro proof is not as dense as the previous blanks of English, but it will take twenty-four lines per inch checkering and possibly twenty-eight. Having already completed two projects, this one will stretch what you have already learned, and will need additional attention to detail, but the end result will be worth it. A simple answer to the quality of your work, is to lay the proof out on your bench when friends are over and see how many of their guns need checkering!

The first thing to do is to obtain an outline of the proof. The easiest way is to place a piece of copy paper over the proof, hold it in place with finger pressure, and use the flat of a soft leaded pencil to rub around the outline. The purpose of this exercise is to obtain a working surface measurement of the area of the proof which could be checkered. The result will be something like …

With the work area determined, I like to make several copies of this paper just in case. With one of the copies I fold it in half, splitting the outline of the proof. I have found that by holding the paper up to the bench light and then folding it over until parallel corners match and then creating a crease is the easiest way. A straight edge and extra fine point of a pen will mark the center of the area down the crease. I then make several copies of this paper, just in case…Of course, you can always use a ruler to determine the center of the outline or even a pair of dividers: your choice. I do recommend a very fine line down the crease.

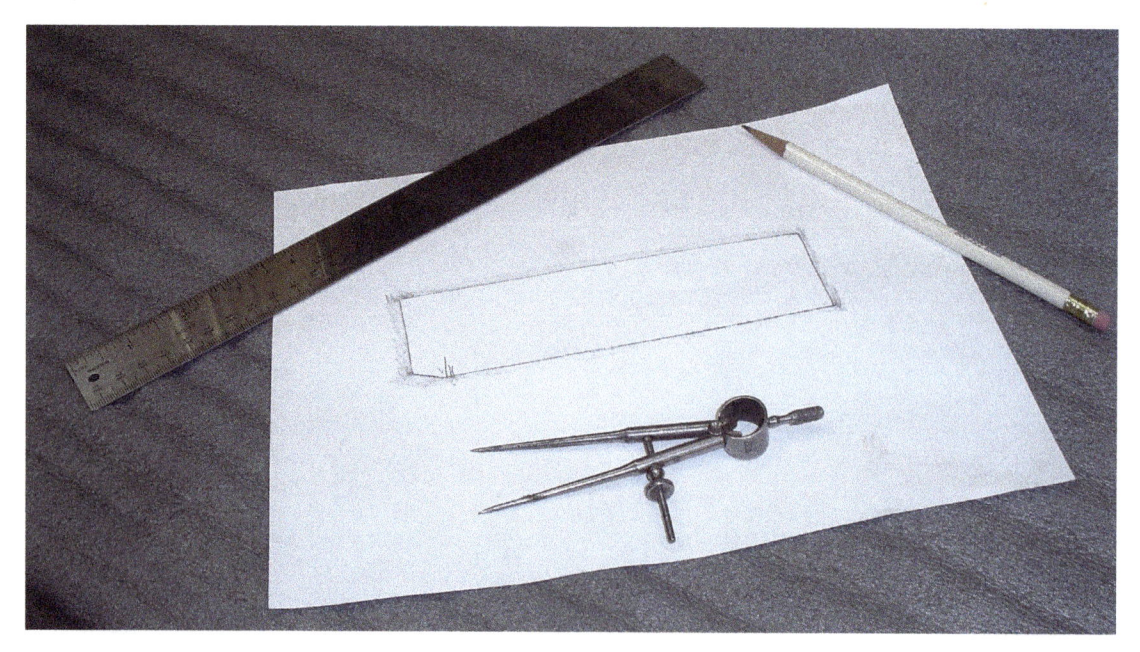

The design I will create here is one I call the *Half Diamond*. I begin by establishing the end – or shoulder – of the pattern. On a shotgun with the raised wood near the receiver, this would be the area closest to the face of the stock or receiver. I draw out half of the shoulder on the paper. I do this free hand, but have watched others use the French Curve to do it. I could just never master that instrument, and thus do it free hand.

I then fold the paper over, covering what I have drawn, and trace the half of the pattern through the paper. I then unfold the paper and trace the tracing through the paper, completing the shoulder. Just a few notes at this point use "thin" paper, onion skin paper if you have it, but using thick twenty pound bond paper will be difficult. In this case, cheaper is better. To insure you are seeing the complete portion of the drawing, place a line at the widest point of the drawing and another at the furthest portion of the drawing. There you have the shoulder of the pattern.

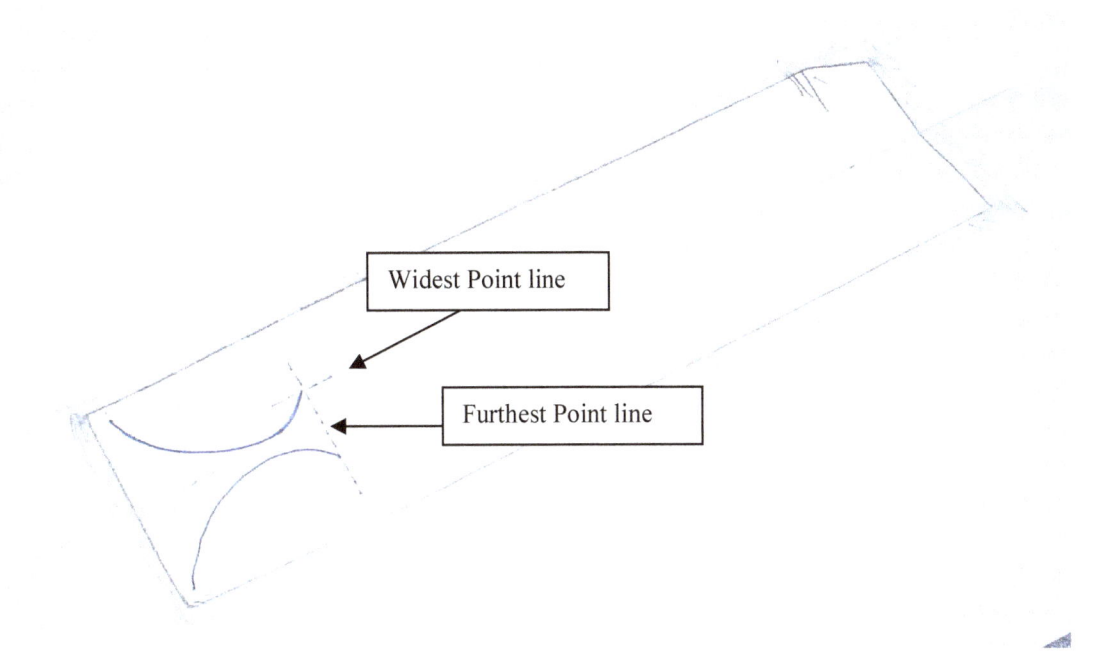

Widest Point line

Furthest Point line

At this point, what I call the "center piece" of the pattern can be a variety of figures limited to your imagination or just bring the halves of the shoulder together. I have cut patterns such as this with variations of the fleur dis lie as well as others, but for this exercise I want to cut a simple half diamond with a four to one ratio.

With the widest point line, and the furthest point line on the drawing, place a small piece of paper on the furthest point line, and make a tic mark at each of the widest point lines. This then is the width we are to use when creating a ratio for the point

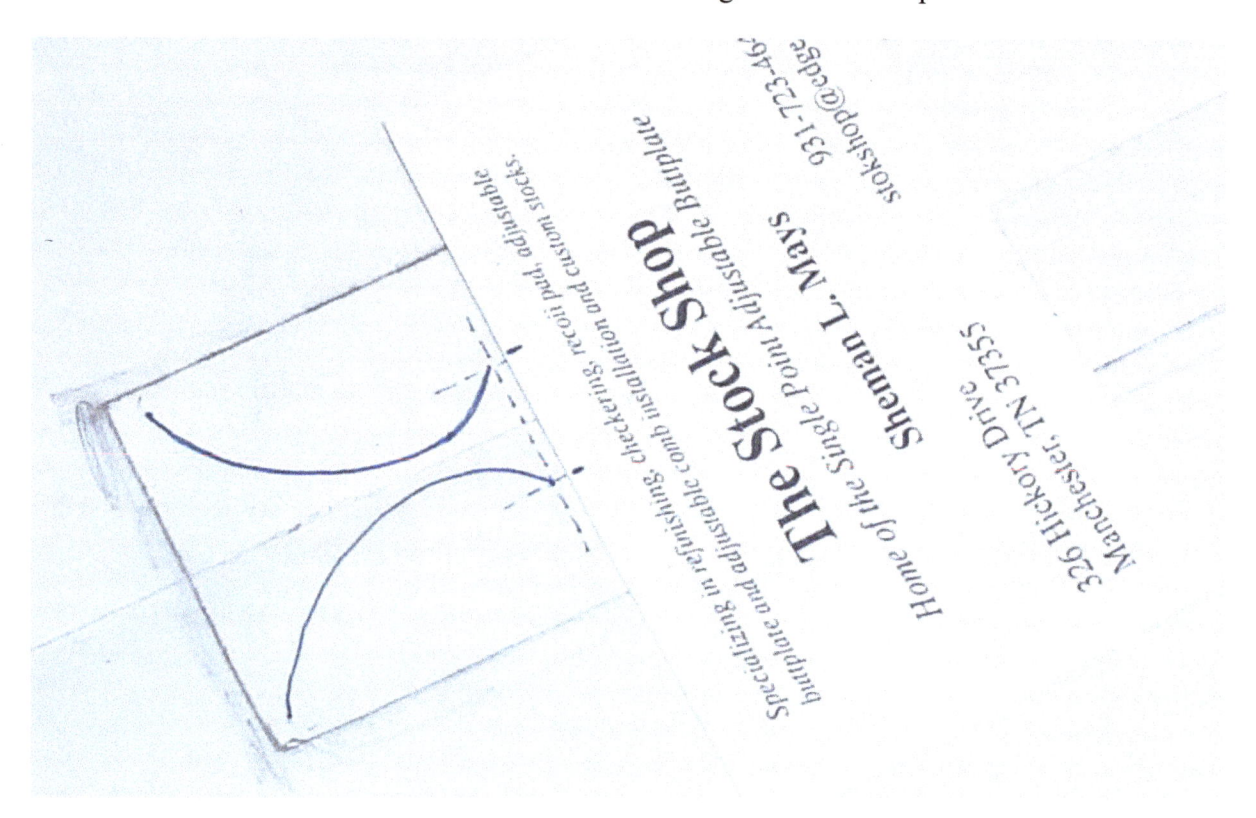

Using this measurement and starting the diagonal line from the center point indicating the furthest point, make the point twice as long as it is wide and place a tic mark on the centerline of the paper. If the point was whole rather than just half as we are working on, the entire diamond would be four times as long as it is wide – thus, the ratio of four to one. With a short straight edge connect the tic marks to form the point of the pattern.

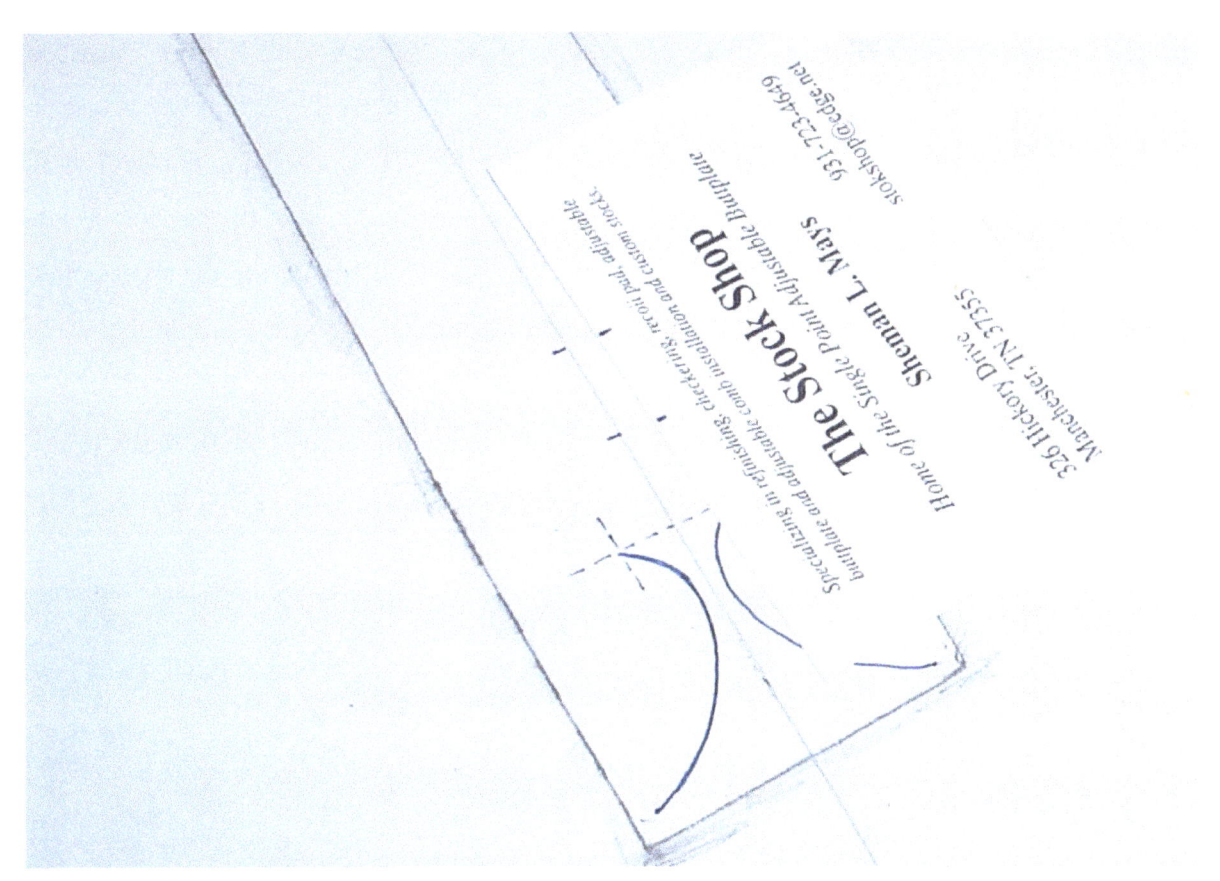

Using a straight edge, complete the half diamond by connecting the points at the widest point line to the second tic mark from the furthest point line on the crease or center point.

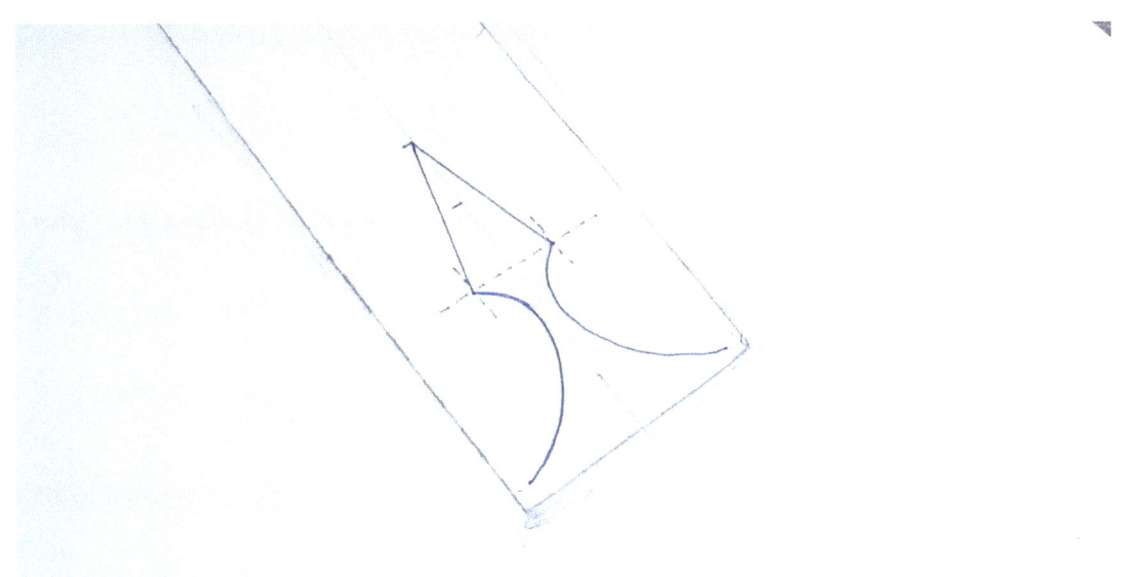

Now is the time to transfer the pattern onto the proof. I first trim the pattern to the size of the wood, being careful to cut just inside the lines on the paper. As I am cutting the pattern to size, I also cut a couple of small diamond shapes in the pattern to be used to secure the pattern to the proof with tape. Placing the pattern over the proof, I use a small narrow piece of tape to position on end of the pattern to the proof, and then slide a piece of carbon paper - Yes, it is still made, a little hard to find, but available - under the pattern.

A very good substitute for carbon paper is the strike over tape used to correct typing errors. Several of these little inch by three inch strips can be placed under the pattern. While the carbon paper transfers a blue or black imprint to the proof, the strike over correction paper transfers a white imprint onto the wood. For dark wood I much prefer the white imprint to the blue or black.

Once the carbon paper is in place tape the remaining end of the pattern to the proof. If the pattern is a large one, the sides can be taped as well, or a couple of rubber bands can be used to hold the pattern in place.

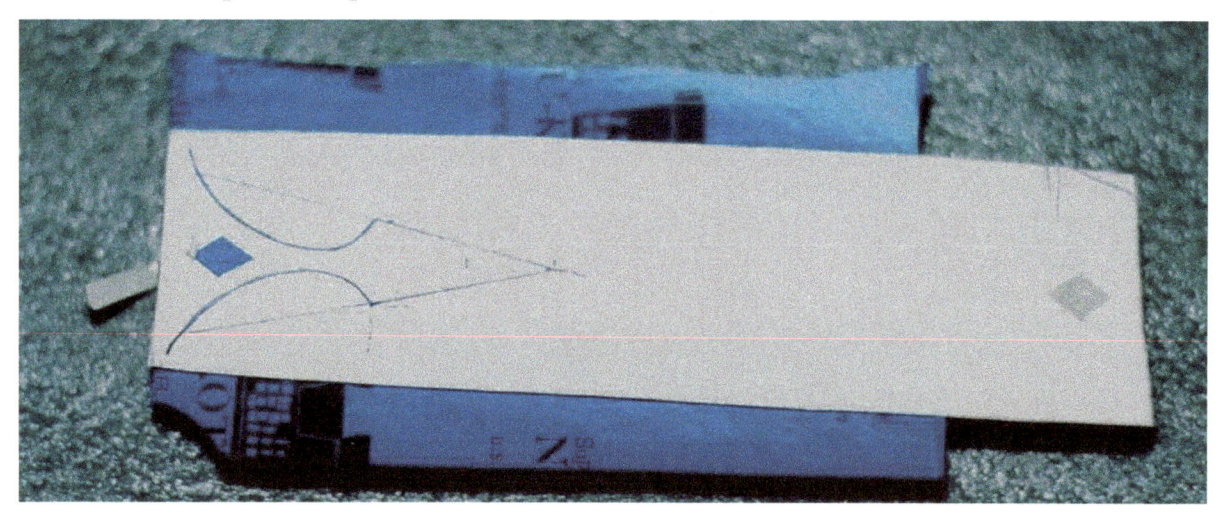

With everything in place, use a soft lead pencil to trace over the checkering pattern making the transfer onto the wood. Using the shortened sixty degree pointer, carefully cut the carbon lines on the proof. Extend the two lines of the half diamond out to form the master lines, but do not take them all of the way out to the edge. Use the tip of the tool primarily, with one hand providing mobility and the other guiding the tool.

See the little white tic mark on the right end of the proof? That's a center line mark and is used for lining up the paper pattern on the proof. With the pattern on one end of the proof, the same paper pattern can be used to establish the pattern on the other end of the proof, in the same way as we did the first. The reason for the centerline is to get you familiar with the assumption that one should never make assumptions about a proof, much less a stock, being the same. Always have and use a uniform procedure to insure you are right.

Centerline Mark

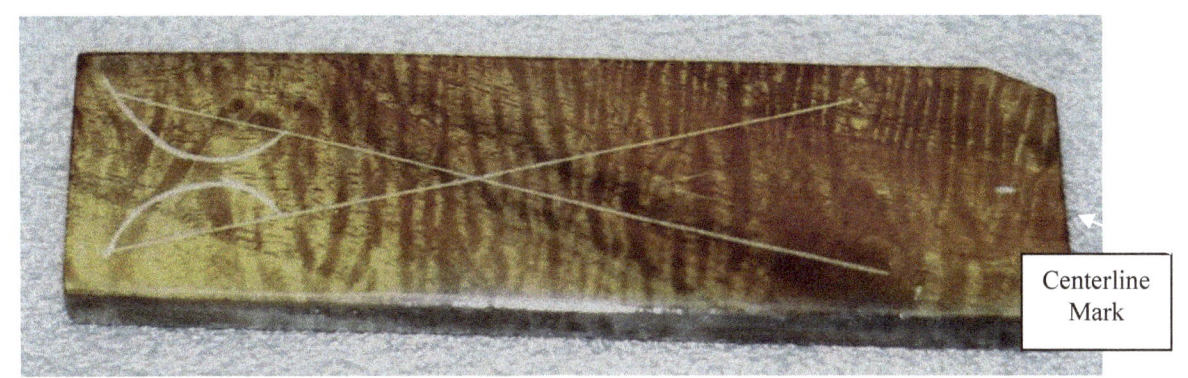

After transferring the pattern to the proof, I cut the pattern with the sixty-degree pointer. I then used the width gauge to track in the border lines, being careful not to extend them all of the way to out. They terminate at a point at which I feel the shoulders of the pattern will come out to the border lines.

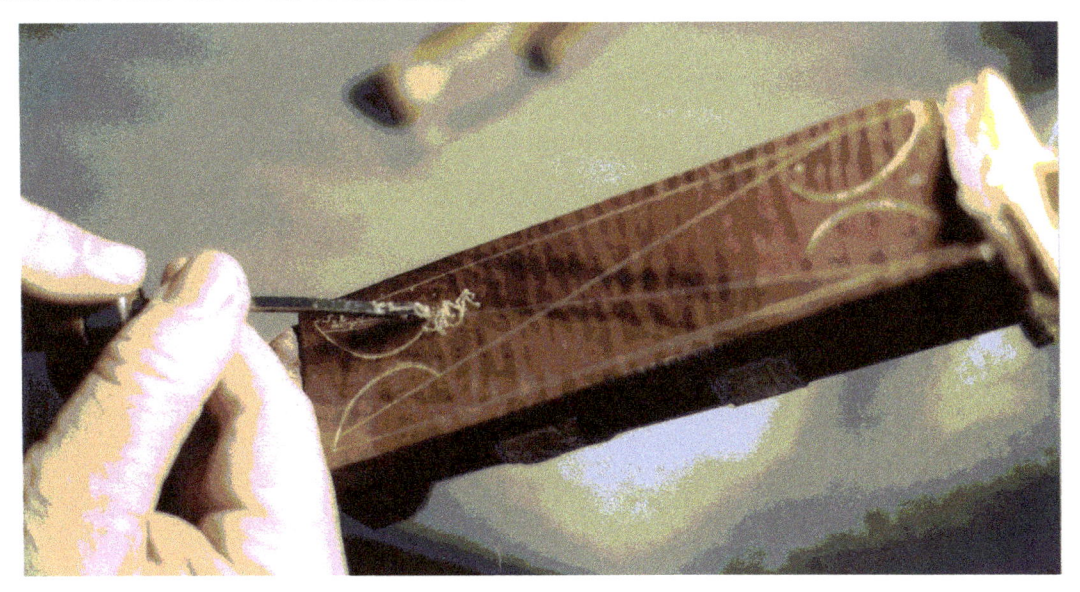

Please notice that I DID NOT cut the lines of the half diamond. I did not do it because the lines extended from the master lines of the first half diamond will come across and form the point lines of the second half diamond. As I track in the checkering lines on the proof, I will take them across until they meet the shoulder of the pattern, and thus form the point lines of the second half diamond.

Again, the preceding is how I accomplish a given task, you may choose to do it differently. Whatever works for you is right. There is no set right or wrong way to accomplish any task in this text, just the way I have chosen to accomplish them. Use it as a start for developing your own.

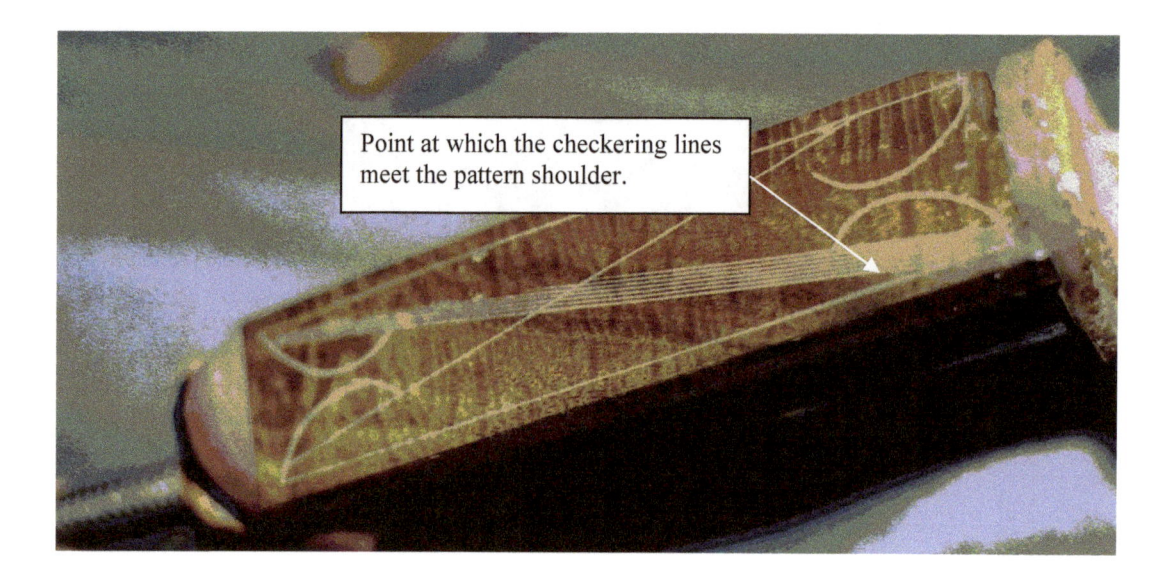

Point at which the checkering lines meet the pattern shoulder.

This is another case of not getting in a hurry. Take your time, cut one or two lines, then reverse the proof and complete the lines. You do not want to cut too many lines and actually go into the half diamond. I have done it – got in a hurry – and ended up having to reduce the size of the half diamond to compensate for the error. The Customer was not aware of it. The pattern looked nice, just two line widths smaller than I intended, but I knew, and it bothered me- still does. Each time I cut a similar pattern, I remember the errors and do not repeat it.

A good practice to get into is to cut available lines while you are "in position" to do so. In this case, after I completed the long lines, I tracked in the short checkering lines along the shoulders of the checkering pattern. In doing so, I have found there is less likelihood of a difference of angle between the two lines. Develop the habit. It is one that will pay dividends.

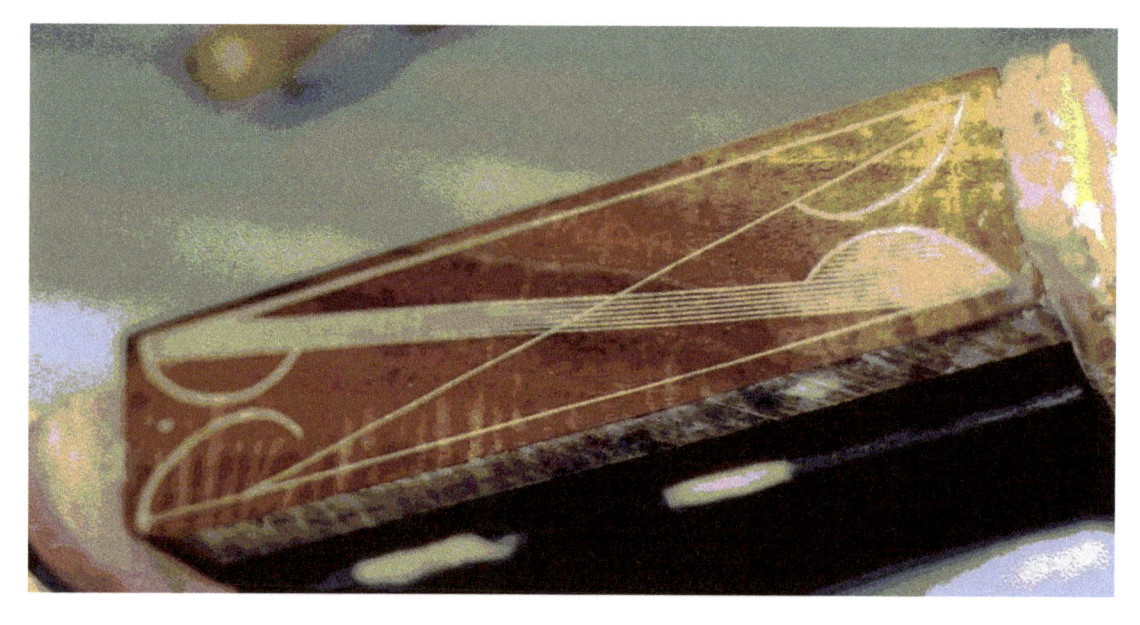

Now do the same thing for the other side. Follow the master lines and track in the checkering lines a couple at a time, reverse the proof, and complete the lines. Do this until you have brought the checkering lines over to the second half diamond, essentially completing the second half diamond as illustrated in the following picture.

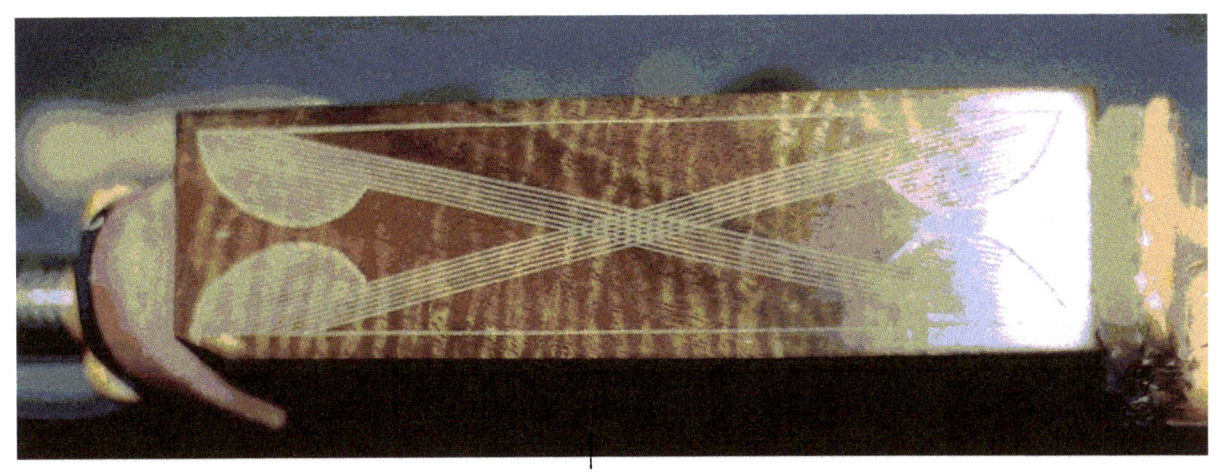

On patterns such as this, with "points" meeting on the same plane, if the checkering lines do not follow the same ratio very closely, it really detracts from the appearance. For this reason I use one of my plastic strips to draw in "approximate lines" of where the subsequent lines should follow. The presence of these lines serve as a reminder of the correct spacing of lines being tracked in, and quickly show if they do not.

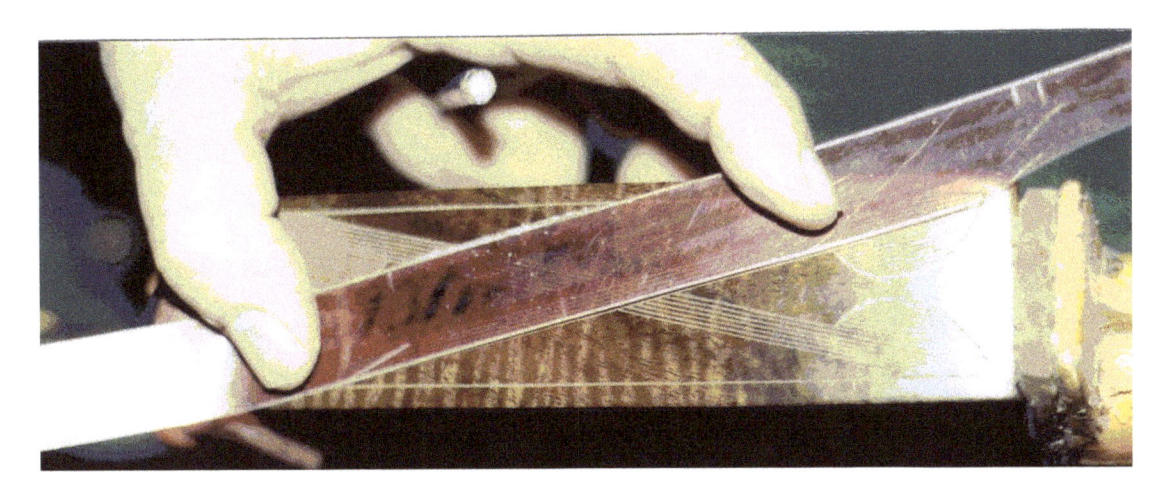

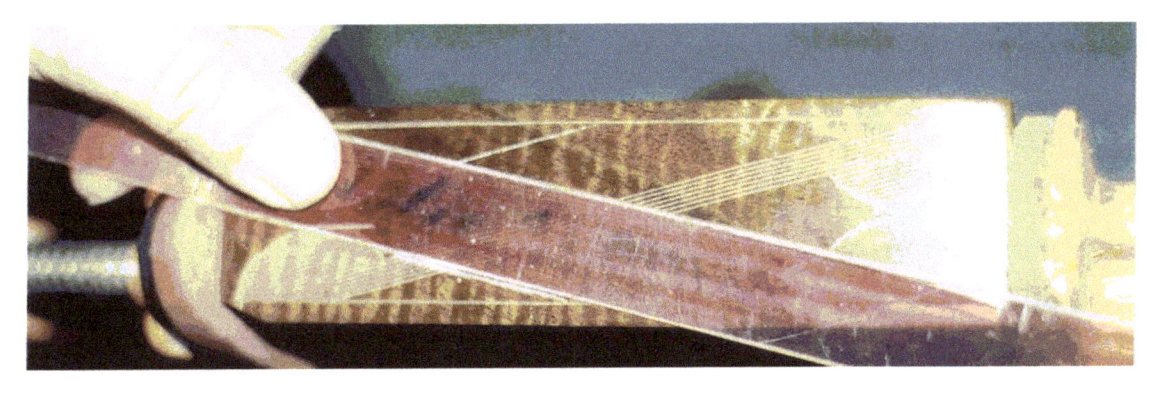

Section 3

Recutting Old / Factory Checkering

Very seldom will a customer want the checkering on a stock recut without the wood being refinished, but it happens. At the base minimum, before recutting checkering on wood that is not to be refinished, I use a mild liquid soap and a tooth brush to scrub the checkering thoroughly. This often reveals the checkering to be in better shape that anticipated. Just as a note, when I refinish a stock, I scrub the areas checkered with the stripper agent and a stiff bristled brush to remove all of the old finish.

Some of the checkering may be as fresh as the day it was cut, other areas may be worn smooth, and still others may reflect errors or poor workmanship. Often times, especially on rifle forearms, the wood is compressed and / or gouged out. Several rifle stocks I have worked on have had wire imprints imbedded into the checkering where the forearm was used to hold a fence down when crossing it.

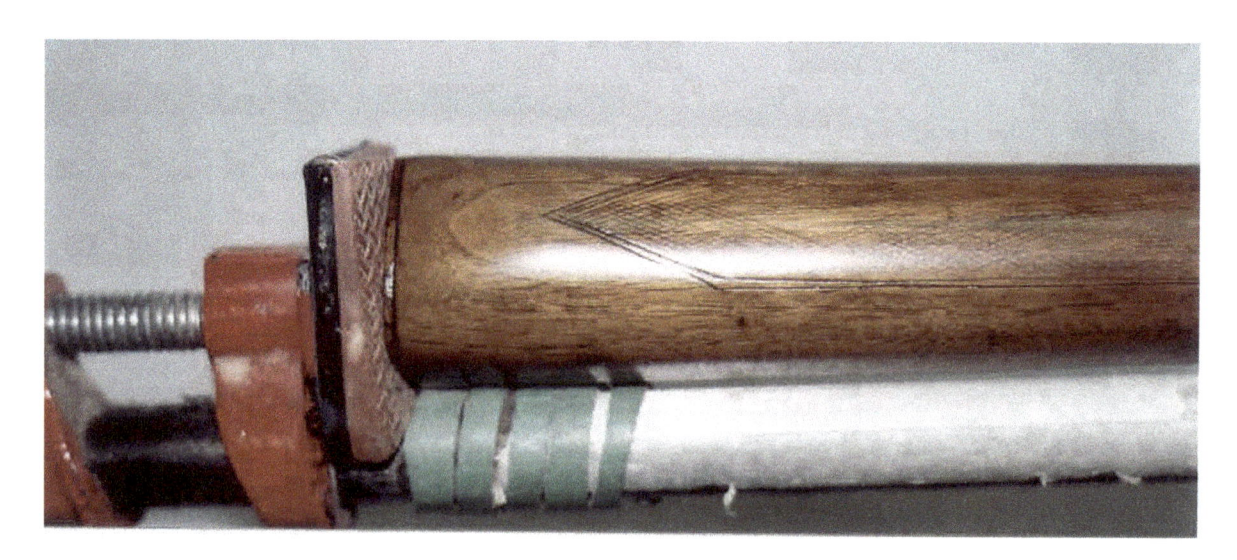

The first thing I do when recutting old or factory checkering is to re-establish the boundary lines of the checkering pattern. To do this I use the short sixty degree pointer. However, if the borders are not straight, or the border lines have been worn smooth, I use the long pointer in 60 degrees. It cuts a defined line, is easy to control, and can later be widened and deepened with a ninety degree cutter for final appearance.

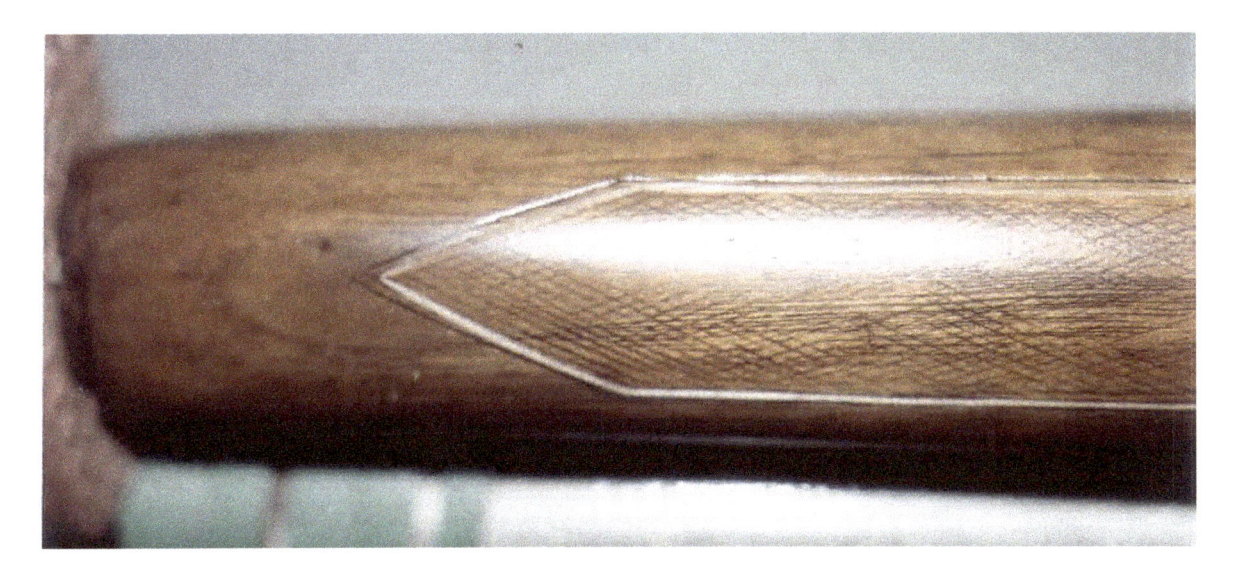

As a general rule, if lines are visible, I recut them. Only when there is an absence of lines do I resort to a two or three line spacer. Why? Because many of the checkering lines on the older firearms were often cut with spacers which often did not conform to a measurement of lines per inch. These spacers were sharpened and that sharpening further changed the lines per inch measurement we rely upon today when making and selecting our tools.

With the border lines cut, a decision on where to start comes up. One can either start at one end, following the ratio established by the end border lines, or one can create parallel lines in the middle of the forearm, using the lines from the end of the pattern. The second option is perhaps the easiest and allows for greater corrective action required by crooked lines and lines not parallel. So, let's go with the first option and start from one end…

I will be using a three line spacer in twenty lines per inch, which according to my research, is the line spacing Winchester used in checkering the Deluxe Model of the Winchester 71. I use the three line spacer as it has proven to provide me with the ability to track TWO previous lines when cutting the third, a feature which helps in keeping the lines straight. I begin by tracking one of the border lines and cutting new lines each shorter than the previous.

With the start made, and don't attempt to carry the lines out full length, be satisfied that you have started the lines in the correct spacing, and then REVERSE the piece. Yes, reverse it. Just turn it around 180 degrees in the checkering clamp, and you will have the same angle to cut the lines back to the border as you did when starting the line. From this point you can complete the lines you had started, and using two of the three cutters on the spacer to track the cut lines, use the third cutter to start a new line and progress over with each new line getting successively shorter. Notice the only lines that are complete are the ones I started before reversing the piece.

When the fresh lines have become too short to accurately gauge if you are cutting parallel lines of going off on a tangent, reverse the piece again. Feeling pretty comfortable with the lines being cut on this piece, I have started more lines than I normally would. In the average situation I seldom cut more than ten lines before reversing the work and completing them.

I will proceed with cutting new lines and then reversing the piece until I am within an inch of the other end of the checkering pattern. At this point I want to check how parallel my lines have been, and get an idea of how the lines will mate up to the border lines on the end of the checkering pattern. With an inch of space remaining, I would be able to slightly widen one end of the lines to bring the fresh lines into harmony with the border lines.

I accomplish this task with one of the plastic strips I keep under the counter. There is a variety of widths, ranging from a quarter inch up to almost two inches, graduating in one-eighth inch increments. By aligning one edge of the strip with one of the fresh lines, I can use the other edge of the plastic strip as a parallel and determine its proximity to the border lines.

Continuing to use the three line spacer, I will bring the lines over to the border, reversing the piece to complete partial lines several times before the pattern is completed. As you get closer and closer to the border watch closely to insure you are keeping the lines parallel. No, your hair isn't going to fall out if you don't, and probably no one will ever get a magnifying glass out to inspect your work, but you will know the results of your work.

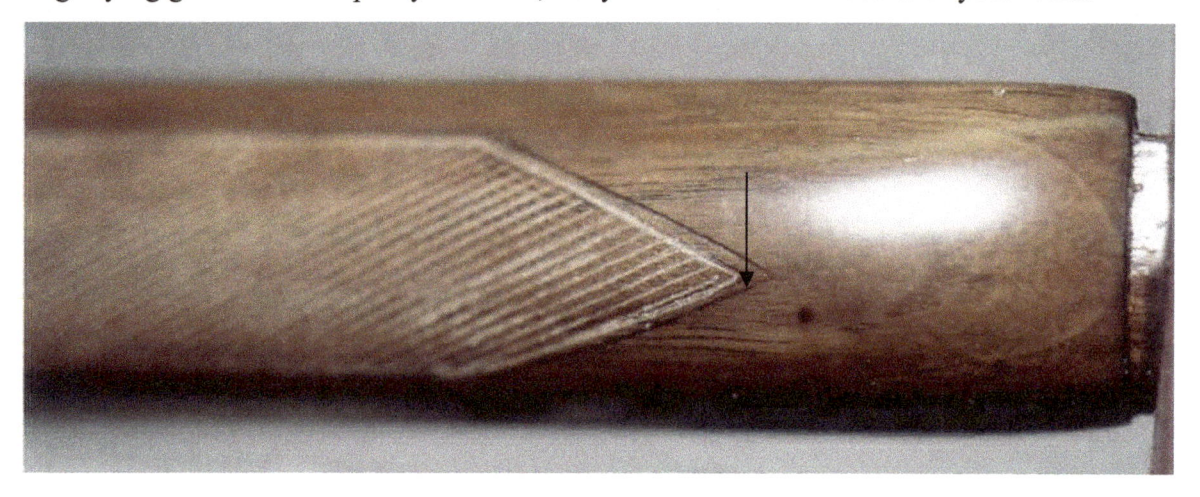

Notice the small "leftover" line at the arrow? That is one of my errors in insuring the last inch width of lines cut were not exactly parallel, but I can live with it. I would like for it to come out perfect, but I consider the results to be very good. At this point it is time to cut the lines running across the lines just cut, which will form the diamonds of the checkering.

We start out in the same manner, starting lines, reversing the piece and completing them, and starting more lines and reversing the work. Repeat this process to a point several inches from the end of the pattern, and then use the plastic strip to determine how the angle of the checkering line compares to the border line. In this case, I used a one inch wide strip, lay the edge on the last line checkered, and used a "Marks Everything" white pencil to run a line down the other edge of the strip. Moving the strip, I used it to form another parallel to the border, and determined everything looked pretty good.

Check the angle of the lines being cut several more times as you cut more lines and get closer to the border line. Be very careful, such as in this project, of the old lines – they can lead you astray and really cause some problems. When cutting over old lines, I like to use a short shank on a spacer, and being left handed, guide the tool with my left hand and use my right to determine the amount of downward pressure on the cutter. My right hand also serves as a brake when cutting close to the border.

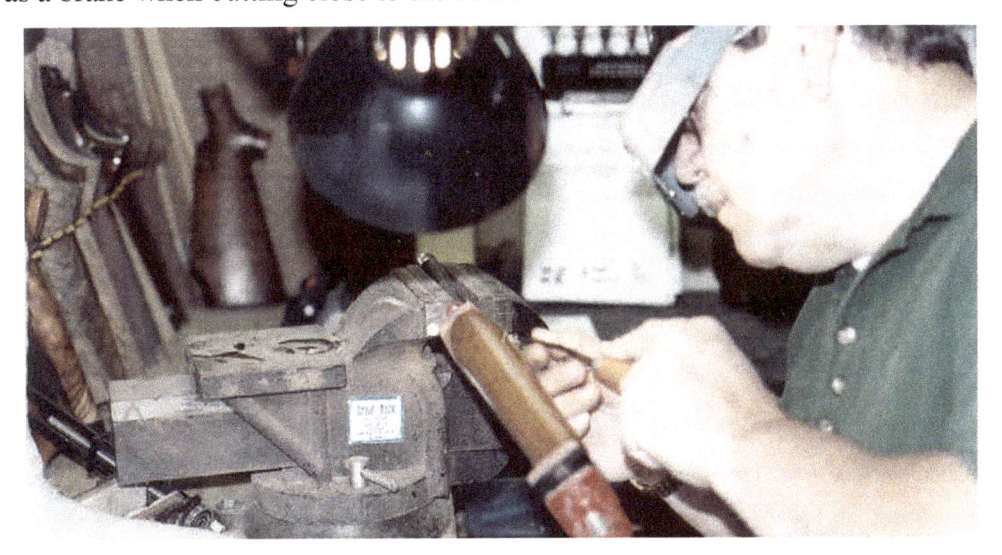

Continue on until all of the lines are completed. While we have worked towards insuring the angle of the lines being cut is the same angle as the border lines, there is little we can do when we end up with a "narrow" line at the edge of the pattern as is illustrated below.

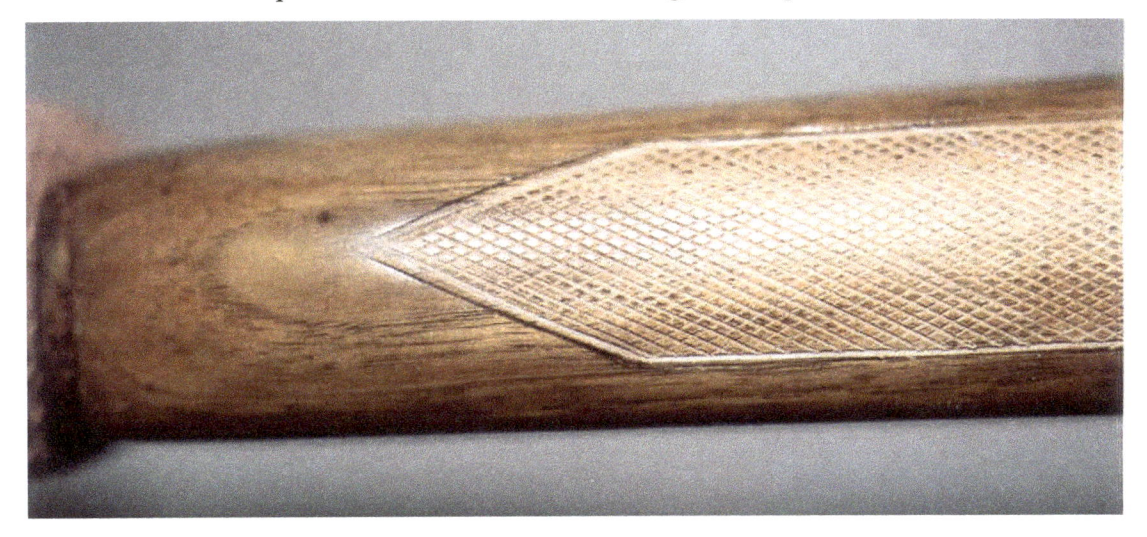

With all of the lines identified, it is time to deepen them. For whatever reason, I like to bring the lines at the ends of the pattern to a point first. You can start at any point – purely personal preference – so I like to start at the ends.

From the ends I proceed down the sides, starting the deepening of the lines about a half an inch from the border line, taking it to the border, and then go to the next line. I will do one side, reverse the piece, and do the opposing line on the same side. I will do this several times before the lines are deep enough to bring the diamonds to a point.

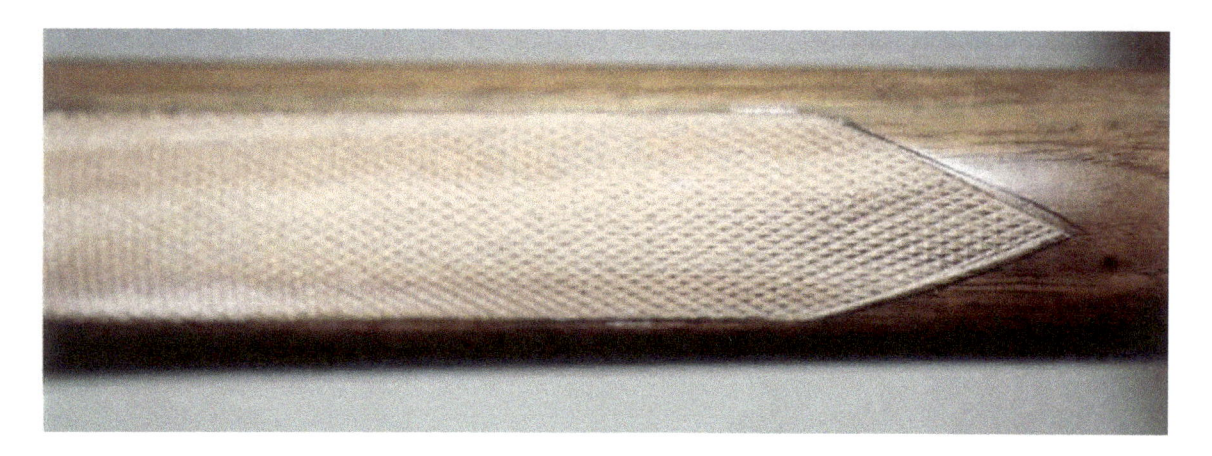

Please, do not attempt to deepen the line to full depth in a single pass, take your time. Deepen them a little, reverse the piece, deepen the opposing angle and reverse the piece and do it all again. On very figured English, I have reversed the piece a half dozen times, taking the lines a little deeper each time. The end result was a series of neat lines the same depth, with no chipped tips from the diamonds. Remember, you are cutting around very small pieces of wood, and the deeper the lines, the more fragile the diamond. Take a big bite of wood with the cutter, and you may end up with some chipped diamonds for your trouble…

With the checkering complete, or so it seems, it is time to cut the borders. From the previous photographs, the condition of the border lines indicated the lines were not cut with any kind of spacer – probably with some form of pointer, freehand.

BREAKTIME: Little boy was up in front of his third grade class telling them all about the great rifle his father had had a stock maker checker. Completing the description the little boy said, "And when I get to heaven, I'm going to ask him how he did it."

The teacher, being an anti-gun, tree hugging activist, asked the little boy, "What are you going to do if he didn't go to heaven?"

The little boy thought for a second and responded, "Then you can ask him!"

I am going to use a narrow convex border tool for the border. This tool will leave a narrow rounded border around the checkering pattern, and it has one really nice characteristic

– it hides errors well. And in this case, there are several errors – narrow lines around the borders – than we need to minimize.

When cutting the border, one edge of the tool must ride in the inner border line cut earlier. Just to be sure we are going to have a good line to follow, run the sixty degree pointer around the checkering pattern. This is time well spent.

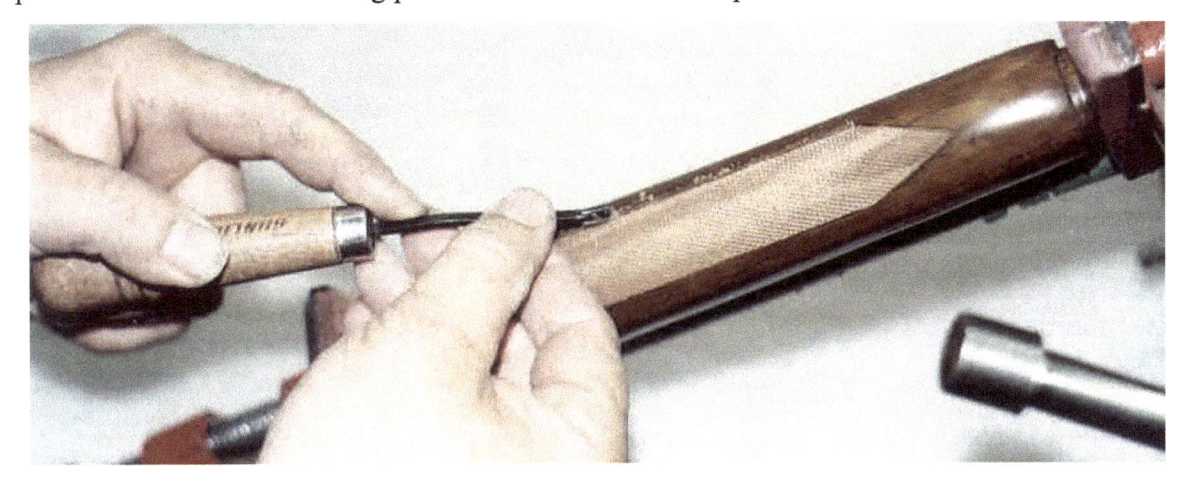

With the narrow border tool in hand, tilt the cutter in towards the checkering pattern and start cutting the border away from the end of the pattern an inch or so is good. By tilting the tool, one edge will be in the border line just "freshened" with the sixty-degree cutter, and the other edge will leave a faint track on the wood, creating the second line. Cut using short strokes mine are about a half-inch forward and then a quarter inch back.

With the faint track of the outer cutting edge on the piece, check it out. Is it straight? Will it encompass the older line? Does it compliment the existing checkering?

With the faint track established, and satisfied it serves the purpose intended, begin deepening the lines with the same short strokes. Take your time. It is easy to get to one side or the other and cause yourself more work, which you don't need.

As the lines become deeper, you will be able to see the top of the rounded bead appear. You will also see places in the rounded bead in which an older darker "ghost" line appears. No problem! Just cut the border lines a little deeper and the "ghost" lines will disappear – simple solution.

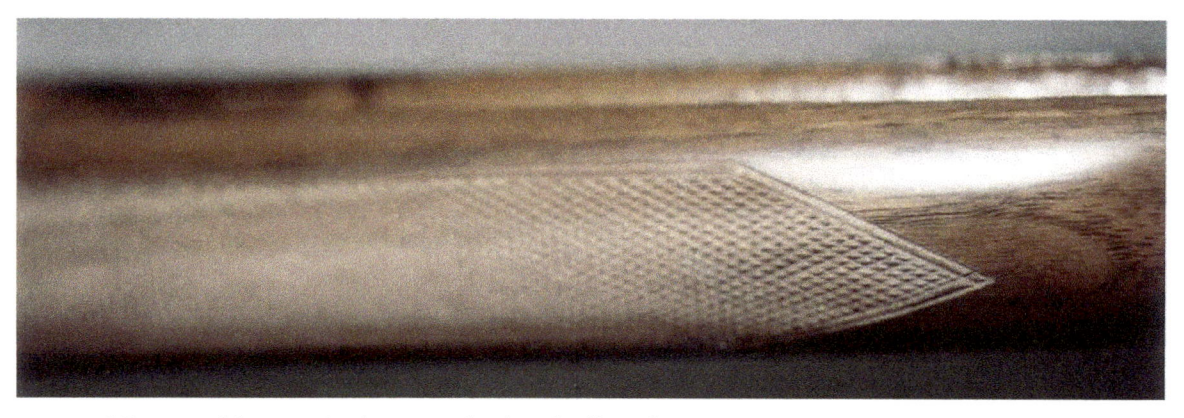

Next problem – As long as the borderline does not make an intersection, you will do all right, just take it slow, use short strokes, and monitor your progress frequently. However, when you come up to a junction, such as we have where the top and bottom lines meet the lines forming the ends of the pattern, a little "extra" work is involved. Use the tip of the border tool for the last half-inch of cutting leading to the junction be careful. Don't run the cutter over onto the adjoining line. Cut only as far as you can without running over the adjoining line. This will leave a very short space, which will require deepening and contouring it to match the rounded bead of the border.

Set the border tool aside and pick up a Short Sixty Degree Pointer or a long pointer ground to form a shortened pointer, and slowly and carefully extend the borderline up to the junction.

Slight problem, the border tool creates a rounded bead when it cuts. The Sixty Degree pointer cuts a "V" in the wood. As the cut will be less than an eighth inch, the difference should not be noticeable. However, I lean the short pointer over slightly creating a cut of about one hundred and twenty degrees, and slightly round the area along the cut.

I have in the past formed a "left" line border tool by grinding away the right half of the cutter, and similarly made a "right" line border tool. Yes, they worked, and worked well, but were a pain to keep up with. I use the short pointer to accomplish the same task now.

So, everything is great. Well not so great. We cut into one of the junction lines and left a run over that stands out. So, let's use solution number three – we skipped number two.

Use the sixty-degree pointer to cut through the junction bead as well as form the outer line into an extended point of the pattern. Thus, you have cut a small diamond on either end of the pattern. It looks good, and observers will marvel at your skill and vision, but we will know the truth…

Almost done. Use a stiff bristle toothbrush to really clean out the checkered and border areas. If everything comes clean, great. However, sometimes, depending on how the grain flows, cuts from one direction or another will not be as clean as cuts from the other direction. Some of the cuts appear to have grown fuzz. When this happens, there is a simple solution, which will lead to a product that looks nice.

Determine the direction of cut which leaves the wood clean and no fuzz, and lightly, and I do mean lightly, recut all of the line displaying the fuzz. Yes, it will take a few minutes, actually just a little longer than it would take for you to explain that the dog gone wood just didn't finish out and look nice.

With the fuzz cleaned, look for small imperfections at the junction of lines on the border. Sometimes, the tip of the cutter was use to "plow" through a cut at the end of the line, and the wood is pushed into a small lump at the end of the line. When this happens, raise the tip of the cutter. I use a long fine cutter and lower the tip onto the "lump" and PULL BACK on the cutter just enough to remove the lump. You might have to do this several times, but it will really provide a neat junction of lines.

Done! Well, almost done…

The checkering must be sealed, and the edges of the checkering lines near the finished wood must be thoroughly sealed. Yes, there are all kinds of sealers that can be used, and most of them will probably do the job. But the sealer I have used for many years, and have found to work very well, is thinned down TruOil, about one part thinner to five parts TruOil, and use a fine bristled toothbrush to apply it. The excess rubs off quickly with a soft cloth.

An hour later, I apply a second coat, and consider the wood sealed, the piece done, and have a cup of coffee before assembling it onto the rifle.

BREAKTIME: A Stockmaker, deathly ill, laying in bed, waiting for the grim reaper. Into his bedroom comes the smell of chocolate chip cookies baking. So out of bed he climbs, barely able to walk, he makes it into the kitchen, dreaming that his last meal on earth would be one of his wife's chocolate chip cookies. Entering the kitchen, he sees a platter of cookies fresh from the oven on the table. As he is reaching to get one, his wife slaps him alongside the head with a hot cookie sheet, telling him, "You can't have any, those are for the funeral."

Section 4

Copying Patterns

Somewhere between *Recutting Factory Checkering*, and *Custom Checkering*, is *Copying a Checkering Pattern*. The example I am going to use for the most part is from a nice Winchester model 71 in 348 Winchester, and I am going to duplicate the pattern onto a standard grade Winchester Model 71. The two rifles belong to friends, and I was asked to refinish the higher grade gun and recut the factory checkering and to duplicate the checkering from the higher grade gun onto the standard grade gun.

My first task is to establish the outline of the checkering pattern. The easiest way of doing this is to place a piece of typing paper over the checkering pattern and, with the flat of a pencil lead, rub over the checkering pattern. Not only will the borders of the checkering pattern come through clearly, but the individual checkering lines will also come through.

When cutting the checkering pattern from the piece of paper, be sure to cut slowly and right on the border of the pattern. With the checkering pattern cut out, place in on the wood to be checkered. In this case I had an original stock to refer to for placement of the pattern. At other times, I have used a pattern created years before and brought out of my archives to use.

On a task such as this, copying not only the pattern is important, but the ration at which the master lines are cut is equally important. I won't go into the angle of the cutter to be used, except to say that I have edgers and pointers in 60, 75 and 90 degree angles.

Place the pattern on the wood to be checkered and move it around – referring to the original stock – until you are comfortable it is in the correct place. If you do not have the original stock available for reference, and want the pattern placed correctly, refer to gun catalogues, gun magazines or one of the different books providing pictures of current and antique guns. I have a reference library built up over forty years, as well as several three ring binders full of tracings and original checkering patterns. I have used all of them at one time or another.

Another excellent way to "collect" checkering patterns is to copy the checkering from every gun you come across, to include asking Gun Shop owners for permission to copy checkering patterns of guns on their shelves. I have a pattern from an Ithaca 4E obtained in just this manner. I also took a bunch of pictures of it while I was there and just happened to have a camera.

At this point I use very short (3/4") and narrow (1/4") pieces of masking tape to secure the pattern, and transfer the pattern to the stock using a Marks Anything White Pencil to trace around the edge. When the white line has covered all of the exposed area around the pattern, I remove one piece of the anchoring tape at a time and draw in the absent line. With the removal of the last piece of tape, I have a checkering pattern on the wood ready for "editing."

Yes, I "edit" my checkering patterns once transferred to the wood. By editing, I "wet out" thick lines I drew in, and replace them with narrower lines obtained with a sharpened white pencil.

If I am not satisfied with how the patterns lays on the stock, I may make a couple of tic marks where a certain juncture / corner of the checkering pattern should be. I then wet out the entire pattern, reset the paper pattern to the tic marks, and draw the lines on again. On one stock, several years ago before I was "blessed" with the infinite patience of a Grandfather, I drew the pattern on five times. I don't remember stopping. I was satisfied with the placement, or just tired of drawing lines.

I use a 60 Degree pointer to cut the pattern lines into the wood, cutting right down the middle of the white line. I have found that this works for me, but there may be better ways.

Please notice one thing on the following pictures, I have continued the two lines forming the upper forward portion of the pattern, allowing them to become the master lines of the pattern. This is a common practice when a simple point pattern is used, and one which is very common on Winchester manufactured rifles and shotguns. The drawback to using this type of arrangement is that often the checkering diamonds look "square," and I like mine to look long and graceful.

Although this section is on patterns, I am enclosing a picture of the rife with the "upgraded" checkering on it. Your thoughts, please.

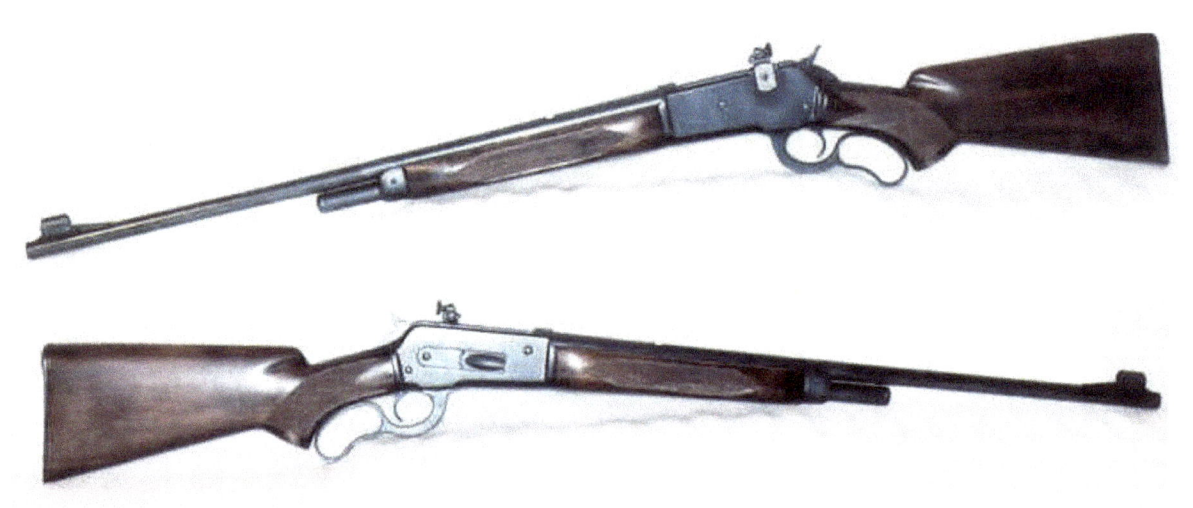

Sometimes I get to do something the factory should have done or offered to do years ago. I grew up with a Springfield Model 5100 20 gauge with a Plastic "tenite" buttstock and forearm, and hated them. When I was a little older - about fourteen - I managed to acquire a Stevens single barrel 12 gauge, also with a "tenite" buttstock and forearm. At sixteen, I acquired another firearm with the plastic stock and forearm, a neat little 22 rim fire over 410 gauge. Over the years, I managed to trade all of them off, but thought about finding another one some day and putting some nice wood on it. Well, lo and behold, along comes just such a job.

I wanted to do something special to the gun, but quoted a reasonable price for fitting the customer's wood – he had had it in his possession for many years – finishing and checkering it. He did not have the budget for what I wanted to do, so I did it because I had always wanted to. In this case, I think the customer really got more than he bargained for.

The forearm was a standard issue semi-finished forearm available from Reinhart Fajen's many years ago. I would have graded it at a low fancy or high semi-fancy. I will skip over the fact that I have always hated the wood screws Stevens used for securing these little forearms to the iron and replaced the wood screws with machine screws and established bushings – from a Krieghoff K-80 forearm – in the bottom of the forearm wood for them.

The plastic forearm did have an interesting checkering pattern on it, and I thought I could maintain the general pattern design but enlarge it for the beaver tail forearm. Using the forward forearm bushing as a marker point, I explored several different variations of the basic pattern for several days. I have a habit of leaving "tasks" for which I have not made a decision on top of my work bench. Sort of a constant reminder of something that needs doing.

The one facet of the design which kept me from making a decision was how to compliment the rear of the forearm where the wood narrows for the forearm iron. I wanted something functional, but which flowed into the remainder of the forearm. I forget how many days the forearm gathered dust on my bench, but everything clicked one day and resulted in a paper pattern which I considered worthy of being copied onto the wood for a long time look see.

Normally, I will white pencil on a pattern I have had difficulty developing, and let it sit a day or two to see if I really like it when the idea becomes cold. I will pick it up, look it over, hum and haw, maybe change a line or two, perhaps tighten or loosen a radius, and put it down only to pick it up an hour later to hum and haw some more. However, in this case I let the forearm sit long enough to get a couple of pictures of it, and started to cut the pattern outline and master lines.

If the job had just been for a customer, I might have made the decision a little quicker, but I was living out my fantasy of putting wood on one of my long ago guns, and I wanted it done right, and I wanted it to be something that would draw attention.

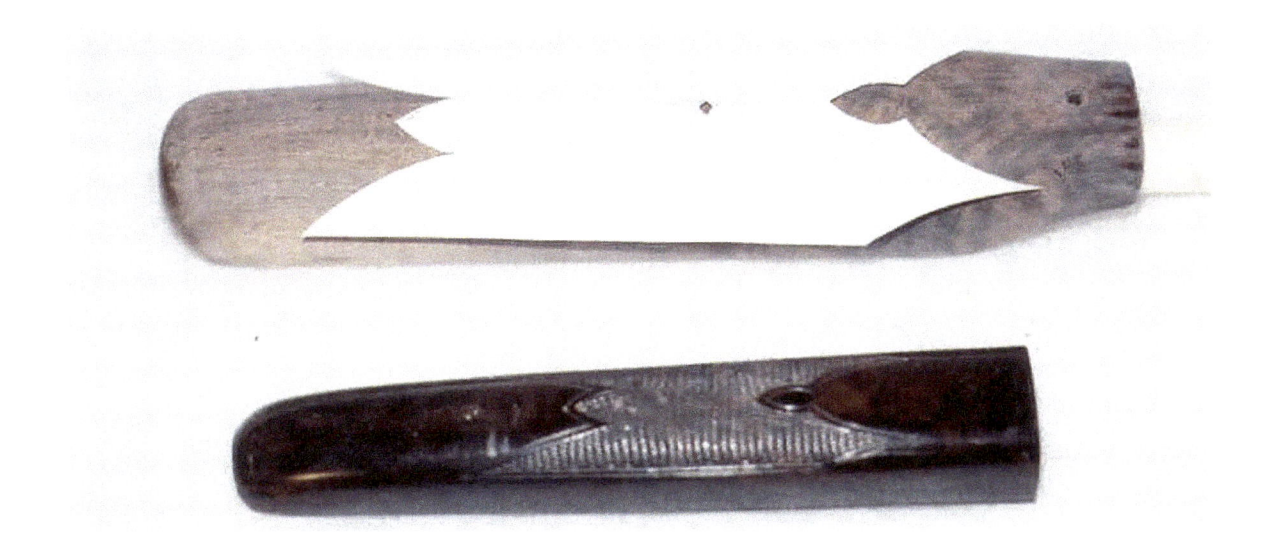

I have read of Stockmakers and other similar professions using a variety of special paper to copy or transfer a pattern, I use plain old, cheap old, typing paper. With the pattern on the paper, and cut out, I place it on the wood.

Depending upon the size of the pattern, I may cut small quarter inch diamonds in the pattern and use tape on the pattern to anchor it to the wood showing through the small cutout diamonds. Most often I will use short (half an inch), narrow (quarter inch wide) pieces of tape to secure the pattern in place. On multi piece patterns, the taping and holding arrangement can become a mess and difficult to get a line on the wood.

In this case it wasn't necessary. I held the pattern in place and used a white pencil to trace around the pattern.

There are times when a piece of wood just checkers well: The lines space out easily, there are no run overs, the wood cuts cleanly and the figured grain shows through, and everything goes like it is supposed. The Springfield forearm was one of those jobs. True, it was a fill in pattern, but …. Well, take a look at the next picture, and you decide.

Sometimes, I just put the piece of wood on the bench, and periodically glance at it, trying to decided what kind of pattern to create to compliment the wood coloring and grain structure. A Customer in Indiana, who later became a good friend, allowed me a free hand in creating a pattern for the stock I built for his ASE 90.

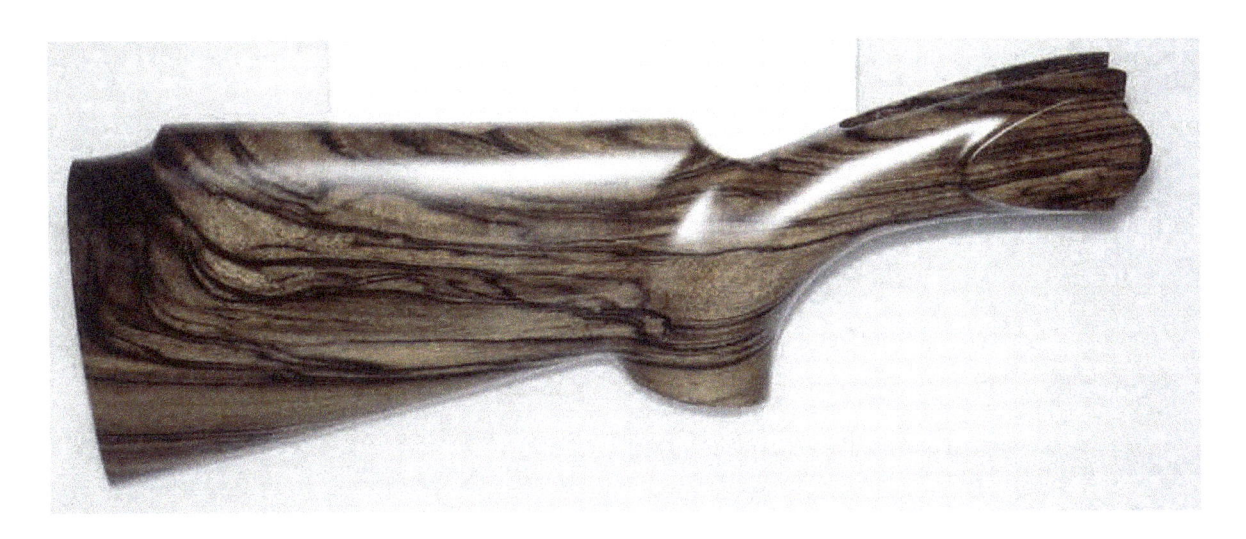

This stock lay on the bench for several days before it surrendered to my white pencil. When all of the "wet out" was over, I had a nice fill in pattern which I felt complimented the stock.

There is a young lady in Indiana that asked me to refinish and checker the stock on her Beretta 682. After looking over a multitude of checkering patterns on guns passing through the Gun Club where she shot, and then looking at books illustrating checkering, she chose a pattern from a very old Reinhart Fajen catalogue, but she did allow me to suggest a few minor changes that met her approval. While at the club, over the old finish, I used a white pencil to sketch in a draft pattern, one she approved of.

Once the wood was refinished, I referred to my notes and a couple of digital pictures and pulled out my white pencil. What had been so easy to draft onto the wood in her presence, turned out to be a bit more difficult. With a series of different size fleur dis leis on clear plastic transparency stock, I selected one that would appear right on both the buttstock and forearm.

I spent several hours one afternoon drawing the fleur dis leis out, copying it onto transparency stock, enlarging it on the copier, and making a copy of the larger version on transparency stock. That was the easy part! Cutting them out with an exacto knife was an experience, but in the end I had a set of patterns of different sizes. Because the buttstock was one of Wenig's New American styles, I did not have to worry about the sides matching. One side was deeply inletted for the pad of the shooter's thumb.

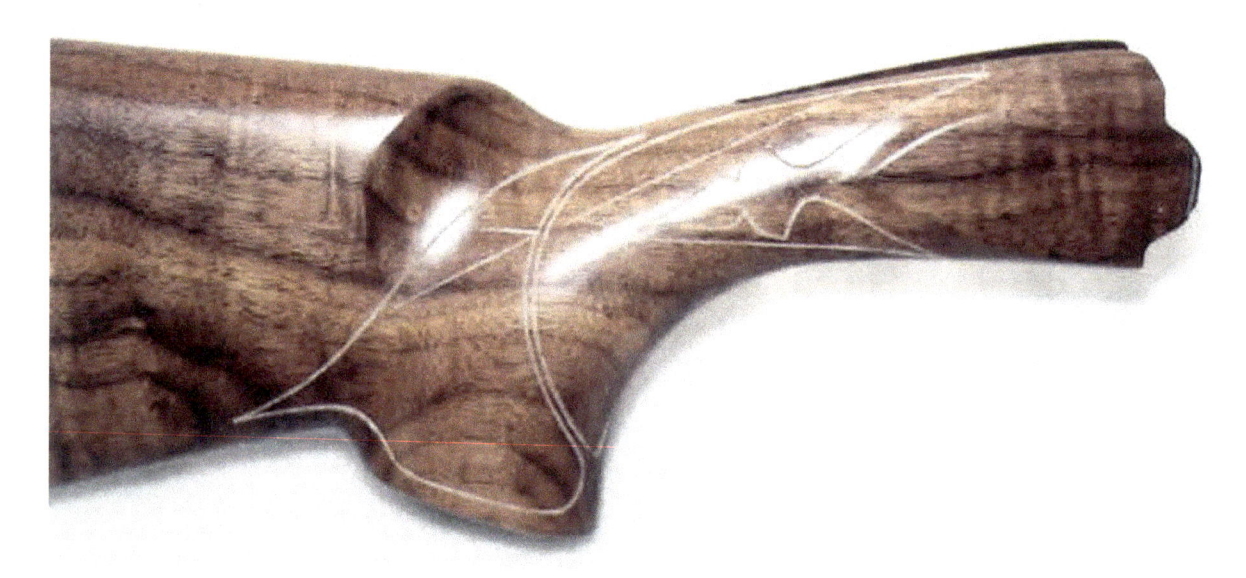

Feeling like I was on a down hill role, I plunged directly into laying out a pattern on the forearm. The Customer had some ideas on what she wanted, but I wanted to take it a little further. It is amazing how far one's talent/ability can be stretched when there is a white pencil in one's hand rather than a checkering tool.

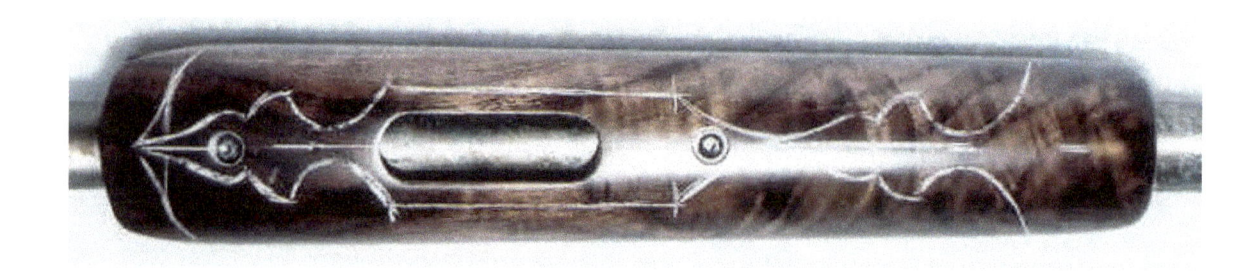

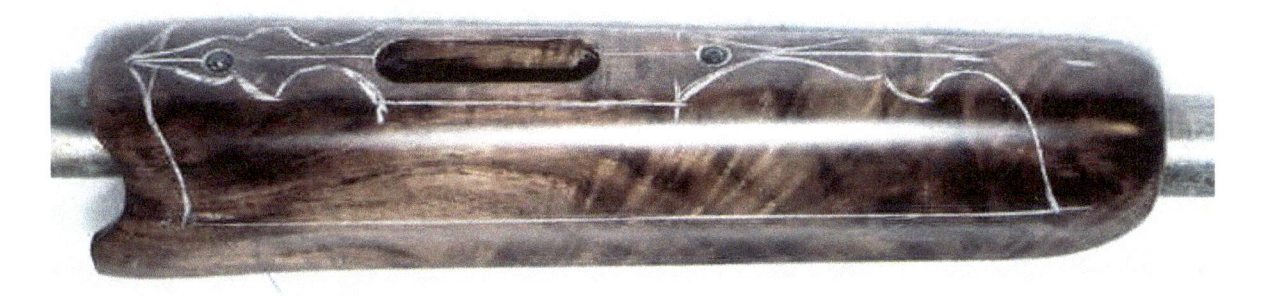

I spoke earlier of having a collection of paper checkering patterns, well, after cutting the border lines of this pattern with a shortened 60 degree edges and a vernier, I made a tracing of the pattern. I may never cut it again, but it resides in the checkering pattern files with the name of the customer written across it.

So above is the end result but getting there is half the fun. To achieve this pattern I positioned the fleur at the bottom using the line I had drawn down the center line of the forearm as a guide, and used a sharp white pencil to draw it in. I then moved the fleur to the top of the forearm, again using the centerline, and drew it in.

Notice the tic marks at the four corners of the hole through which the forearm latch will come through: Those are my boundary marks. I use them to establish line junctions, or the start of a curve. Certainly not rocket science, but they work. I draw the curves of most of my patterns, such as this one, free hand. I could never master a French curve well enough to depend on duplicating a line. I have several I use for specific purposes but using them to lay out checkering is an art I have not mastered.

Once satisfied with the pattern, I then edit it. The lines that are heavy are wetted out and replaced with a thinner line. Lines that do not match, when there are two or more similar junctions, I double check, and usually end up thinning or slightly repositioning them. Changing the position or thickness of a line is a matter of a minute or less at this stage. Tracking in a border line that does not match an opposing border line can occupy an hour correcting.

I would advocate the use of creating different sized fleur dis leis onto transparency stock. It is easy to do, and it is cheap. And there are other "figures" which can be of use when transferred to transparency stock as well.

When all of the work was over, I thought the wood came out very nicely. I just wish my skills with a camera were a little better!

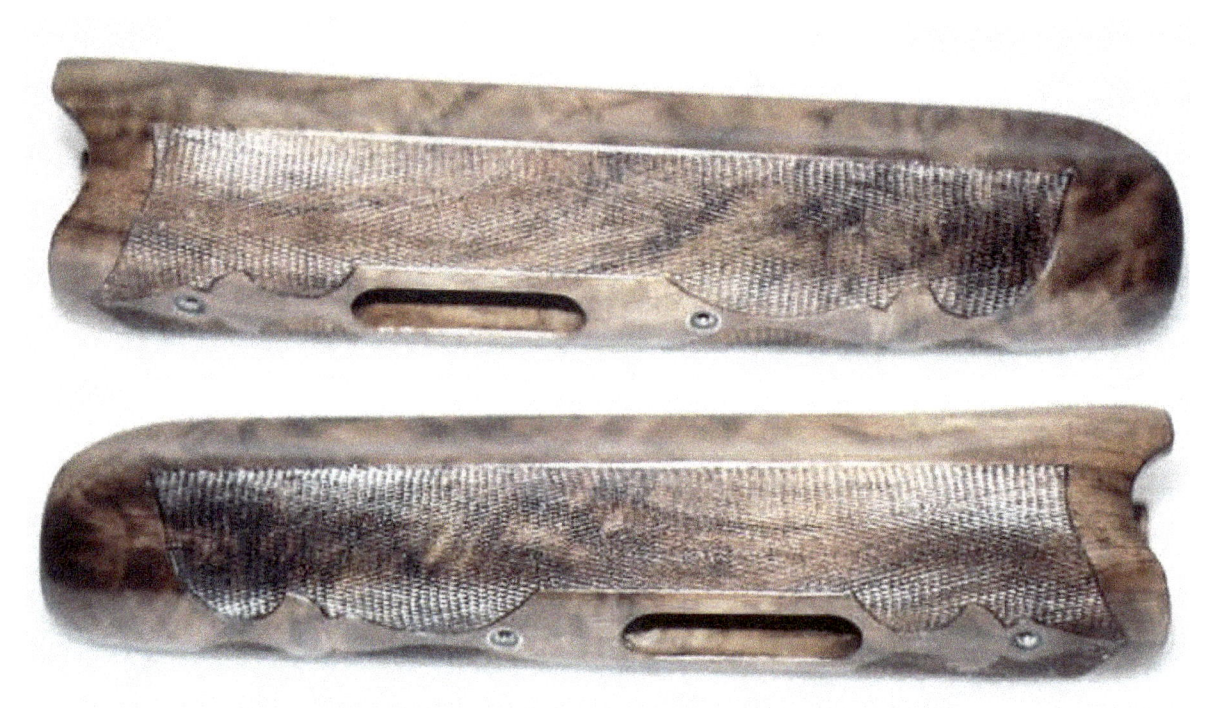

I was lucky enough to have followed a very fine Skeet Coach in doing the final fitting of the stock. I firmly believe that the Wenig New American design stock helps shooters stay in their gun and keep their head down. Notice I did not extend the checkering pattern up into the area at which the thumb pad comes in contact with the portion of the stock inletted for it. I did it once, and later modified it when the checkering ate through my glove.

I have heard, "I'll bet you can't do that again," so many times I now just smile and answer, "Probably not." Such was the case with the forearm for an LC Smith 12 Gauge with auto ejectors on which I had free rein to checker the buttstock and forearm. The forearm was from some extremely dense and highly figured Claro Walnut obtained from Cecil Fredi, Las Vegas, NV. After completing the application of the finish, I felt the wood would take twenty-eight lines per inch with ease, if I was slow and careful.

The pattern I wanted did cause some problems, I just couldn't decide what I wanted to cut. Now this is not a unique problem for me, for a cure I sit back with a stack of Double Gun Journals and thumb through them until I find something that I want to cut. The idea of the "pinnacle" design on the LC Smith forearm came from several sources and was then modified to fit the shape of the wood at hand.

Once the forearm was completed, I realized the fun had just began, the buttstock was yet to be cut. Deciding the pinnacle portion of the pattern was all that I really wanted to transfer to the buttstock, I used my time proven method of transferring a pattern, or in this case, a portion of the pattern. I used a pencil and paper rubbing.

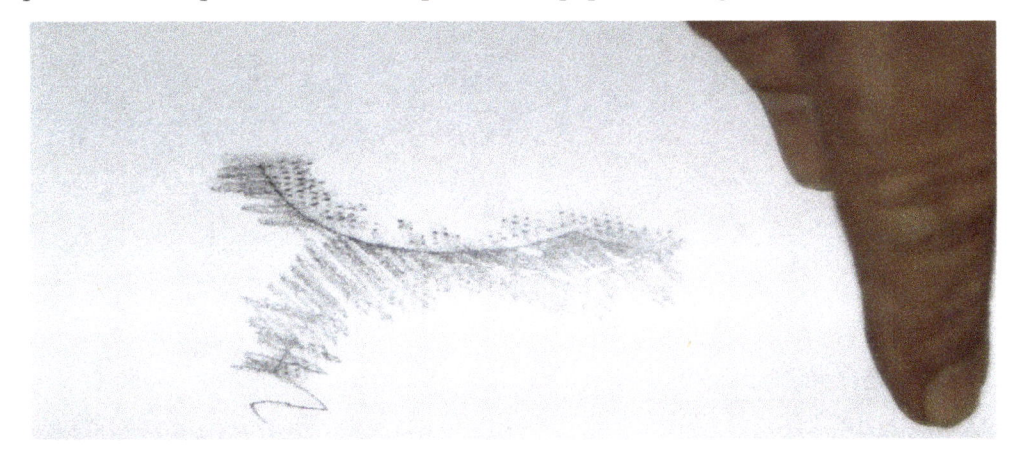

Cutting the correct outline of the pattern is the hardest part of the transfer to me. However with the help of a sharp pair of scissors – I had to quit cutting paper with my shop scissors – and a little patience, I manage to complete the task. In proofing the pattern on the paper, I place it over that portion of the pattern copied and determine how close is the copy.

With the paper copy of the pinnacle, I determine the correct position on the grip area of the buttstock. In this case, my guide line is the centerline down through the grip area of the stock. I feel that it is important to keep the pattern balanced. No, it is not a checkering law chiseled into wood and placed on a mound somewhere, it is just my feeling and the way I checker. I transfer the pattern onto the buttstock with a white Marks Anything pencil with a point I file to a sharp point. If I need to change it, just a little moisture on a finger tip...

With the pattern on the buttstock in white, I use a shortened sixty degree edger to track in the outline of the pattern and then the master lines. Please note that the Master Lines are at a four-to-one ratio, in duplication of the forearm.

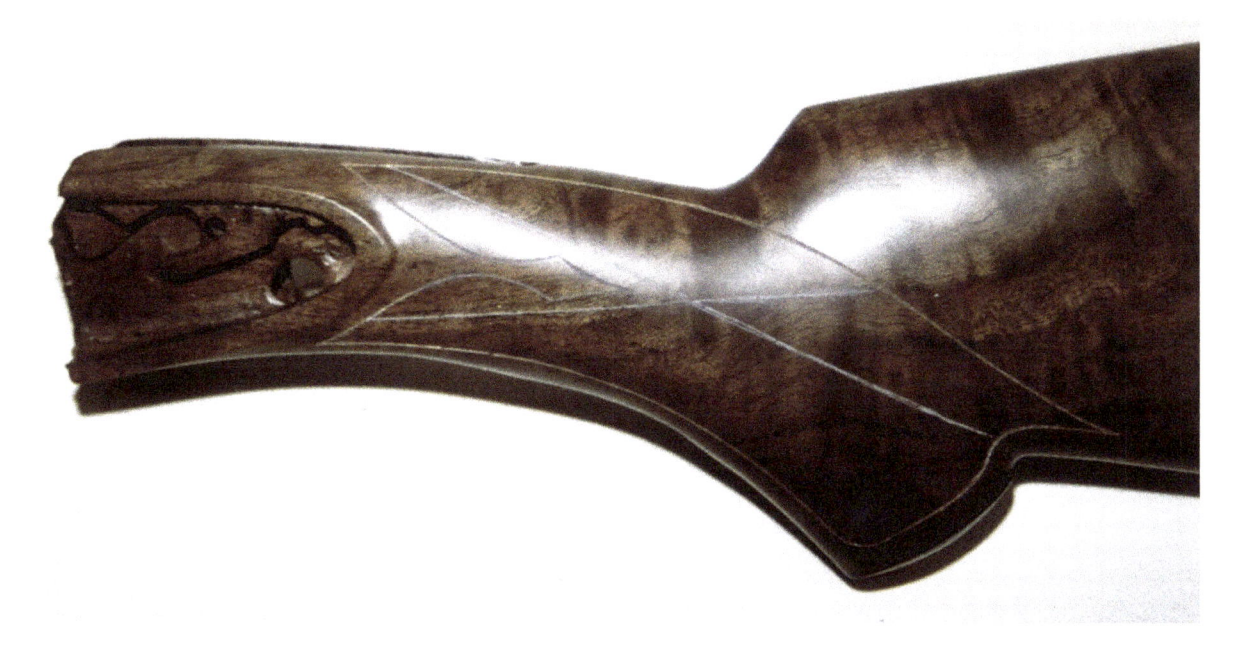

Just a little note here, in most cases my checkering is unique, and for me, and a growing number of others, is easy to recognize as checkering coming from my shop. I have recently provided pictures of the completed work to several customers wanting to include the pictures with the appraisal of the weapon for insurance appraisal. Last week I received an inquiry from an insurance company wanting a quote on replacing a stock I had made several years ago. The gun had been stolen. I don't think the insurance agent was a shooter, he certainly had no appreciation of fine wood or multi-panel checkering!

Once the checkering was laid out and the checkering lines tracked in on the left grip, I wanted to transfer the checkering patter to the right side. To do this, I used the pencil rub on paper to establish the placement of the sidelock. I then notch the paper to allow it to seat on the wood below the sidelock.

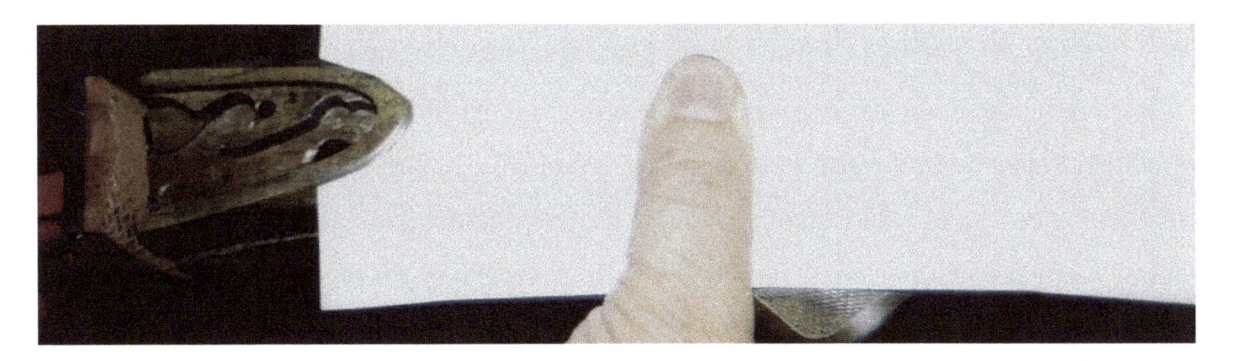

Holding it in place, I use a pencil to rub over the pattern. Since all I wanted was the pinnacle, I held the paper in place with my thumb. Had I wanted more of the pattern, I would have taped the paper to the stock by cutting small diamonds in the paper and applying tape over them, establishing the bond I would need.

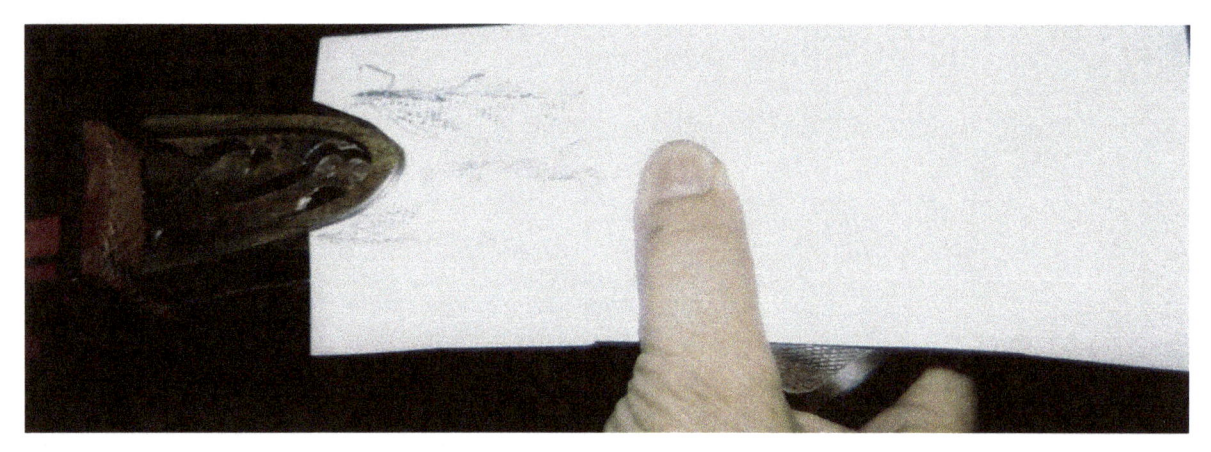

When cutting the rubbing from the paper, be very careful. Most times, unless I am feeling foolishly brave, I wear the magnified visor. Also use a good pair of scissors, but I believe I have already stated that. When the pinnacle is cut out of the paper, lay it over the original which was copied. If the paper copy is exact, or very close, great, if not, do it again.

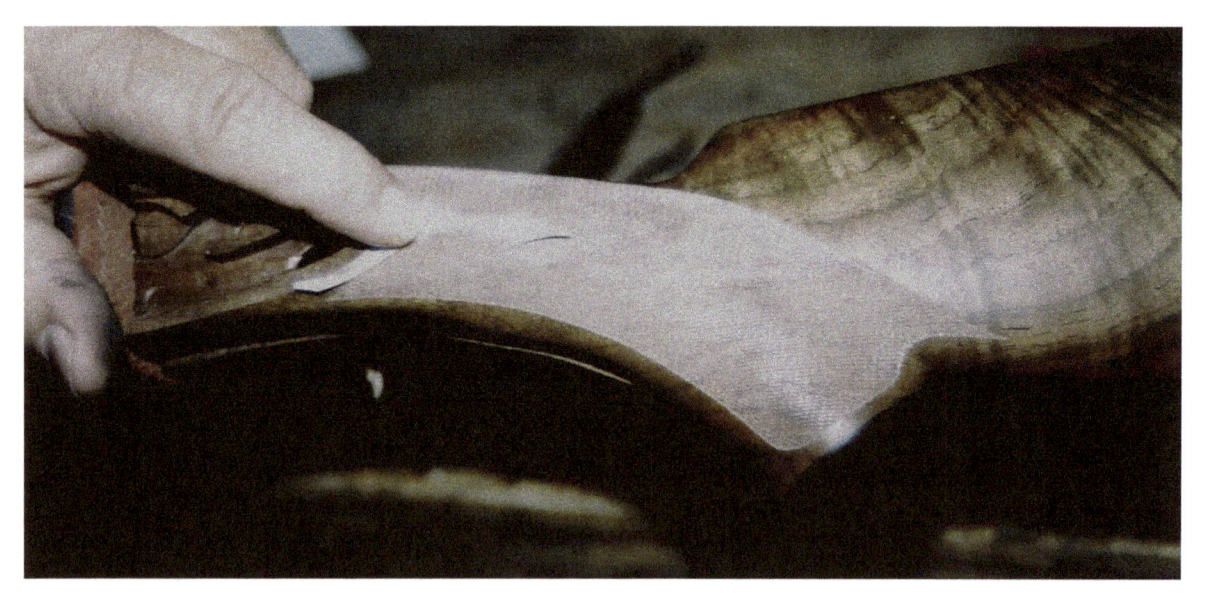

If you are satisfied with the copy, place it aside. You want to use the piece from which it was cut. Place the larger piece in position, letting the tip of the pinnacle fall on the centerline drawn in on the grip area as shown. Once it is in place, and you are satisfied, use small strips of tape to lock it into position. I use very narrow pieces of packaging tape, but masking tape does in a pinch. I cut the pieces from the end of the tape, about an eighth inch wide. Just a few of these will secure the pattern in place.

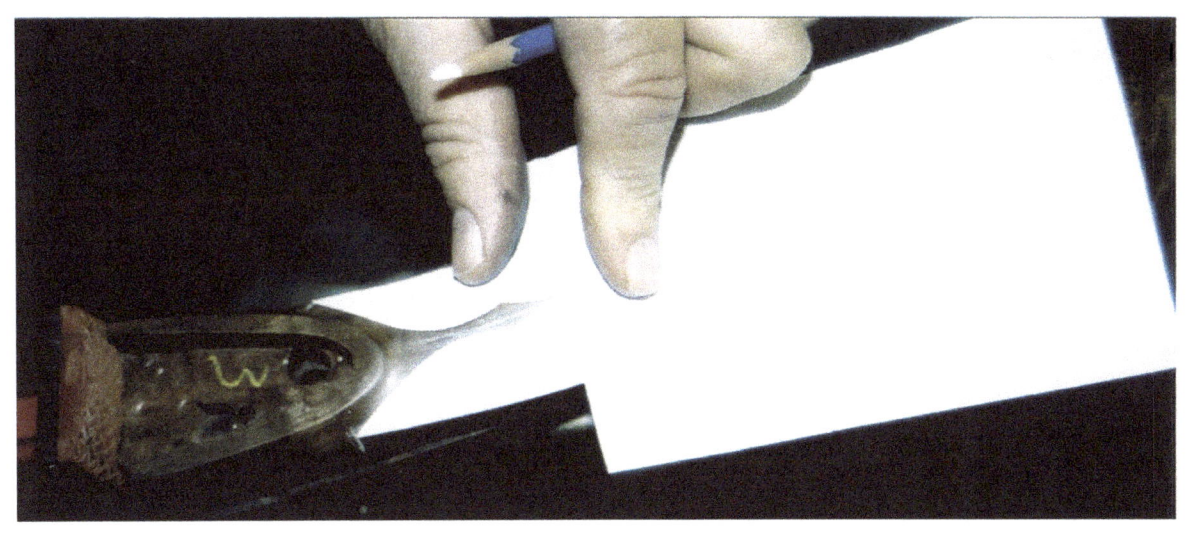

Now use the white pencil – filed to a very sharp point – to carefully outline the pinnacle on the stock. As you are doing this, remember that when you begin cutting the lines of the pinnacle, you will be cutting <u>outside</u> of the lines, not on the line!

Section 5

Developing Patterns

Sometime in the early seventies, I believe about '74 or 75, I first used a checkering pattern which I continually modify and still use. Somehow over the years, and I cannot explain exactly why, I refer to it as the "Turnip Seed" pattern. I have cut it on both one and two piece rifle stocks, one and two piece shotgun stocks, and three sets of pistol grips which the owner wanted to match his rifle stock.

The pattern is unique, and I know of no one copying it. Many times, I have recognized my work at shooting events and gun shows and tried to remember who had commissioned the work. Several times I have informed the present owner of the work of its origin and have received additional work with the condition that the same checkering pattern be used.

This is the pattern which I now call the Stock Shop Standard Pattern.

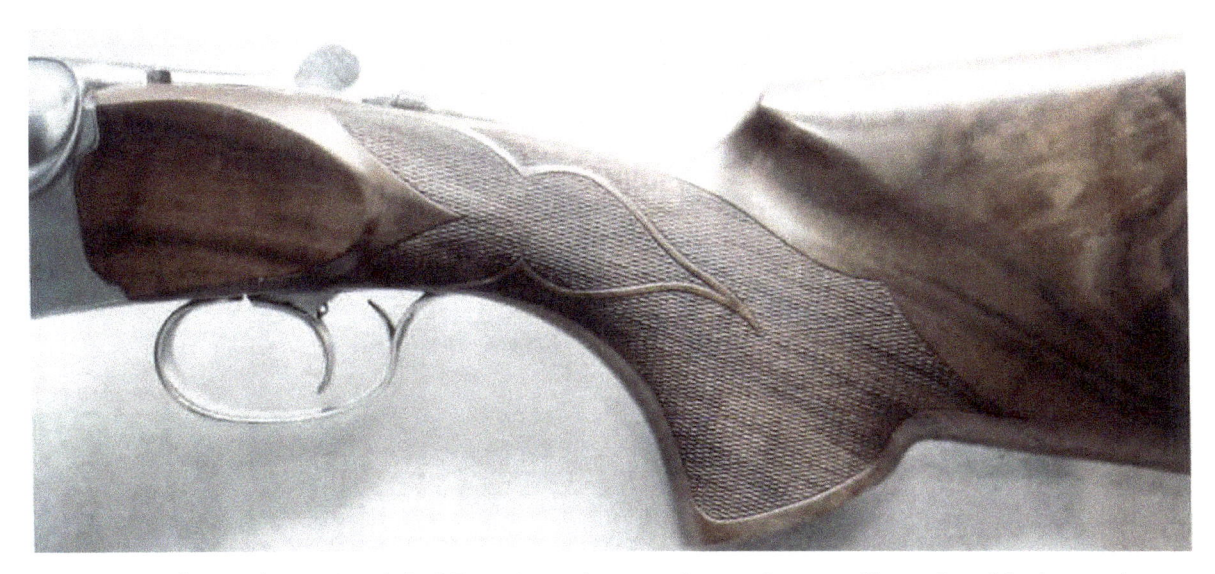

Stocks such as Wenig's New American style stock as well as thumbhole stocks, or those with altered contours to accommodate whatever, present a challenge in developing a checkering pattern because both sides of the stock do not have the same contour. A trap stock for a Browning I received from a Customer presented such a challenge. On Wenig's New American style stock, one side of the grip area is deeply scalloped to accommodate the shooters hand, while the opposite side of the stock is pretty much normal. In creating a checkering pattern for the first New American stock I checkered, I decided to maintain something which would show on both sides of the grip area. First concentrating on the right side – the buttstock was for a right handed shooter I drafted out my pattern, then cut the master lines in, and then tracked the checkering lines in before approaching the left side of the buttstock.

With the right side pattern cut in, and waiting for the lines to be deepened, I used a piece of typing paper to trace the upper part of the pattern by rubbing over the pattern with the flat of a number two pencil.

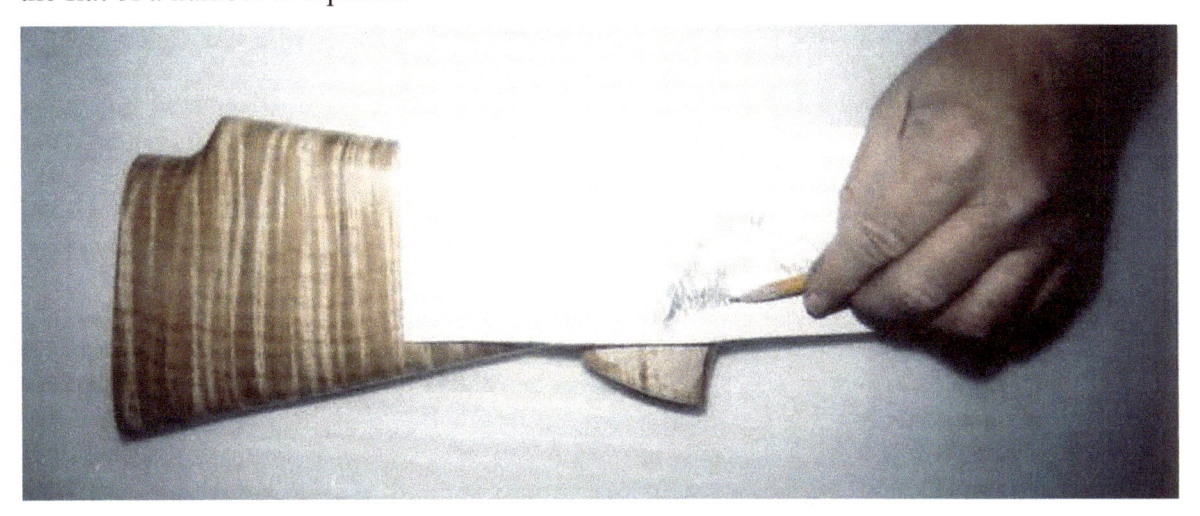

One of the secrets to obtaining a pattern in such a manner, is to be very carefully to cut on the inside of the tracing. You will be using your white pencil to trace along the outside of the pattern. Just to double check your accuracy, lay the cut-out pattern over the original and see how good you are. If it is off to any measurable degree, do it over.

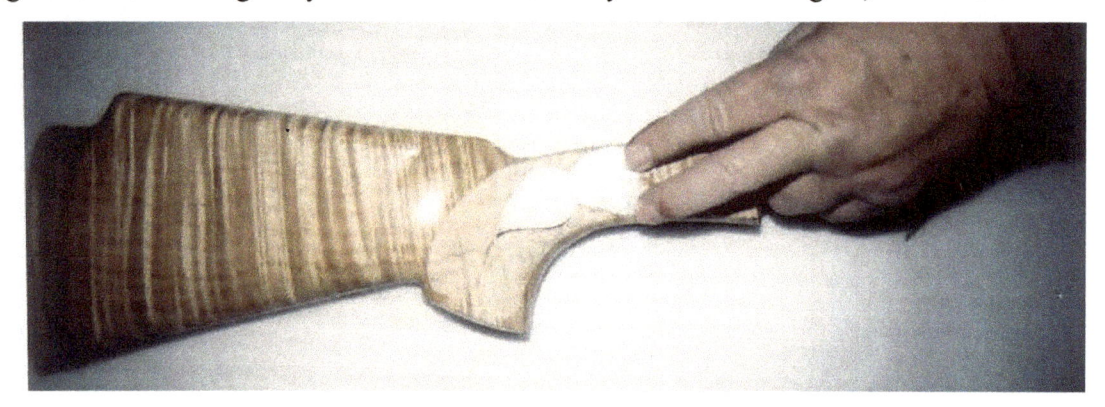

Once you are satisfied with the size and shape of the copy, try positioning it on the other side. I have done this little exercise many times, and have a small selection of the "Turnip Seed" of the pattern on clear transparency stock. It really helps in that you can see through the transparency and see how the pattern is placed on the grain and figure of the wood.

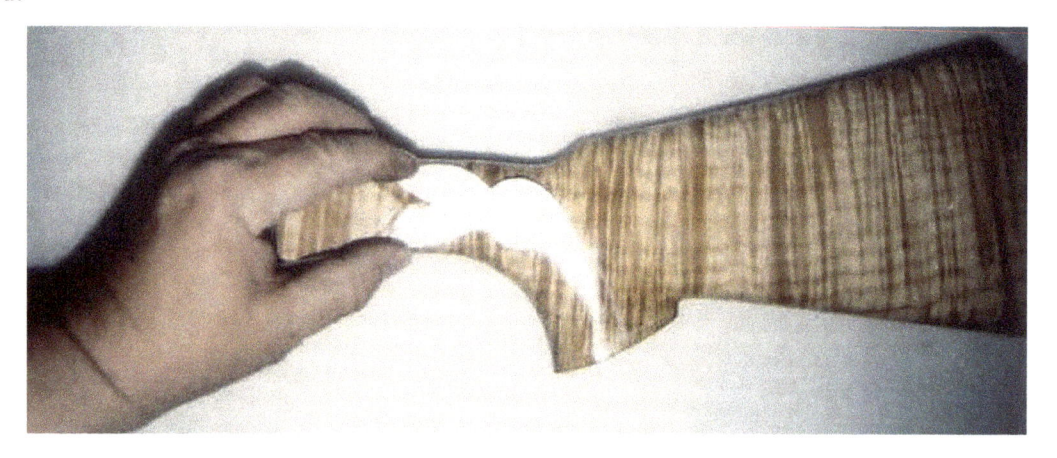

Because the contours of this design of stock are so different, I use a while pencil to draft in the outline of the pattern rather than try to exactly duplicate the pattern from the opposing side. Because I wanted the ribbon of the pattern to show up on the maple buttstock, I used some stain on the ribbon to illustrate how the two patterns, over differing contours of the same buttstock, can compliment one another. Oh, the stain was later eliminated from the checkering diamonds and lightened on the ribbon. The contrast was appealing.

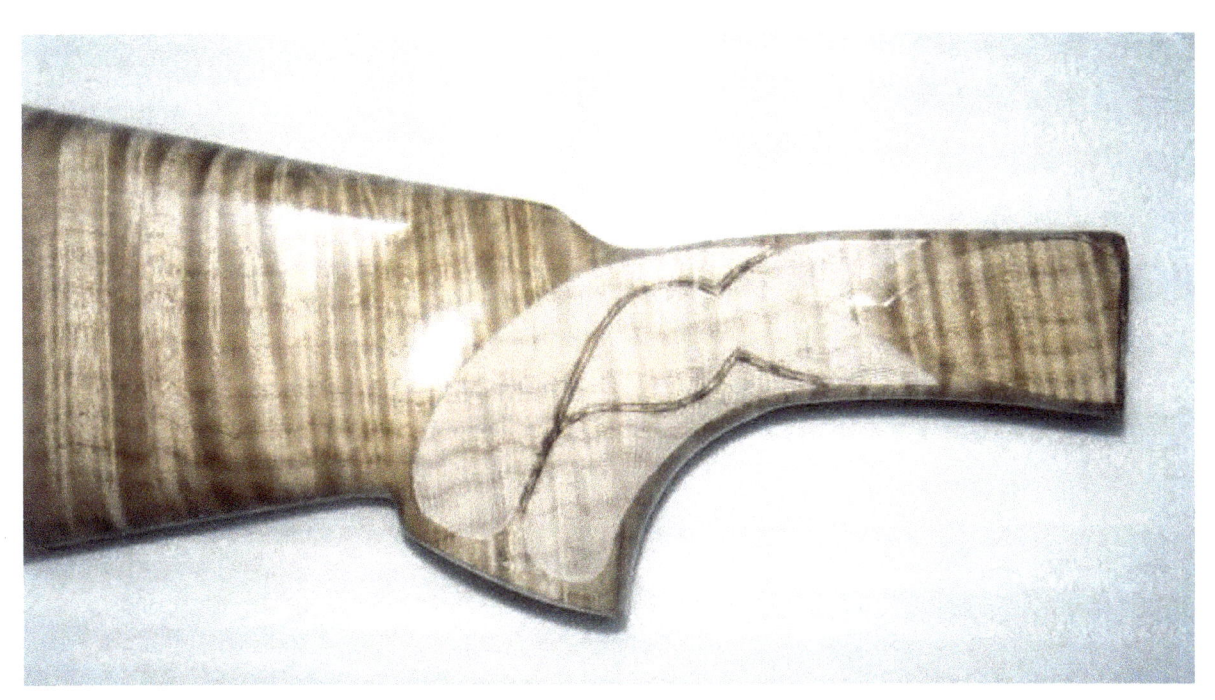

On the forearm accompanying the preceding buttstock, I had a basic idea of what I wanted to do, and on the third or fourth pass settled into a pattern I would later cut. It was a little more elaborate than the buttstock, but clearly something that could be identified in a gun rack from a distance. If I come to a point where I just want to get some lines on the wood – called anal frustration – I put the piece aside and plan to pick it up another day. A beavertail forearm for a twenty gauge L.C. Smith lay on my work bench for almost a month before I was able to develop a pattern I liked.

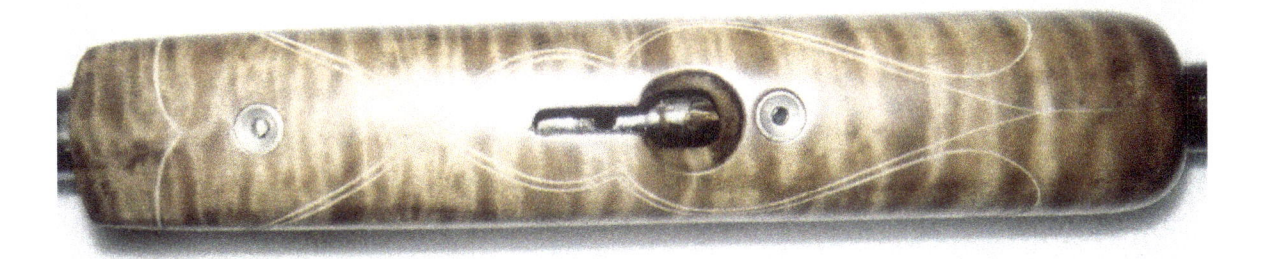

This piece did not spend but a few minutes on the bench between the time I drew the pattern on and when I began cutting it. This was one piece of work I wanted to see done.

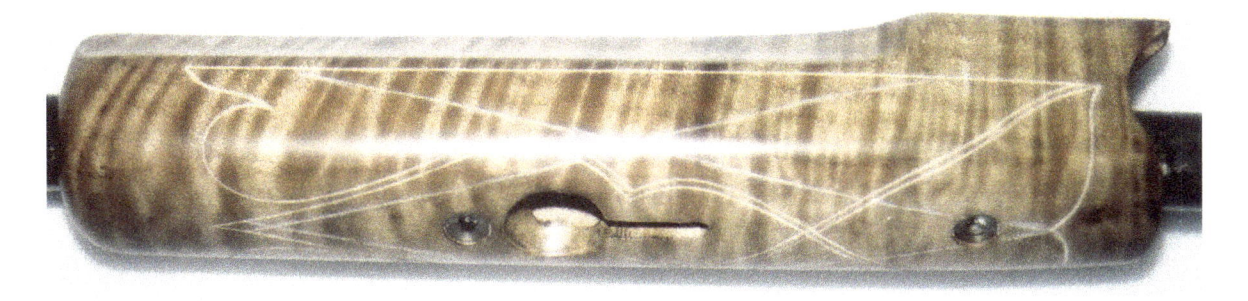

When laying out patterns such as this one, use the checkering ration guide to determine how the master lines, and thus the checkering lines will fall in relationship to the ribbon of the pattern. Having failed to do this a few times (few? Ha) over the years, I can vouch for the surprise when the error jumps up off of the pattern and screams "*Screw Up*."

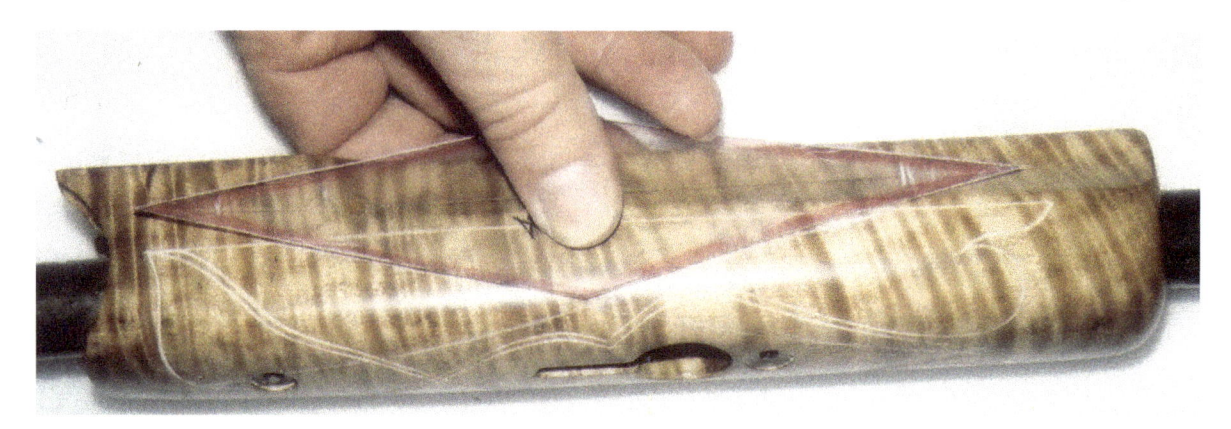

One thing you will quickly discover is how fast, and with so very little provocation, the diamond template can move around on the surface of the item to be checkered. I have yet to find a transparent material that does not slide around. Thus, there are small strips of masking tape always available on the rim of my checkering lamp.

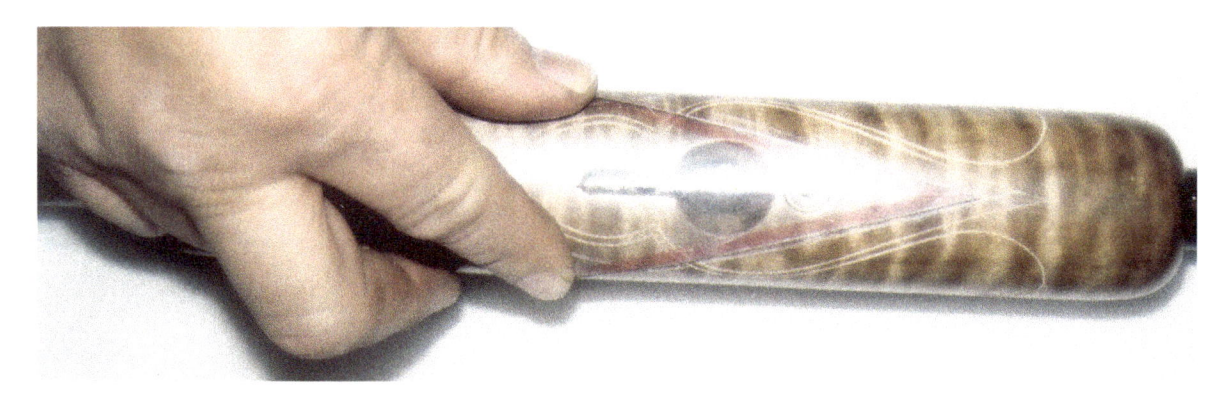

The stain was used to make the ribbons of the pattern stand out. This photo was taken before the ribbons were cleaned up and the excess stain removed in the cutting process of taking the checkering lines to full depth. The work shown on this and previous pages was done for a very special friend. An avid shooters, in his mid-seventies – I wanted the work to look nice, but more important than anything, I wanted it to fit him like the proverbial glove. I have since watched him shoot his K-20 with this wood on it, and it fits, and he shoots great. And if he happens to miss a bird every once in a while, it's the fault of the stock maker.

As I do with most stocks, I settle back with my trusty white pencil and began drawing in "what if" lines. Needless to say, the lines are easily removed, and leave no mark on the stock, and I have removed a lot of lines before I finally settled on a design I like.

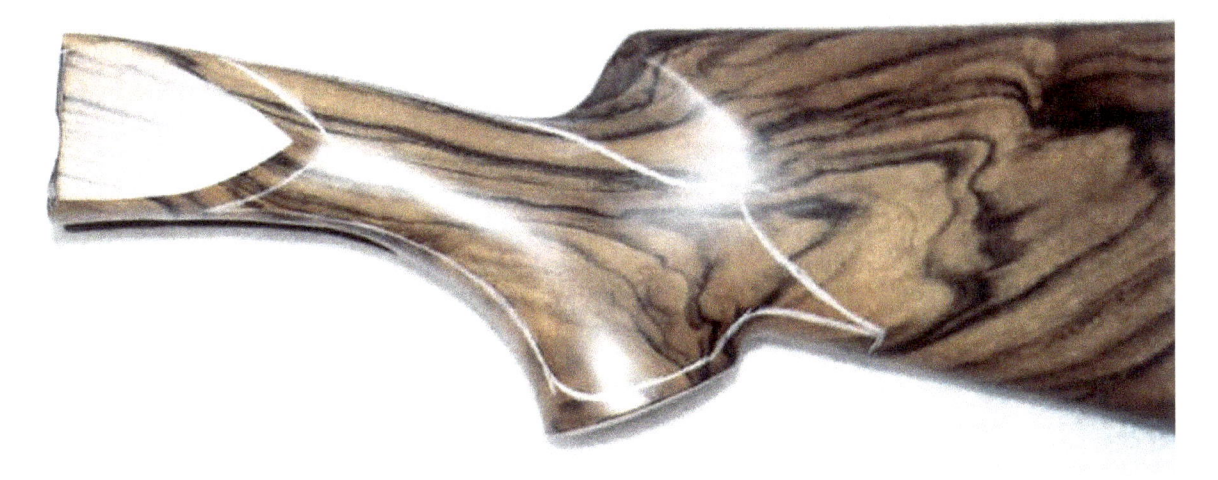

As shown in the preceding picture, the pattern originally selected for this piece was replaced with a fill in pattern following the contour of the stock. I felt the point pattern made the grip area look too short, and went for the fill in pattern. As the stock was a nice grade of English walnut, and was well finished, I chose to cut a 3 ½ to 1 ratio diamond in 24 lines per inch. I find this ratio looks nice when cut 24 lines per inch. With the master lines and outline of the pattern cut, a moist paper towel quickly removes the white pencil lines and leaves me with my work.

In most cases, I checker the forearm first. Usually during the process, I will play with the forearm a little to lay out some ideas for a pattern which will match the buttstock. In most cases this process works pretty well, but sometimes it can lead to an absolute nightmare. Especially when there is a large opening for the forearm latch, such as in on a Browning and Kolar over and under.

The forearm to be checkered is for an LC Smith, Ideal Grade, 12 Gauge, single trigger, automatic ejectors. The wood for the forearm was an excellent piece of American Walnut obtained from Cecil Fredi Gun Stock Blanks. After filling to the forearm iron, and then to the barrels, the wood was finished with in a Satin Finish FullerPlas, this gun is no closet Queen, but a gun that has gone afield and will be back in the fields when complete.

The first step in ANY checkering job – regardless of what is to be checkered – is to define the area to be checkered.

To begin with, I like to establish a center line on forearms, and what I call a flow line on grip areas. Start with the forearms. When establishing a center line the length of a forearm, first be sure that points of reference such as forearm latch inletting and forearm bushings and screws are centered. You may find that they are not. I use several methods for determining the centerline of a forearm. One method I have used for years is perhaps the most simple and requires the least amount of effort.

First, near one end of the forearm area to be checkered, place a small tic mark _across_ the forearm. This is to be used as a reference mark for future acts. Next, get a piece of typing, copy or tablet paper and cut off a strip about an inch wide the length of the sheet. Place the strip of paper across the forearm _at the tic mark_. Grasp the ends of the strip of paper and pull then taunt around the forearm. Make small tick marks with a pencil on the paper at the point at which the side of the forearm ends and the top flat begins, or in the case of a forearm with a rounded top, at the point at which the barrel channel begins.

Remove the paper strip, and fold the paper lengthways with the two lines just made matching. The crease caused by the fold should be an equal distance between the two lines. Place the paper strip back over the forearm at the same point - tic mark – on the forearm. At the point of the crease, make a tic mark on the forearm. This is your centerline. Repeat this process for the remaining end of the forearm.

With a centerline established at each end of the forearm, use a straight edge to establish a line between the two, and that is the centerline of your checkering reference.

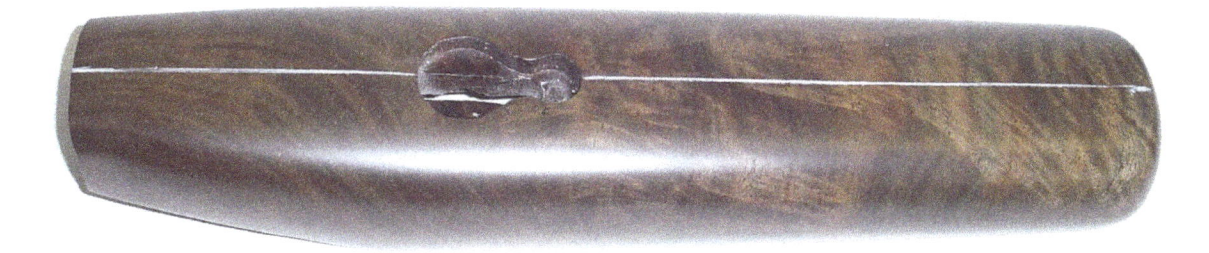

With the centerline established, use a clear plastic template of the checkering ratio to establish the master lines. Yes, it does seem early to establish the master lines, but wait, the purpose will become apparent.

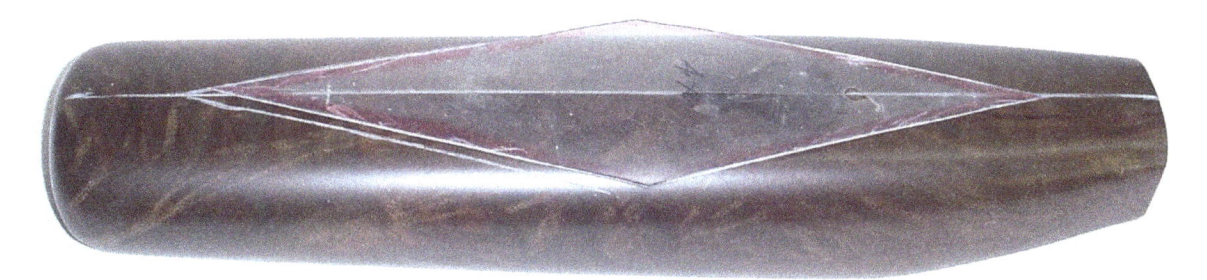

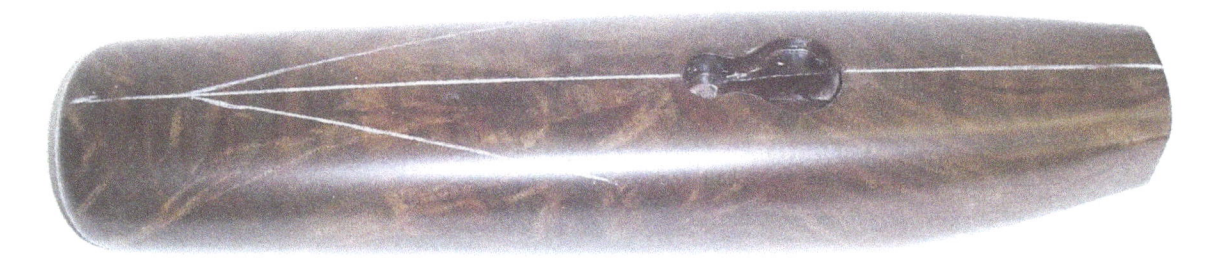

Make a small tic mark on the side of the forearm, to identify the boundaries of the checkering pattern on the sides of the forearm. These small marks will provide the location of the "ends" of the checkering pattern.

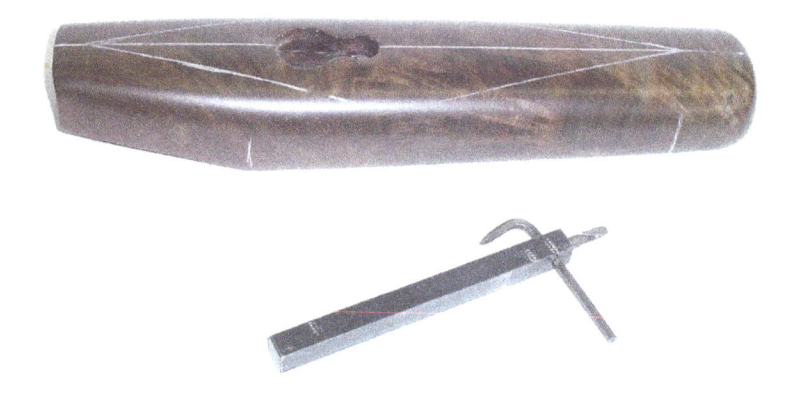

The border lines which parallel the top of the forearm are the easiest to make and can get you in a bunch of trouble. Rule number one when making these lines. Do not extend the lines all of the way out to the anticipated end of the pattern. Draw them short of their intended destination. I use a small parallel gauge to make these lines. Adjusting the scribe to the length desired, lay the scribe holder across the forearm, and lightly drag the scribe across the forearm. I start the scribe line in the middle of the area I am identifying to be checkered and scribe the line about two thirds of the way to where I think the pattern will end. Then I do the same for the opposite end and then the other side of the forearm. I do not attempt to scribe the line deeply, that is not the task of the scribe. The scribe is to mark and identify the proposed line. In the past, when I have attempted to used the scribe to make a deep line, the scribe point had often followed the grain of the wood on the forearm creating a crooked line that needed attention to correct later.

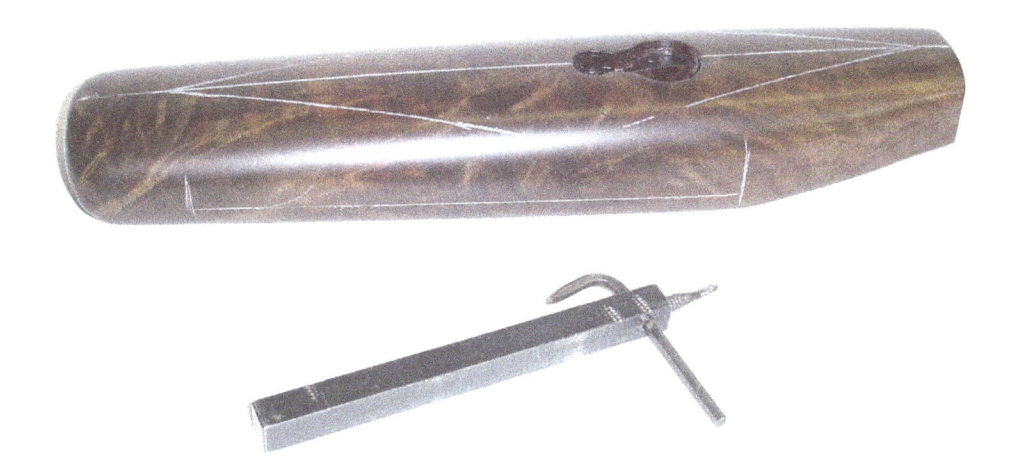

We are not ready to do any serious work until the forearm is mounted onto a fixture - in this case a piece of black pipe.

With the pipe alongside of the forearm, with equal amounts of the pipe excess to the ends, I use a white pencil to mark the pipe at the point I want to drill and tap a hole for an anchoring screw. In this case, because of the current hole in the forearm, I drill and tap the pipe for an 8 x 32 socket head screw.

Once the pipe is prepared and the screw installed, it becomes obvious the mount is unsatisfactory – the two pieces need to be leveled. Ideally, the pipe would ride on the ridge in the forearm separating the two barrels in the center of the forearm.

A small scrap of wood is slipped under the pipe, the pipe centered, and the screw tightened.

Even up side down, it is leveled and ready for placement in the vise. Please note at this point, only the two borders and the master lines are drawn in. I have found when drawing the tentative pattern outline in, having the piece on a pipe and capable of being placed n any desired position is an advantage.

There is another manner in which patterns are developed or created for a specific task. I call it Half and Half. As in all checkering jobs, the first task is to determine the centerline of the forearm to be checkered. With this done, I use the white pencil to lay out the checkering pattern on half of the forearm. When I am satisfied with the pattern I have developed, I use a shortened sixty degree edger to cut the border lines for the half of the pattern I have drawn in. One of the secrets in cutting this part of the checkering pattern is to cut the lines only deep enough to "react" to the pencil rubbing to take place.

Once the outline of the half pattern has been cut, I tape a sheet of copy paper in place right on the center line of the forearm. I then use the flat of a soft lead pencil to rub over the cut lines of the pattern to bring it up onto the paper.

Remove the paper from the forearm, and using a sharp pair of scissors, No, not the ones used to cut sandpaper! Cut the pattern from the sheet of paper. However, we have to have a method of placing the second half of the pattern to the first half, so using the white pencil make a tic mark on the forearm and at the same location, make a tic mark on the paper with the pencil. I do this at two locations. Thus, the edge of the paper at these two locations can be placed at corresponding locations at the centerline of the forearm and the pattern placement will be exact.

Being sure to cut down the inside of the pattern as you will be tracing around it with a white pencil. If you cut down the middle or the outside, the second half of the pattern will be larger and not match the first half.

Reverse the paper pattern, line up the tic marks on the forearm and on the paper, and tape the paper half pattern in place with several thin strips of masking tape. Be very careful in the placement of the paper pattern.

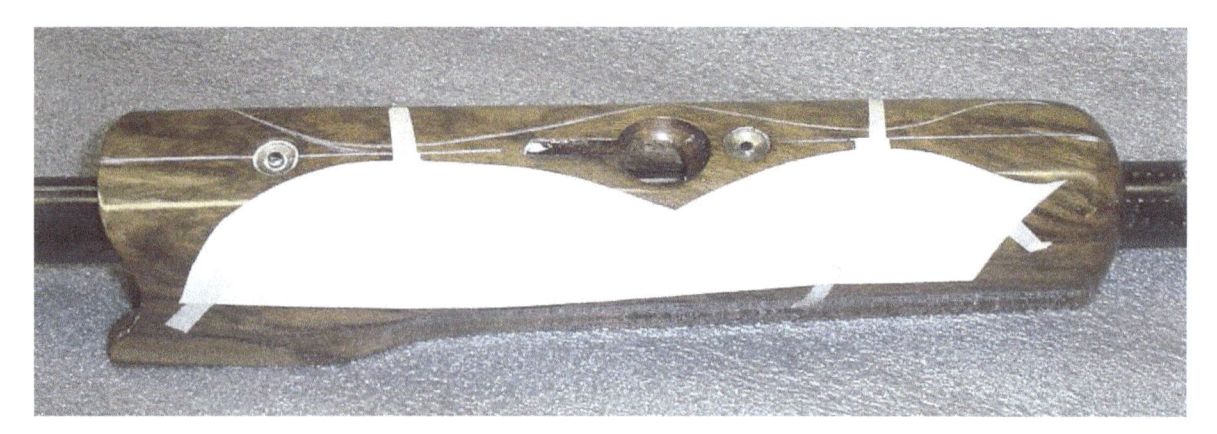

With the pattern in place, carefully use the white pencil to trace along the paper onto the forearm. Before starting, please sharpen the white pencil. The finer line you leave around the pattern, the fewer problems you will have in establishing a line in the correct place. Go very slow and concentrate on laying down only a fine line not a wide conglomeration of lines which will prove impossible to follow. I have stated it earlier, and will repeat it now, patience is an absolute necessity in checkering. And if you feel you are making a mistake and should stop and re-do something such as a sloppily drawn line, STOP and re-do it.

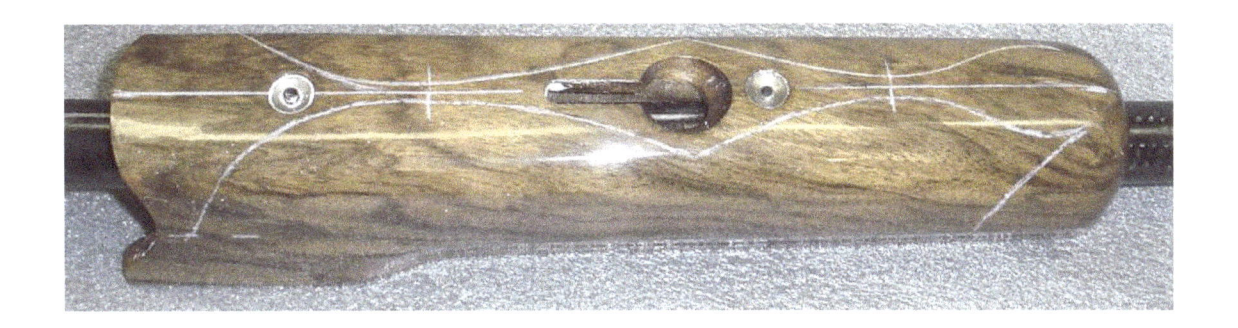

Again, using a shortened sixty-degree edger, cut the border lines. Remember, we traced outside of the pattern. To be sure the patterns will be the same size, cut on the inside of the line. Don't cut deeply just enough to establish the border of the checkering pattern.

The next chore is to lay out the master lines. As we are going to cut two separate panels, we want the master line angle to be the same for both sides. To insure this is so, center the plastic template of the ratio you are going to use – in this case a 4 to 1 – on the centerline of the forearm. Because I will be rotating the forearm around, rather than try to hold it in place while I use the white pencil to trace along the template to form the master lines, I use short pieces of masking tape to secure the ends of the template in place.

The corners of the template can be taped in place with small pieces of tape – as you have done the ends – or they can be held in place while the master lines are drawn. I do it both ways. However, if you tape the corners of the template, be sure to trace the line up to the tape from both sides, and then moving the tape back away from the corner, draw in the line at the corner. Not a big deal, but it can save a few problems if you are doing a short line. In this example we have a nice long line to deal with.

The next step is to extend the master lines to the border lines. To do this a "straight edge' made from transparency stock is used. It is very flexible and will follow the contour of the forearm. Laying an edge of the straight edge along the master line, hold it flat and use the white pencil to trace in the extensions of the master lines. When I first started doing this, I use thin strips of masking tape to insure the straight edge was held in place. Depending on the length and angle of the line involves, I sometimes still do.

The end result will be master lines extended from border to border. To check your accuracy, as both sides of the pattern should be identical, how close to identical do the master lines intersect the border lines on the patterns? They should be almost identical. This is always a good check to determine how the halves of a pattern are laying. Most times measuring the distance is not necessary. Any noticeable difference will rapidly be seen with the naked eye. A double check to extending the lines is to establish a tic mark where the master line should intersect with the border line, after having drawn one in, and checking the position of the straight edge before tracing the line. It is sometimes reassuring to know you are right before committing.

Early in my career (sometimes referred to as *the other life*) I was away from home and my small shop in the garage a great deal – try 152 days a year average for six years – but used the nights of this time to my advantage. I checkered small items, especially forearms and buttstocks and drew out checkering patterns in motel rooms across the south and east. I still refer to these drawings periodically. I developed what I call "reference sheets" of the outline of different buttstocks, and the surface area of forearms. I have sheets for a variety of grip areas for shotguns, to include a Hopkins and Allen single shot, several Belgian doubles (both hammer and hammerless) as well as forearms for L.C. Smiths, Knickerbockers, Sterlingworths, American Arms Co, Parkers, Fox, Stevens, Winchester Model 12's, 21's and 24's, Remington Model 11's, 32's, 58's and D and F grade 1100's and many, many more..

I would lay the sheet out, and with a soft lead pencil, sketch in a proposed pattern. If I liked it, I put it away. If I didn't like it, I threw it away. The ones I have kept over the years occupy three, three-inch three ring binders. There is a fourth binder of the set. It contains "rubbings" of the checkering on a variety of buttstocks and forearms. This binder has helped me many times in determining the correct checkering pattern for a certain grade of gun.

The method I used was to fold the paper in half, draw only one side of the proposed forearm pattern, refold the paper, and trace the image of the just drawn lines through the paper. In this way I achieved a "balanced" pattern.

When developing patterns to checker, I remind myself of the tale of the monkey that reached into vase with the narrow top, grasped a hand full of fruit, and then could not remove his hand without letting go of some of his fruit. Lesson: you will have to cut the pattern you draw. Be sure your imagination and ability are both firmly planted in reality or be prepared to call me.

Section 6
Cutting Impressed Checkering

There are stocks on which the checkering is impressed into the wood, or as some would call it, reversed. And while this does provide a very cost efficient way of providing checkering – if that is what one chooses to call it – I just don't care for it. I believe the most common example of this is the Remington Model 1100 semi-auto shotgun, but there are many of others.

For example's sake, I will illustrate the technique I use for "cutting impressed checkering" and while it may not serve everyone's needs, it has worked for me for many years. The object of the first illustration in a Winchester Model 490 rifle I received in, partially refinished, to have the impressed checkering recut.

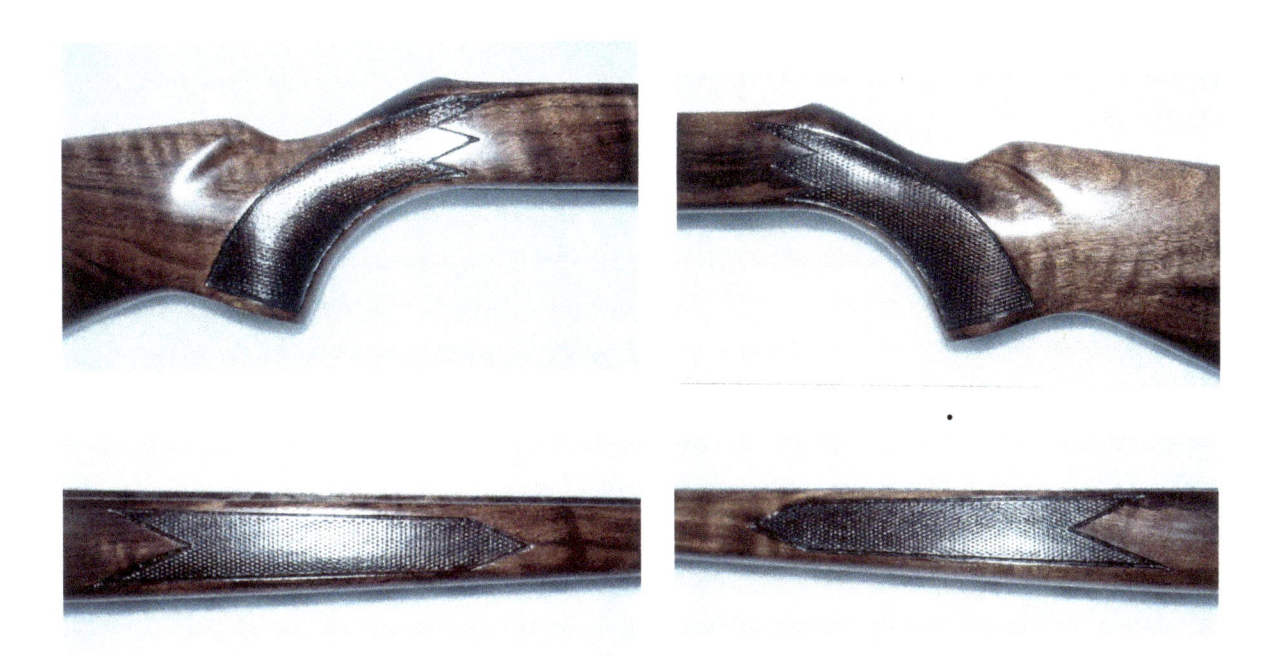

In most cases, using a spacer is almost impossible, and having spent considerable time correcting errors made with a spacer, I use a ninety degree pointer to cut the lines, "eyeballing" the path of the pointer as it cuts one line at a time. For this reason, this task required some experience in checkering.

I start near the center of the pattern and cut a light track down the center of a line of the impressed checkering. Skip a line, and then do another line, and repeat this procedure. After five or six lines, notice that the opposing/crossing lines require some degree of imagination to visualize the line. If one were to cut every line, rather than skip every other line, and then come back and try to cut all of the opposing/crossing, it would be very difficult to maintain the integrity of the pattern. I do cut each of the short lines and several lines closest to the border.

With the lines tracked in one way, continue the process and track the lines in from the opposing direction. After a short while, because you are cutting the same spacing even though it is very wide, you will begin to recognize when the track you are cutting is correct or perhaps a little wide or a little narrow.

I have found it very helpful to begin tracking a line near the middle of what will be the entire line, and after cutting several "half lines," reverse the stock and cut the portion of the line I had left. Inevitably when I do this, I will find a line or two I started a little too near one side or the other. By completing the line from a mid-point I deem correctly located, I can correct the error while it is still a faint track. Try it. It works for me, and may well work for you.

Having cut every other line, it is time to now cut the lines in between. I do this in the same manner as cutting the lines previously, starting near the center, laying a faint track, and carrying it all the way to the border. When all of the lines are completed, I reverse the stock, and complete the space between the starting point I have used and the border.

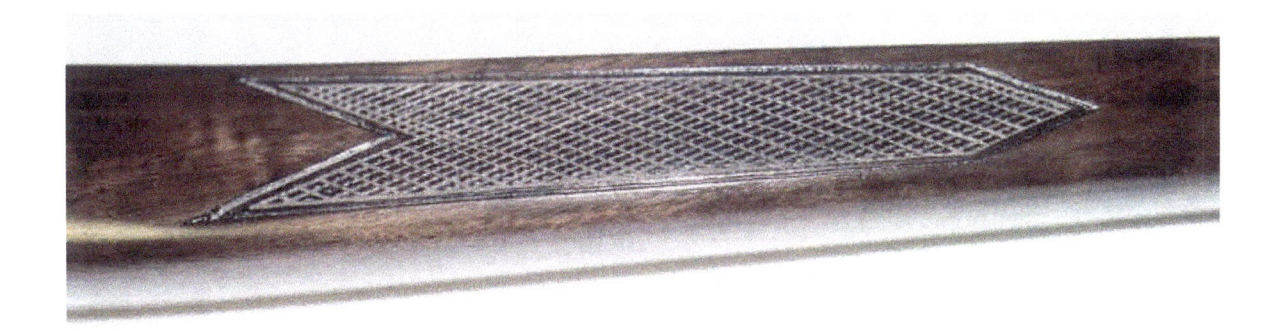

With only one set of lines to be cut from the "every other pattern, don't get over anxious. Don't take anything for granted. It is not easy, and the moment you think it is a crooked line or over travel will bring you back to reality. My son's Skeet coach had a fondness for saying the most import bird to be shot is the next bird, all previous birds shot at were history. It is the same with checkering, the line being cut is the most important line, and deserves your full attention. Take your time. Heck, take a break. And if you are really confident, take your wife shopping – that will bring anyone back to reality quickly!

Start each line the same way. Starting near the center laying a faint track and carry it all the way to the border. When all of the lines are completed in this manner, reverse your work and cut the missing part of the lines.

I am hesitant in saying this, but believe it or not, the hardest part of this checkering job is done. Deepening the lines to full depth remains, and if you maintain your focus to the task at hand, the end result will be something of which to be proud. Remember something from years ago, something about winning a game with offense, but loosing a game on defense? Well, the hard part is done, but if the lines are not deepened evenly, and the track you have laid is not followed, you can really mess up what could have been a good job. So take your time and go slow!

With the entire pattern identified with light tracks, and satisfied the lines are parallel, I begin deepening them. Cutting impressed checkering is very different from cutting checking on a normal piece of wood. The wood you will be cutting on the impressed checkering has been compressed – it is therefore denser – and its pores may be filled with finish or residue of finish. Therefore, in my experience, wood that has been impressed checkered is more likely to chip than other wood.

Do not attempt to deepen the light tracks using the tip of the pointer as a plow! Use the teeth of the cutting edge to gradually deepen the lines. The lines will not only be straighter, but neater, with fewer voids from missing wood.

Depending upon the origin of the stocks being recut, the finish can be a real problem. Some of the older Remington wood was extremely difficult to cut the impressed checkering because "diamonds" were filled with that hard gloss finish that Remington used. I recut a lot of Remington wood, some of it with very nice figure. But I always started with a new pointer, and in several cases, had to replace it before both the buttstock and forearm were complete.

To begin deepening the lines, I start about three quarters to a half inch from the border, and slowly deepen the line to about half depth. I follow this procedure until the entire edge of the pattern is cut right up to the border.

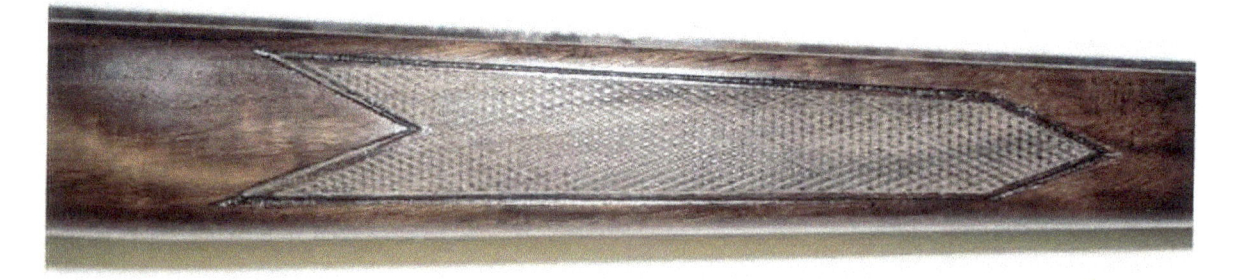

After having cut through several gallons of finish, depending ion the finish you are cutting through, you might consider replacing the pointer on your tool. If it is still cutting well, good, leave it alone. But some finishes, such as the one Remington used for years, will quickly wear out a pointer.

With the line cut to half depth, repeat the process and take the lines to full depth. Do it slowly, let the pointer take away the wood. Don't get impatient and use the pointer as a plow. If you do, it will be easy to detect the lines you are cutting. They will resemble plowed furrows, not checkering lines.

Done! Almost. The lines have been cut to full depth, the diamonds are all pointed and when viewed under a lamp, there is no finish on top of the diamonds to reflect the light.

The borders on this particular pattern consist of a rounded bead of varying depth and width. I use a border tool of medium width to trace over the borders. Unless you really want to dress up your work or intend on doing a lot of checkering, the purchase of a border tool may not be an economical purchase. I do a lot of checkering, and I keep a supply of the border cutters on hand in all three widths.

At this point, I will use a soft bristled tooth brush to apply a little sealer over the checkering, insuring that all of the lines are thoroughly covered.

Now that the forearm is done, it is time to tackle the grip area. The grip area will present some unique challenges when cutting impressed checkering. The grip area is rounded. Most grip areas of the same model gun are not the same outside measurements, but the die pressing in the checkering is the same, and wood can be compressed more or less from stock to stock.

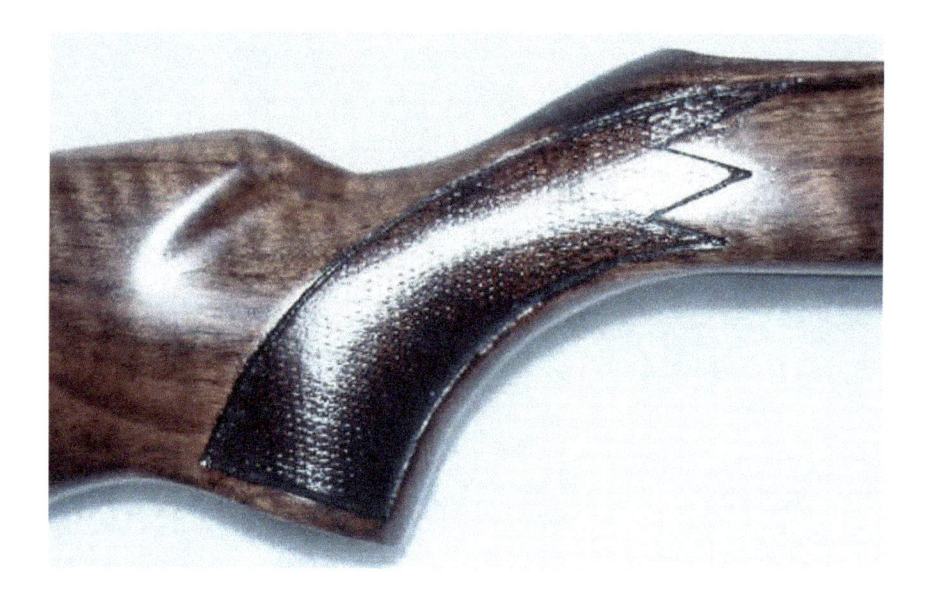

Notice the upper left of the above checkering pattern, how deeply it is pressed into the wood? Now look at the same area on the picture below, same stock.

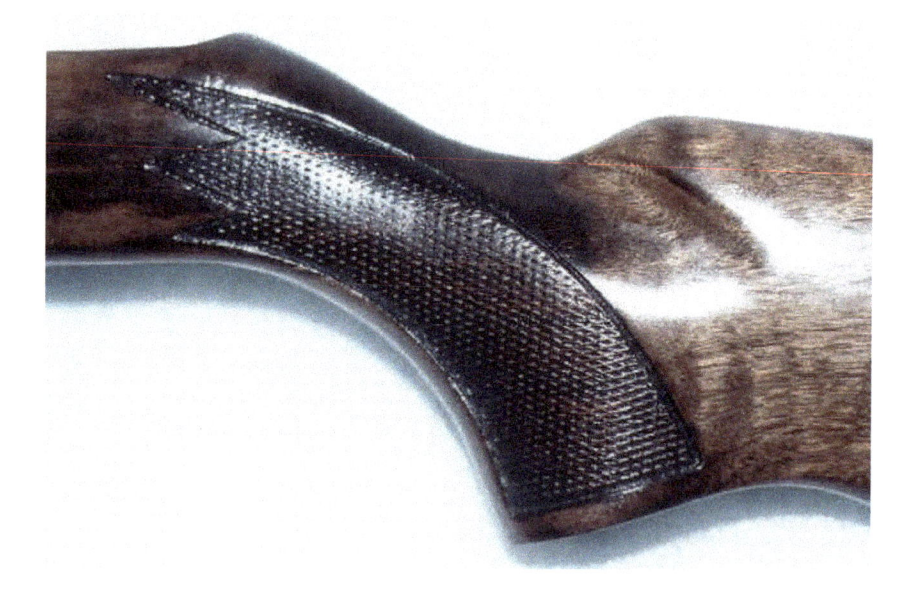

The grip area should be cut in much the same manner as the forearm: beginning with laying every other line throughout the pattern. There will be some areas, such as on the lower rear of the right grip, on which every line was laid out.

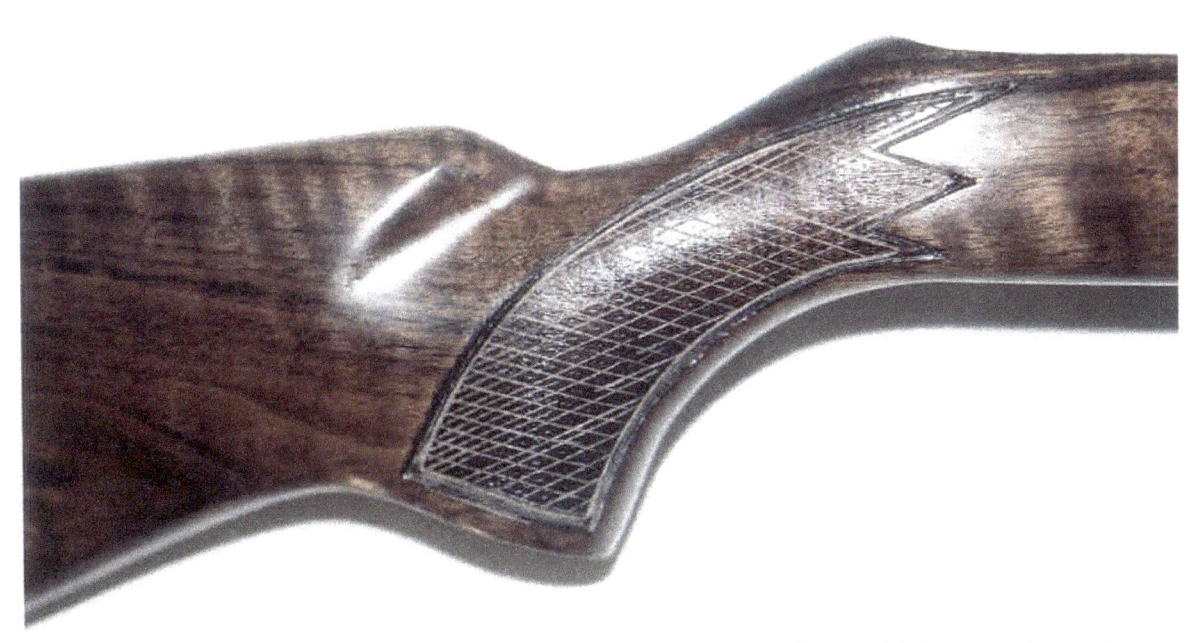

The next step is to go back and begin laying out the lines which were skipped over. Don't get impatient: layout all of the lines before beginning to take them to full depth.

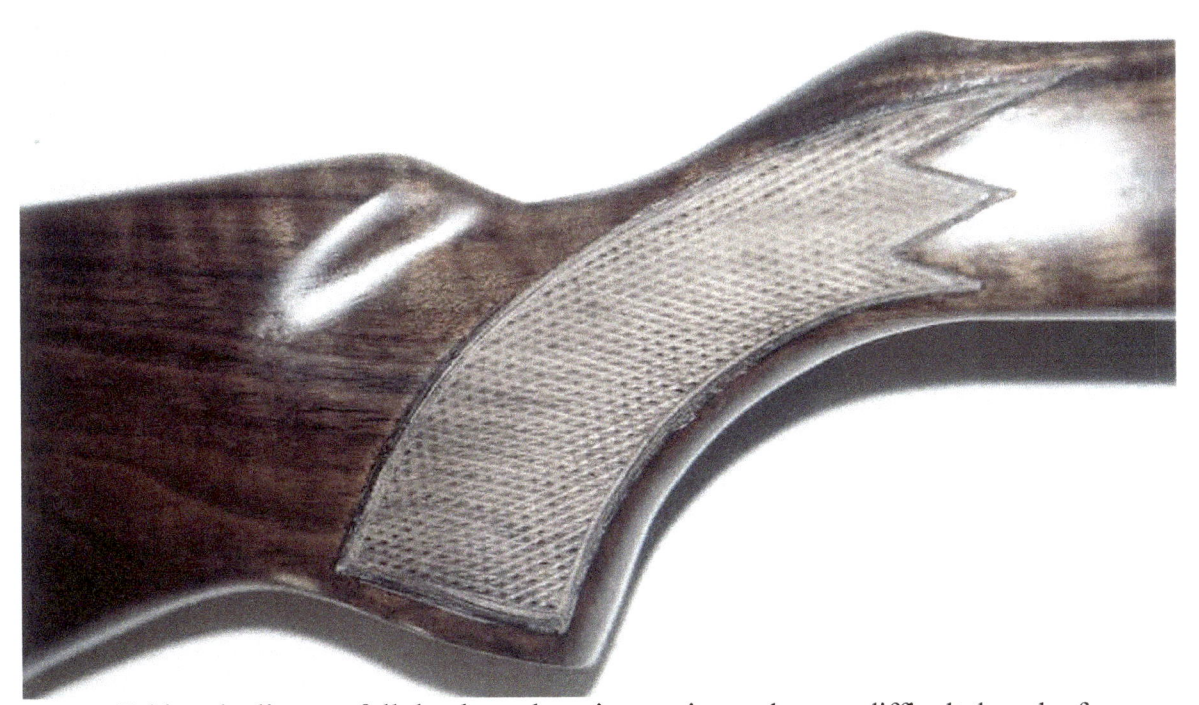

Taking the lines to full depth on the grip area is much more difficult than the forearm. The stock must be reversed many times, and without care during this reversing, the stock can encounter "bench damage." Remember, lay your tools down and out of the way, use both hands, free of anything which could cause damage, then place the stock in the holding devise.

Too many times I have forgotten this rule, trying to same a few seconds, and paid for it in repair time.

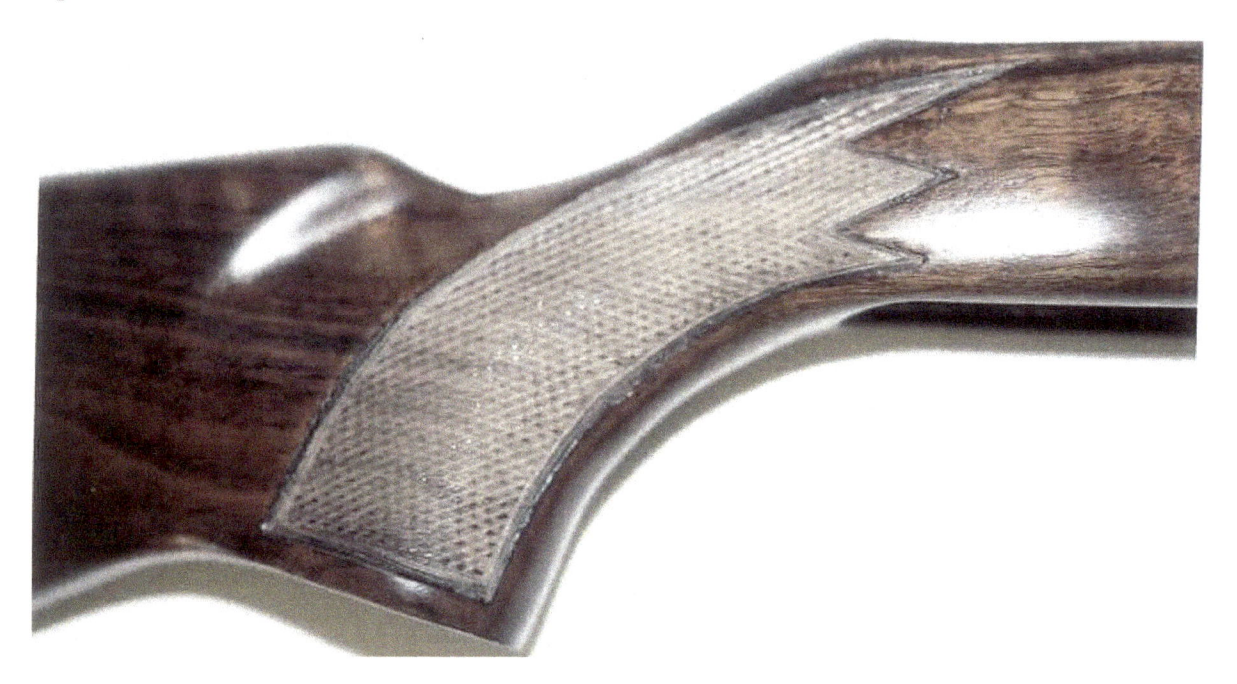

Perhaps the most common job of this type is the Remington Model 1100 buttstock. I have seen some really nice wood on these guns with impressed checkering. But regardless of nice wood or plain, an example of how to "cut" the checkering on these old stocks is a must.

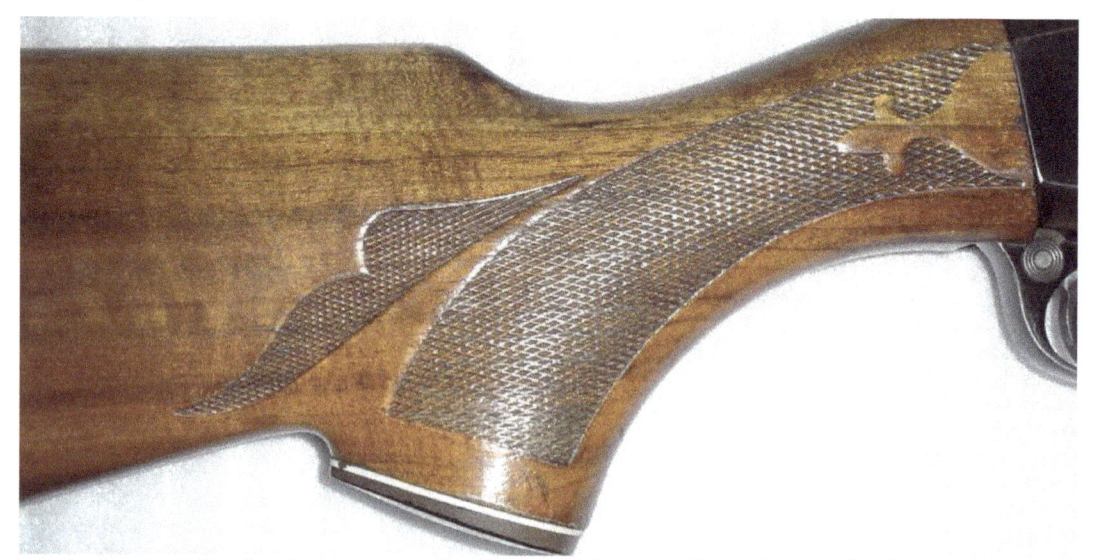

As in any checkering pattern, the first task is to outline the checkering pattern. I use a 60 degree pointer to outline the areas except for the fleur. The pointer has been shortened to about half of its normal length. This allows making the short curves without dragging the rear of the cutter over the wood. When doing this, be very careful and take it slow. Cut just at the juncture of the impressed checkering and the non-checkered wood.

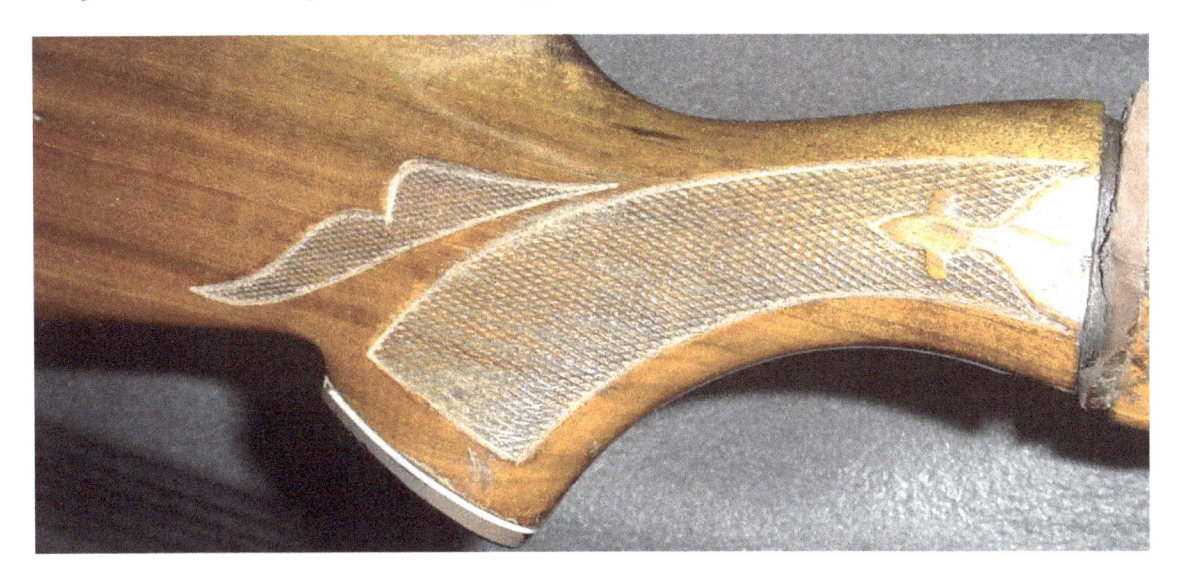

This presents several challenges. The first of which is to determine if you want to keep the fleur. In some cases, the impressed checkering is not well executed, and the decision is more or less made for you. However, on this buttstock the fleur is well executed, and will require a "non-standard" checkering tool to outline it. I use a 6 millimeter skewed wood chisel. I use one hand to apply pressure and the other to guide the chisel point around the fleur.

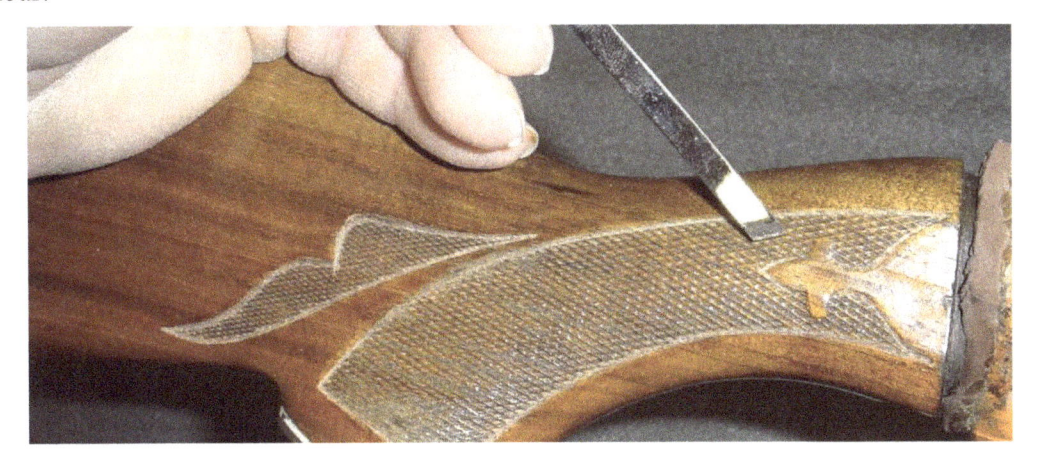

Once the entire pattern has been outlined, it is time to get to the task at hand. I lay a track on every other line, doing all of the lines in one direction, and then the other. In this manner I am sure to have enough imprint in the wood to come back to. Too often beginners cut every line in one direction, and then find they do not have a track to follow when it is time to cut the opposite direction. Just do every other line in one direction first. Take my word for it.

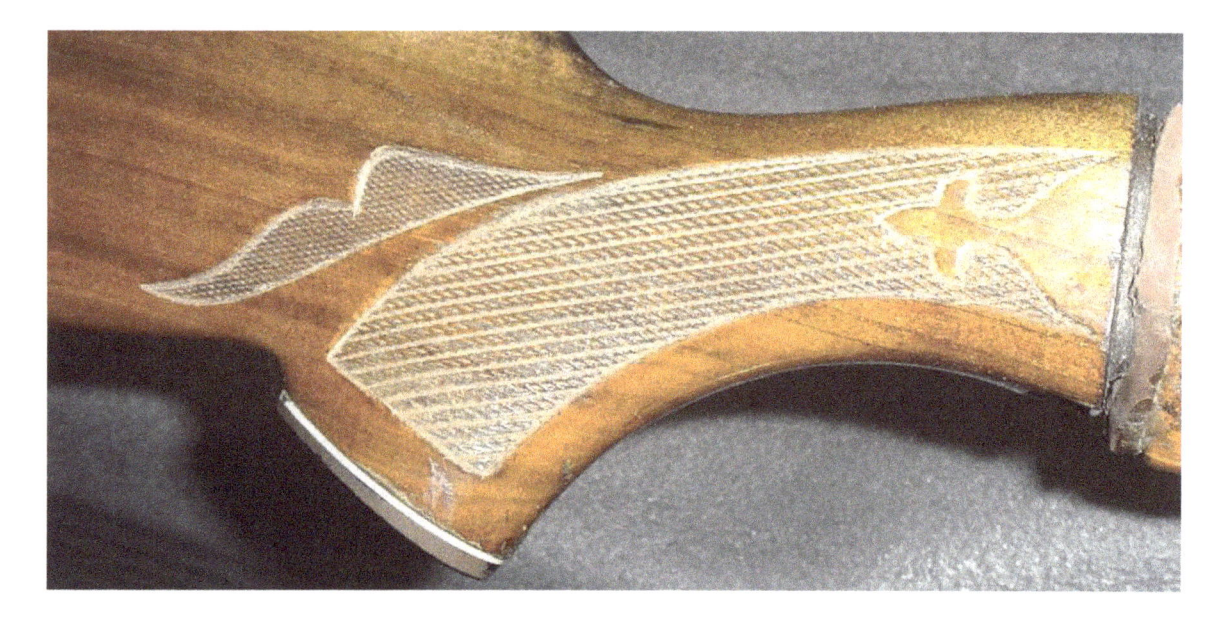

Now lay a track on every other line going the opposite direction. Don't get over confident, take it slow and easy.

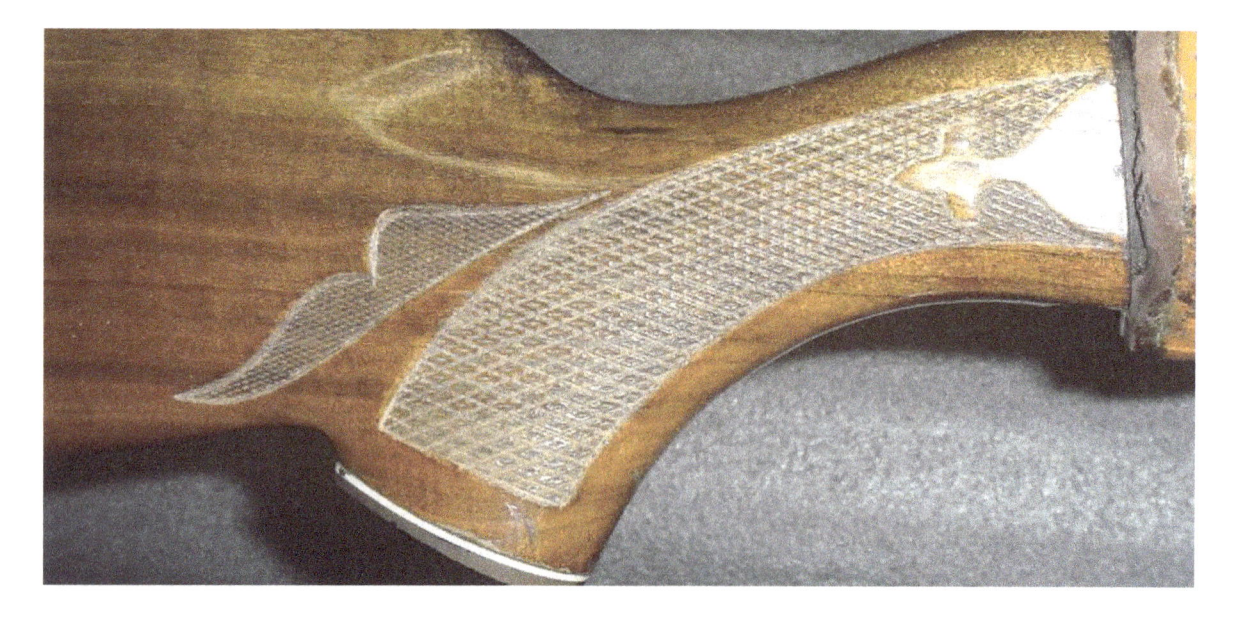

With every other line cut in both directions, begin cutting the remaining lines. Remember to start your line near the center of the line's length. If your cutter is going to favor one side over the other, it usually happens at the start of the cut. By beginning your cut in the middle of the line's length, when you reverse the work to complete the line, it will be much easier to correct any error made.

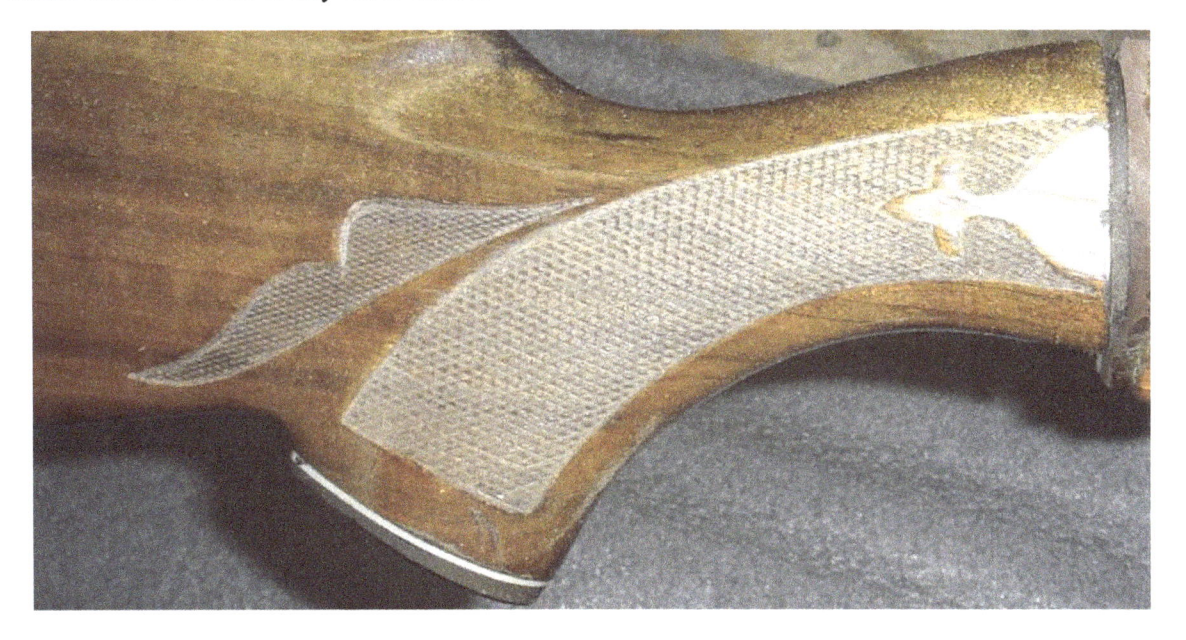

With all of the lines tracked in, it is time to change tools. I prefer to use a ninety degree pointer in the fine cut. I have found – through experience – that it will follow the track better than a medium cut pointer. At this point it is very easy to get over confident, so beware and take your time. With the tracks very apparent, I do not skip lines when making the final cut, but cut every line in one direction, and then come back and cut all of the lines in the other direction.

For cutting the short lines around the fleur, I use a shortened ninety degree cutter, the cutter being shortened to about half of its normal length. After cutting lines to full depth, full depth being when there is no finish showing on the top of the diamonds you are creating, you are entitled to sit back and admire your work.

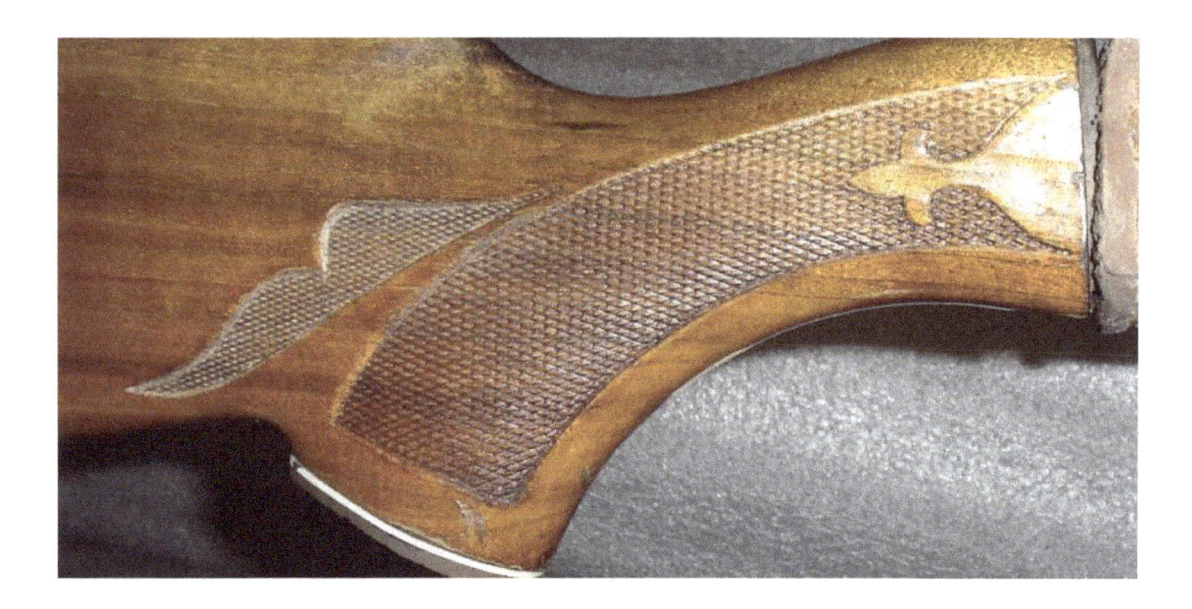

There is a second alternative, one which I use when the impressed checkering is not well executed. I remove the fleur.

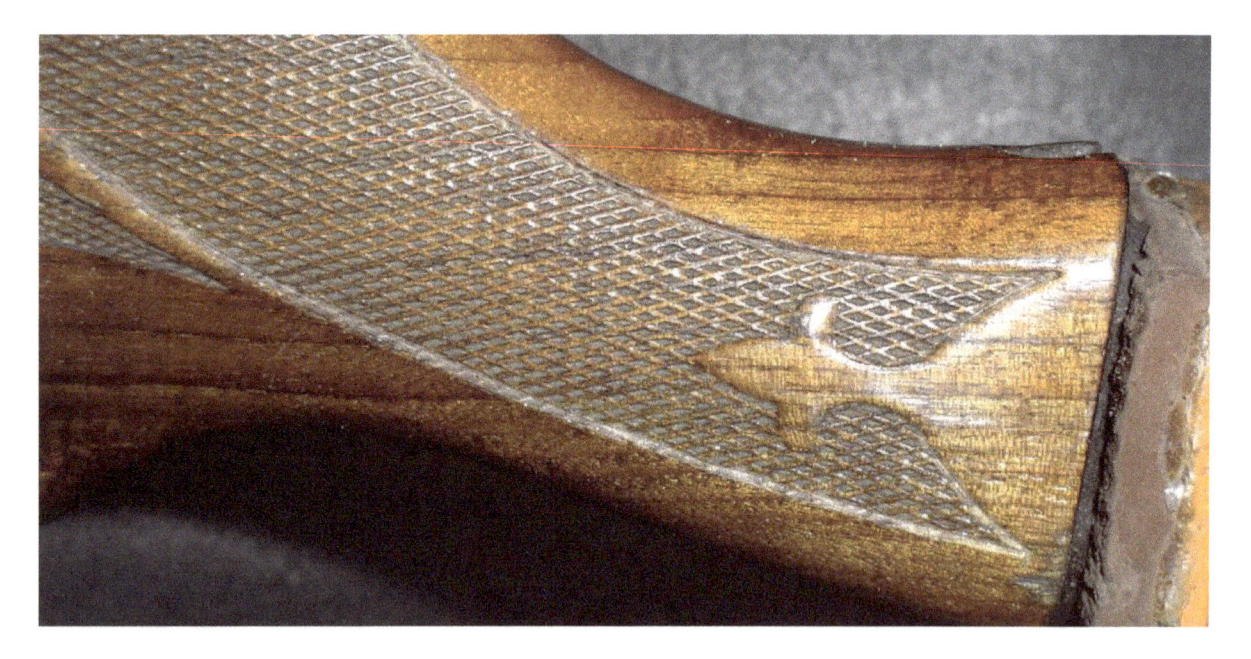

The first thing to do is determine how you are going to "cut off" the fleur. In this case I rounded the pattern, eliminating the fleur. A shallow cut with the 60 degree pointer indicates where I intend the lines of checkering to terminate. Follow the procedure previously described when checkering the other side of this buttstock, cutting every other line. For those checkering lines terminating at the fleur, simply continue the line over the fleur and taken to full depth later.

With all of the lines established, the next step is to take the lines to full depth, but in the case of the fleur, to reduce the wood height down to the impressed checkering height. I do this by using a 90 degree pointer to cut the lines on the fleur first one direction, and then the other. You will very quickly discover the wood of the fleur is much higher than the wood of the impressed checkering. By continuing to cut the lines over the fleur first one way and then the other, the level of wood will quickly be reduced.

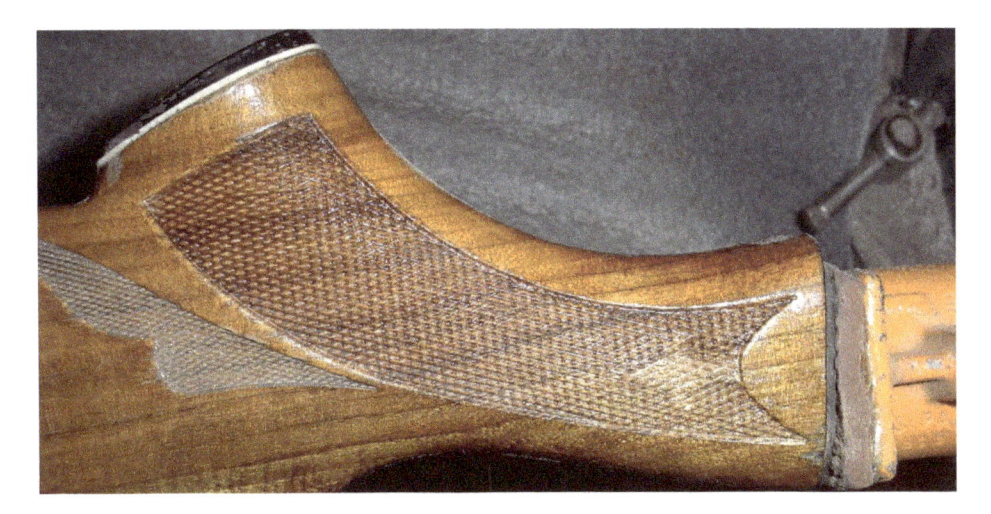

The wood of the fleur is going to be lighter in most cases, not having been compressed. The simplest solution to this problem is a little matching stain on a small brush applied to the light area. With no finish on the wood, it will take the stain very well. Or, you can leave it lighter than the surrounding wood, so your friends will notice, and you can tell them all about your skill in checkering.

SECTION 07

Repair and Salvage

DOUBLE LINE

No, unfortunately, I am not prefect. I make mistakes. Some are the same mistakes I made when just starting to checker. I recently made one of "those" and after saying some words to the wall – it does not answer nor does it talk back, an ideal conversationalist – I decided to record my lack of focus.

It was a simple adjoining diamond point pattern on very nice English for a little Winchester Model 101 in 20 Gauge belonging to a good friend and customer. I had cut all of the line going one way on a side panel in the shape of a half diamond, and then began cutting the lines in the other direction. I do not know where my focus went, but it certainly wasn't on the task at hand. The very first pass with the three line spacer turned into a double line not two inches from the start. I made a small arrow near the error with a white pencil, and determined to use it as a reference point for pictures of the correction process.

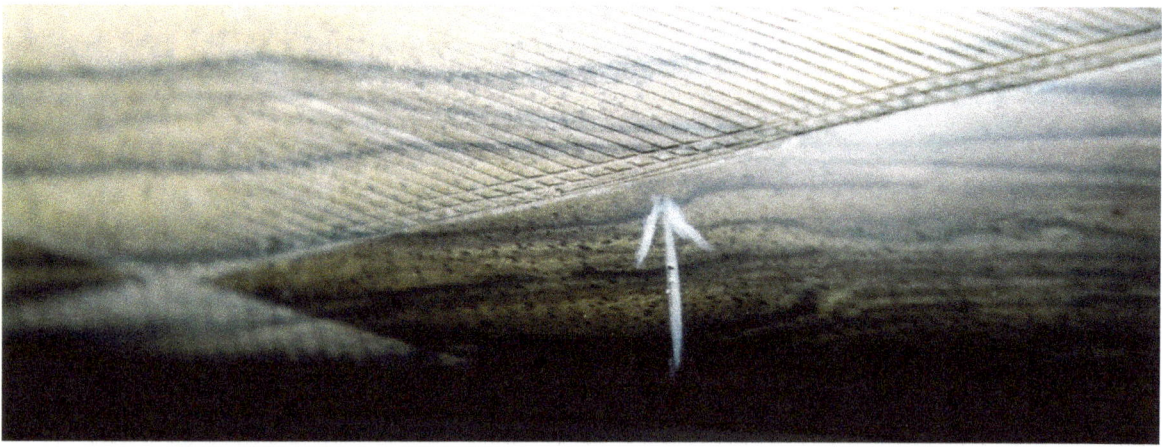

The first step in the correction process, after the conversations with the wall and other inanimate objects cease, is to reverse the work in the vise in order to get to the area above the error which in this case, had not yet been checkered. As I mount forearms such as the one pictured on pieces of pipe, three-eighths inch pipe works well for twenty gauge forearms. By the way, this is an easy task. Use the arrow on the forearm to determine in which direction I have placed the work, as the arrow will stay on the forearm the whole time.

I then use a sixty degree edger to establish a straight line I can be sure the spacer will follow. In this case, it is the border line. If the double line is in the middle of the checkering pattern, use the edger to lightly cut a line at least two lines distant from the double line.

With a straight line for the spacer to follow, I use either a three or four line spacer on the first pass at correcting the line. I am using a three line spacer. I start out above the error, in this case where there is no checkering yet cut, and begin the lines which will lead into the area needing correction. As I get into the double line area, I tilt the spacer cutter sideways. With the spacer tilted to a point at which the teeth of one row are firmly set in the straight line, just cut with the edger, and the other rows are barely making contact with the wood. After several passes in this manner, I reduce the amount of tilt and allow more of the teeth to engage the wood making a deeper cut. It will take several passes to achieve corrected lines. While doing this, FOCUS on insuring the spacer follows the straight line cut with the edger.

If you do this, the other lines will follow parallel – makes sense doesn't it? – and the correction will have begun.

Once the corrected lines are established, continue laying out the checkering lines if you are laying out a pattern. When all of the lines are complete, then come back and complete the correction. Of course, if you create the double line when deepening the checkering lines after the pattern is all laid out, jump right in there.

The first step is what I call insurance cuts. These are cuts I make with a sixty degree edger on the corrected lines and several lines to each side. I do this to insure when I begin taking the lines to full depth with a ninety degree pointer there will be a definite line/track to follow and I will not be creating another double line to correct. Cut very slowly and very carefully, especially if you are cutting on highly figured wood, as I am on this forearm.

Now it is time to cut the lines running in the opposite direction. Continue using the sixty degree edger on these lines in the area near the corrected lines. In this case, I cut the half inch or so of line leading to the border line, passing through the corrected lines. This allows for the same insurance that of the pointer following the desired line and not following a false line or even making a new double line – I've done it.

In preceding picture, just to the right of the arrow, illustrates a double line cut at the border line. To correct this error there are two solutions. First, you can simply extend your pattern over one line and the double cut will disappear when the lines are taken to full depth. On this pattern, because of the interlocking diamond patterns, that is not an option.

The even easier option is to use the ninety degree pointer to cut the border line – remember we used a sixty degree edger to establish a straight line initially. This may remove the double line as the border line deepens. When doing this making it appear natural is more difficult than it seems. If you take the line straight down, your action in increasing the depth will reduce the width of the checkering line adjoining it. My solution is to slightly tilt the pointer toward the side needing correction, effectively making the pointer a one hundred degree pointer on one side, and slowly cut the line. In this manner the line is widened only on one side.

You will notice the area of the corrected lines is slightly lower than the surrounding area, or you may not notice it. It is slightly lower, but when completed and sealed, not noticeable.

As I have said so many times in this book, when the grain of the wood comes through the checkering, the checkering is good. "Cecil, thank you for offering such great wood to make stocks from." And "John, Thank You for allowing me to make your stock and forearm, and understanding why it was a week late."

When I look at these pictures, I am reminded why I became a stock maker and not a Proctologist. Ain't that wood really something great to look at!

Almost immediately after completing this job, I received a new replacement forearm in for a Browning over and under. The order had been for plain, straight grain walnut to match the buttstock. In inspecting the forearm before installing the iron, I couldn't help but notice the flaws in the checkering. The following picture shows the checkering which is either a very poor attempt at correcting an error, or just plain old poor checkering. If you are unfortunate enough to receive a replacement forearm or buttstock with checkering of this quality, I recommend you return it. Browning is especially considerate of making things right with the customer.

Let me sum up these few pages by saying that we are all going to make errors in our checkering. It is the skill and technique we use in correcting our errors that will make them all but invisible

RUN-OVERS

I recently observed a stock on a twelve thousand dollar shotgun that had runovers on the forearm checkering. True, it was borderless checkering, but run-overs. After thirty five years, I knew I had a future in checkering.

Run-overs are one of the easiest mistakes to make and one of the easiest to prevent, and possibly one of the most difficult to correct. Don't believe me? Look at the wood on the guns on the sales advertisements, and I mean for the high dollar guns.

So, I am going to address several ways of covering up run overs. And before you ask, No, not all run overs are capable of being covered up. Some just have to stay there like a sore thumb sticking out and serving as a reminder to do better next time.

The best way to cover up runovers is to prepare for them! Yep, plan on them. And the plan starts when you cut the outline of the checkering pattern, using a 60 degree pointer or edger. I use an edger most of the time - one that has been shortened to half its length.

When cutting the border, I make the line about two-thirds the full depth of what I anticipate the line finishing off at. A sixty degree cutter is very important.

The sixty degree cutter cuts a deep and narrow line at the border, and forms a nice stop for the checkering lines to be cut.

Naturally, the tip of the cutter is going to make small "indentions" in the border when the checkering line meets the border at an angle. Accept it. Just keep the point of the cutter down, not allowing it to ride up over the border line and create a big overrun. This may require bending the shank a little to create the desired angle, and several attempts may have to be made before you get it right and the tip of the pointer cuts. The time required for the modification is much less that the time required in correcting a major run over.

Don't get upset when the small indentions occur. It is a natural occurrence. Just be careful to not cut a line over the border, but if you do, we'll cover that too. But for now, just continue tracking in the checkering lines and then take them to full depth. DO NOT attempt to correct the indention until all of the checkering lines have been taken to full depth.

Indentions caused by tip of pointer

Why? Because you are going to have one chance to remove the indention, and that is done with a ninety degree cutter. The additional angle of the ninety degree pointer will widen the line and remove the remove the indention. Cut with a light touch. Let the pointer do its job.

If the indentions are really apparent, then cut with the ninety degree pointer, lean the side of the pointer into the indentions, really making the pointer angle something over one hundred degrees, and make a few passes over the cited area. This is usually all that needs to be done.

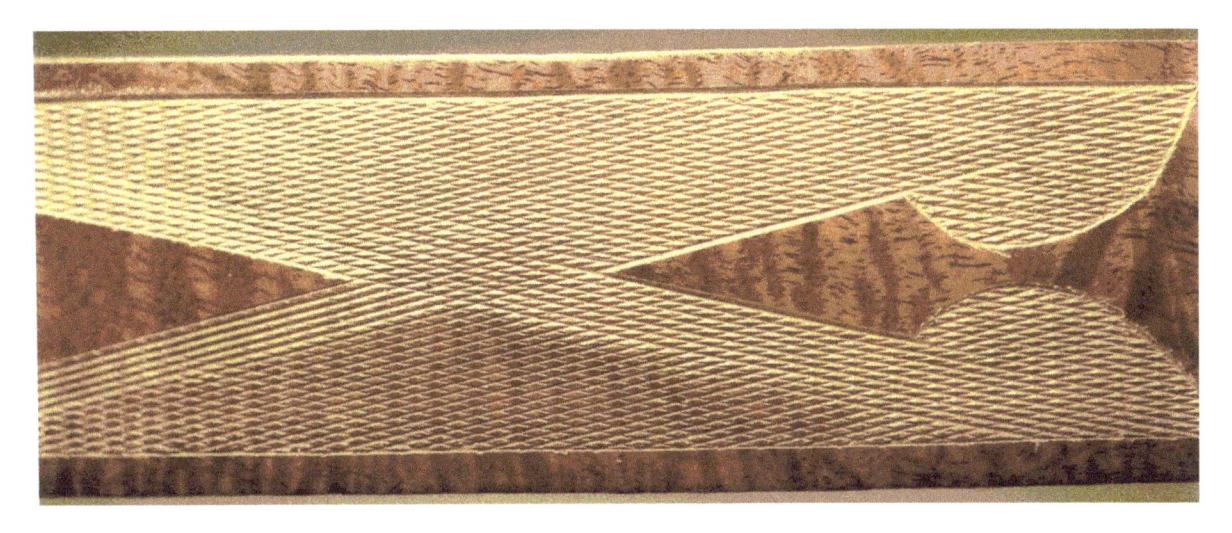

However, if leaning the pointer does not take out the indentions, you have two choices. The first choice is to leave it like it is, and try to explain the indentions on the border to the customer – Good Luck. The other is to cut a border which will remove the indentions entirely.

Make no bones about it, I prefer borderless checkering. But I have added borders because they would dress up the pattern, and I have added borders to remove/cover up errors. Not wanting to let work out of the shop with errors, I would suggest cutting a border. There are many types of borders, but I use two primarily. The first tool is a two line spacer, eighteen lines per inch spacer. The second is a border tool which cuts a rounded bead.

SECTION 8

Ribbon / Panel Checkering

The checkering pattern with a ribbon separating the panels not only looks good, but when properly executed, attests to the level of skill of the person checkering.

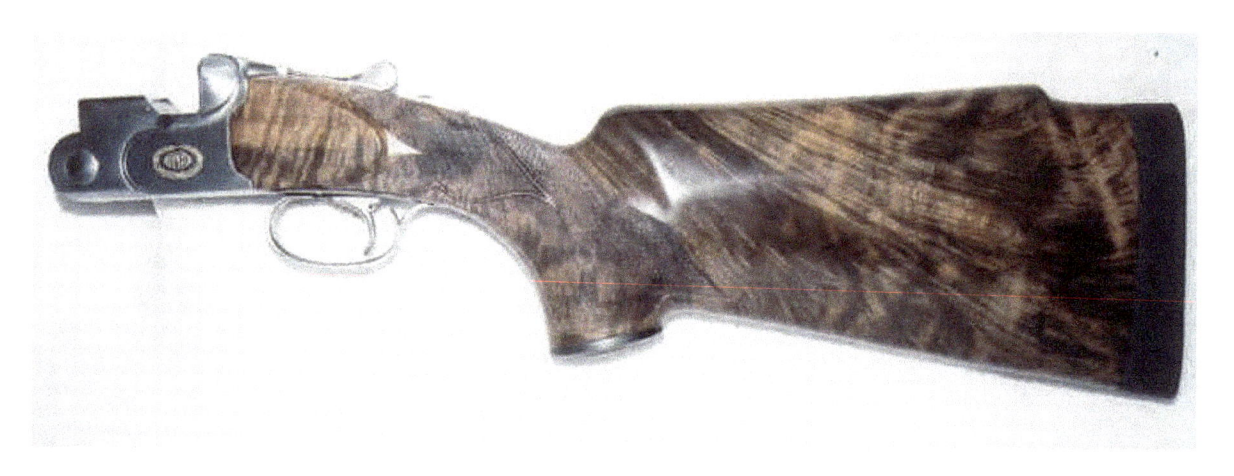

I have seen several ribboned checkering patterns in which the cutting wheel of an electric checkering tool did not cut all of the way to the ribbon, and the hand tool used to bring the line to the ribbon did not match the cut of the wheel. The wood was really nice, but the checkering downgraded it to something just above pine. On several other patterns, the "nicks" in the ribbon caused by the forward edge of the cutting tool was very apparent, making the ribbon appear notched. The times I have seen this on otherwise fine jobs are too numerous to mention.

Cutting a checkering pattern with ribbons does require a higher level of skill than a regular point pattern! What is the difference between a pattern with ribbons and one without? An increase in the area at which checkering lines must terminate. <u>Just more chances for a run over, **that's all**</u>. And believe it or not, and I will illustrate the technique a little later, an accidental run over of the ribbon – if it is not full line depth – is not that difficult to correct.

Laying out the checkering pattern is the first step in successfully cutting a checkering pattern with a ribbon. Select the width of the ribbon carefully: I use a narrow ribbon for 28 and 26 lines per inch, a medium ribbon for 24 and 22 lines per inch and have had few requests for a wide ribbon and coarser checkering. These are my recommendations based on having cut ribbon patterns for over twenty-five years. They are not cast in stone, and can be used or not, depending upon the type of wood and the layout of the pattern. You are the person with the tool.

Over the years I have used a variety of tools and techniques to draw in and cut the lines of a ribbon. I first used a set of dividers with sharp points, but had one heck of a time controlling them. I then tried a multiple line spacer with the center row or rows of teeth removed. That wasn't bad. I have built several special tools which cut only two lines, and I have tried to "free hand" the lines in and deepen them with an edger.

I have four tools of each width, with the handle identifying the cutters as having been modified and how. I have found that there are times when the long cutter is nice and needed (Tool #1), and other times, such as on tight curves, that a shorter cutter is better – (Tool #2). Thus, after installing the cutter on a shank/handle, I remove the rear half of the teeth on a belt sander. In this manner the short section of teeth will not drag over the line when making sharp curves.

When bringing a ribbon into junction with another, I need cutting teeth on just one side or the other. Thus, I have removed the right half of the row of teeth on one (Tool #3), and the left half of the row of teeth from the other (Tool #4), top of next page.

Tool # 2   Tool # 4

You are the boss, and the layout of the ribbon is your decision. The origin and termination, even splitting the ribbon, are all decisions you make, unless your customer has a "drawing" of what they want and are willing to pay for it.

I classify a ribboned checkering pattern as one of three types. The first type is the **freestanding** ribboned pattern. In this pattern the ribbon is self-contained and does not join the outer borderlines. It is, as one customer described it, freestanding!

The second classification is the **attached** ribboned pattern. In this pattern the lines comprising the ribbon originate and terminate by joining the borderlines of the pattern.

The following picture is of a Winchester Model 42 I checkered in 1979 and just recently I came back in contact with it. Long story made short – I received the gun in as a Field grade gun and replaced the wood, added a vent rib, a blue job and opened the choke up to a loose I/C. Look at the lower corner of the ribbon – Yep, screwed up! I cut the outside border lines and then cut the ribbon in – mistake! Cut the ribbon in first, and then the outside border lines, insuring the ribbon flows into the border, not comes into an abrupt meeting.

I did not make the same mistake on the forearm, as shown below.

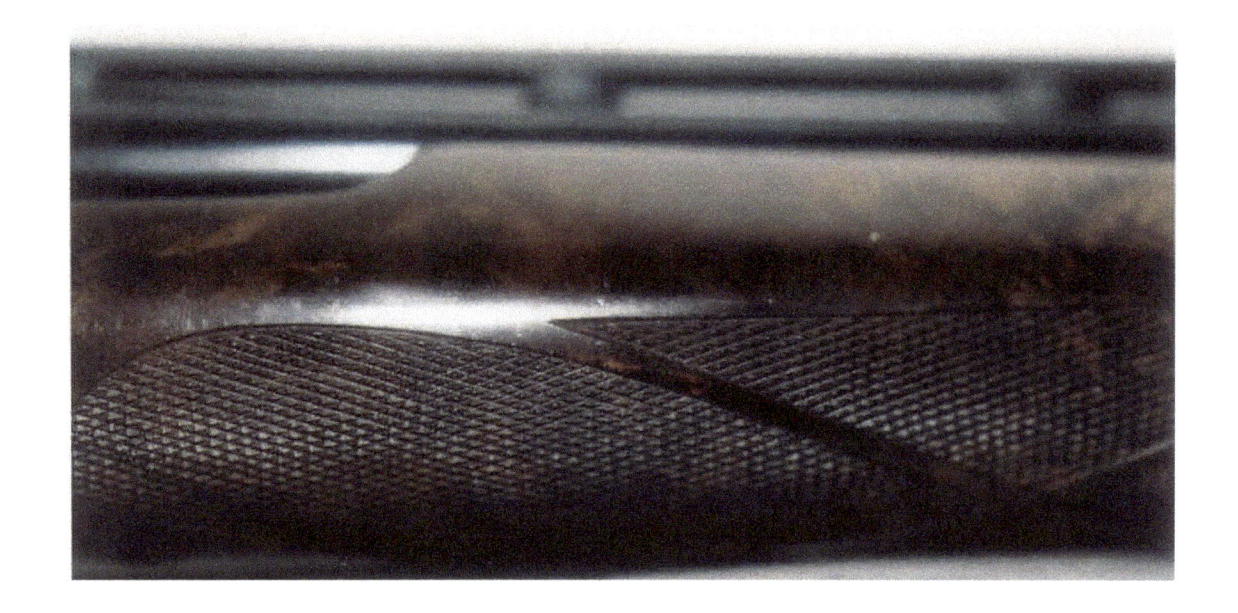

This following picture is the best illustration of what not to do when beginning checkering. Don't make the pattern so complicated the chances or a mistake are not in your favor. In the example, the customer wanted to see all of the ribbon and also the angle – ratio – of the checkering diamonds. I obliged him, and when drawing it out made a few changes to the basic pattern.

Please note the sides of the center diamond ARE NOT confined. They are open just like a road intersection. Later I will determine which lines have precedence.

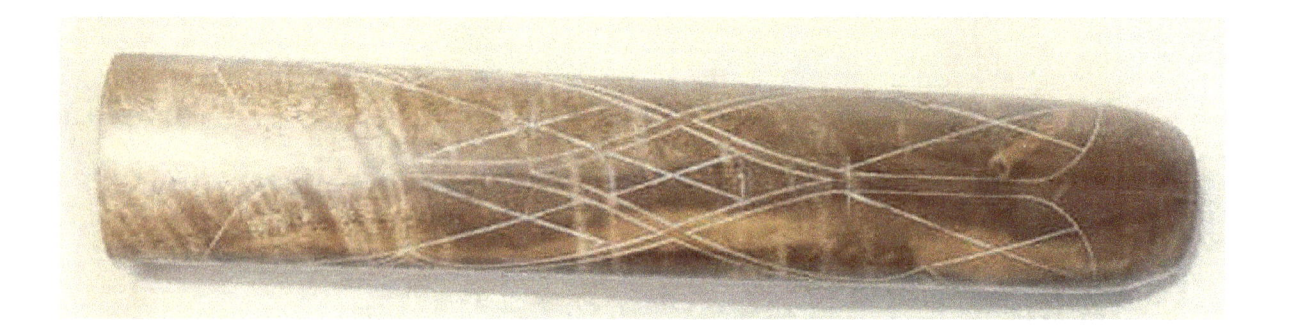

The third classification is a **combination** of the other two. Lines forming the ribbon are both freestanding with others attached. This is the most common pattern I work with. The *Turnip Seed* pattern can be an attached or combination ribboned pattern

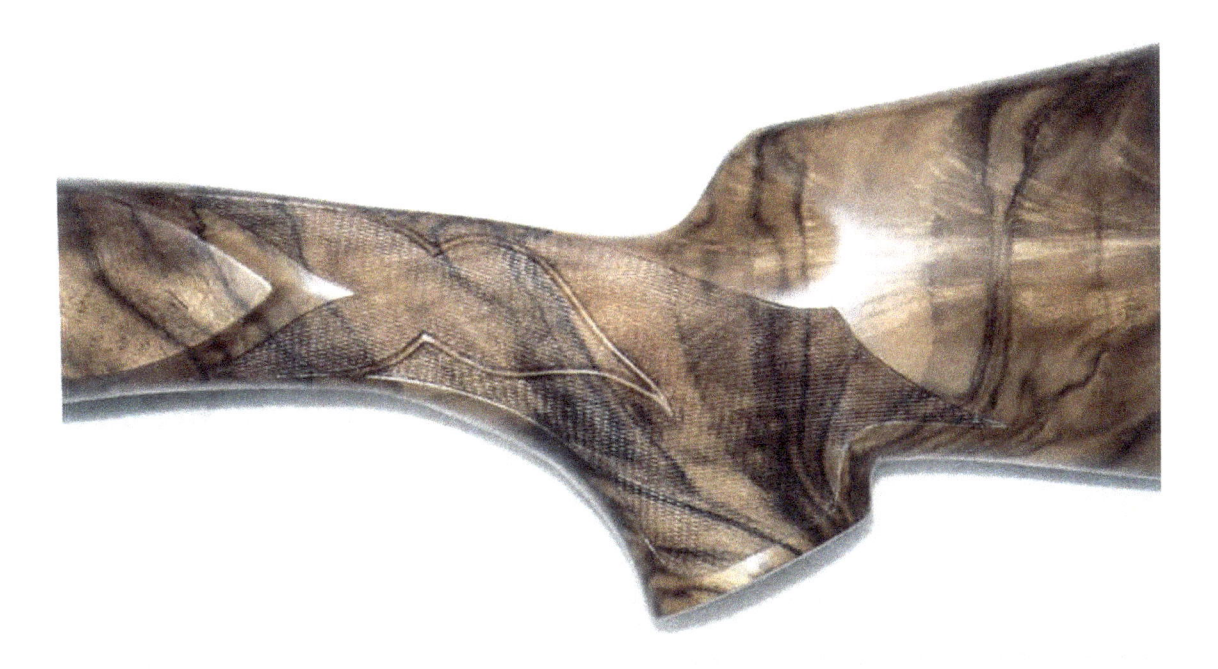

Before you get carried away, and plunk down a substantial amount of money for a fantastic stock you have the ideal ribbon panel checkering pattern for, I suggest you "test your skill" on a few inexpensive proofs. I just happen to have a nice proof of English Walnut from a very nice wood set I put on a Krieghoff K-80.

The first step is to determine the area to be checkered. In this case, the entire proof block. For this exercise I feel the need to focus on the central diamond and leave the ends of the proof somewhat "easy."

The second step is to develop a checkering pattern for the area to be checkered. This is accomplished using the folded paper technique discussed earlier. After obtaining an outline – on paper – of the proof. Once the pencil outline is on the paper, make a copy. Actually, I would make several copies of the paper at this stage, just in case… With the paper folded, begin putting your ideas down on the paper, folding it over and tracing the second half of the pattern. If you don't like it, you have another page to use and try again. I want one central piece – diamond – in or near the center of the proof extending to the ends of the proof, actually splitting and becoming the borders.

The third step is to transfer the pattern from paper to the wood to be checkered. This task can be accomplished in a variety of ways, as already discussed. For this exercise taping the pattern to the block and slipping a sheet of "old fashioned carbon paper" under it is the easiest. Please note, when approaching a clerk in the office supply store to ask about carbon paper, find a clerk old enough to have used it. I have found that most clerks have no idea of what you are asking for.

The fourth step is to cut the border lines of the pattern. Please notice how the lines on the ends of the proof are slightly scalloped, but the lines along the long part of the proof are straight. The ends were curved slightly to follow the form of the central diamond. The two long lines were made with the "edge marker" and then deepened with a shortened 60 degree pointer. It makes a great tool for cutting in borders.

The fifth step is to cut one of the ribbon lines all of the way out to the border lines. In retrospect, I wish I had not extended the diamond out to the border line, but had left about a quarter on an inch space. That space could be checkered – only a couple of lines wide – and might look really good. But that is why practicing on proofs is a good use of time. The next time I cut this pattern will be on a nice stock set, and I will make the "improvement."

The sixth step is to use a spacer and track in the second line of the ribbon. The intention is to checker this proof in 24 lines per inch, and thus I have chosen the Medium spacer. If I had chosen 28 lines per inch, I would have selected the narrow spacer. With 26 lines per inch I use either medium or narrow spacers, depending upon the wood.

The seventh step is to join the ribbon lines to the border lines, where applicable. This is the step from which you can sit back when complete and smile, or, wonder how in the devil you are going to correct your error. In bringing the lines to a junction with an opposing line, remember to stop approximately a quarter inch from the junction and use one of the single sided spacers – either one with teeth on the left side, or one with teeth on the right side.

The eighth step is to lay out the master lines. The aster lines are the lines which determine the ration of the diamonds to be checkered and do not need to be very deep. In fact, if the lines are too deep, they will be difficult to follow with the spacer used to track in the checkering lines. Go easy - just make then deep enough to see well. If you have to come back and take them a little bit deeper, no problem, but you can't come back and make them "less deep". Know what I mean?

Use a plastic template to lay out the master lines, positioning the template from the centerline of the pattern. In this way you are assured that the checkering diamonds you are going to cut will be aligned with the flow of the pattern. I use the three and a half to one or the four to one ration diamonds for most of my work. As previously described, the templates are made from transparency stock - easy to make, last a long time, and are in my opinion, invaluable.

The ninth step is to track in the checkering lines. When tracking in the checkering lines, remember you are laying lines to be followed with a pointer, and you are not taking them to full depth. Notice how the checkering lines below the master line get shorter the further away from the master line. When using the previously cut line as your guide for cutting a new line, each succeeding line will get shorter. When the work has progressed to the point illustrated in the photo, reverse the position of the proof in the checkering vise – just as you would with a forearm of buttstock – and take the lines to termination. Major rule – do not try to start the line near the border using the back teeth of the spacer or you will end up with either crooked lines or run-overs of the border, or both.

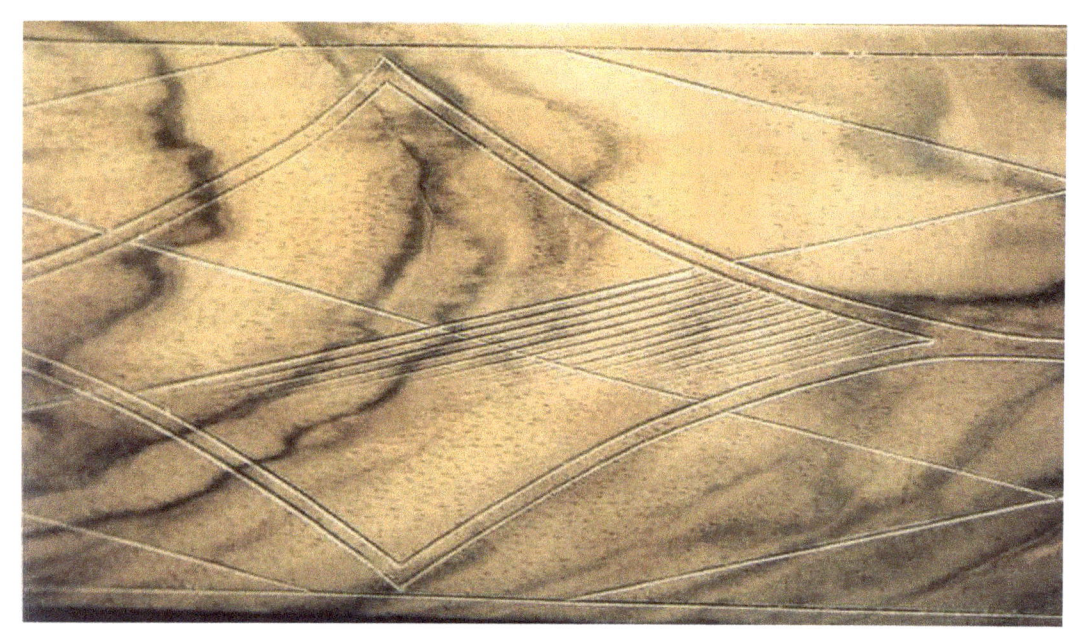

Please note the angle at which the spacer is held.... Notice the cutting end of the spacer IS NOT held so as to act as the bow of a boat? When held as the bow of a boat, the spacer will leave track marks at the borders with the teeth on the end as they are higher than the level of the wood. Just as the bow of a boat cuts through the waves, the front of the spacer will create run-overs. However, with the angle of the spacer positioned to act more like a blunt nosed barge, the line will be tracked onto the wood up to the border, not over it.

In determining the angle of the tool, the first task is to determine at what angle you CONFORTABLY hold the tool. Then, modify the angle of the cutter by bending the shank of the tool to achieve the angle you want. Yes, it will take a little time and some experimenting, but a whole lot less time that would be required to correct run-overs.

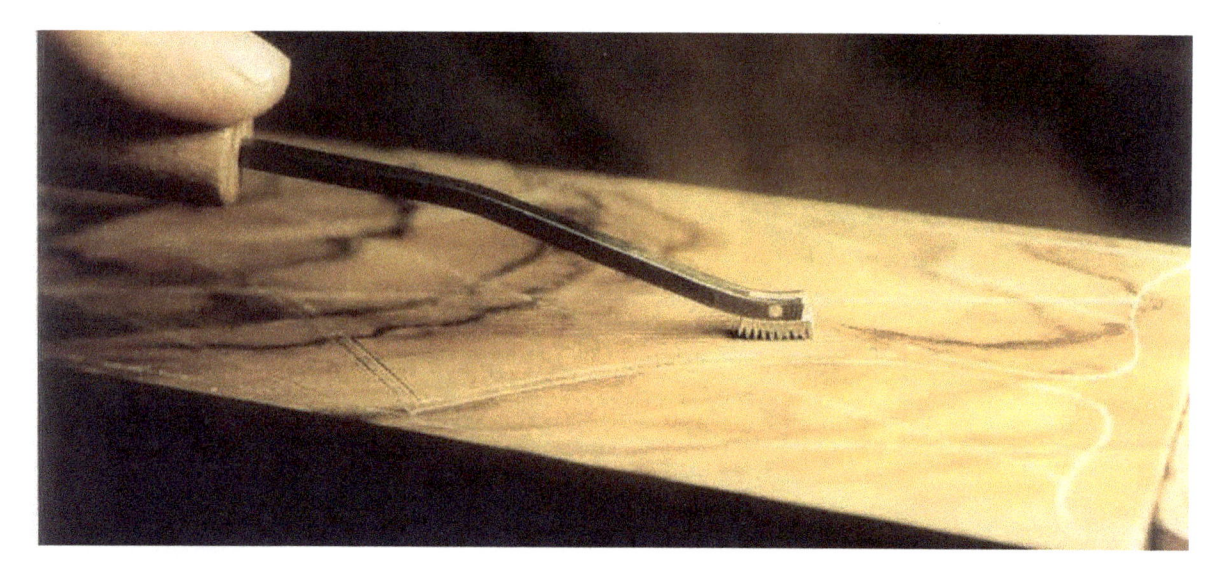

Want to see how good you did?

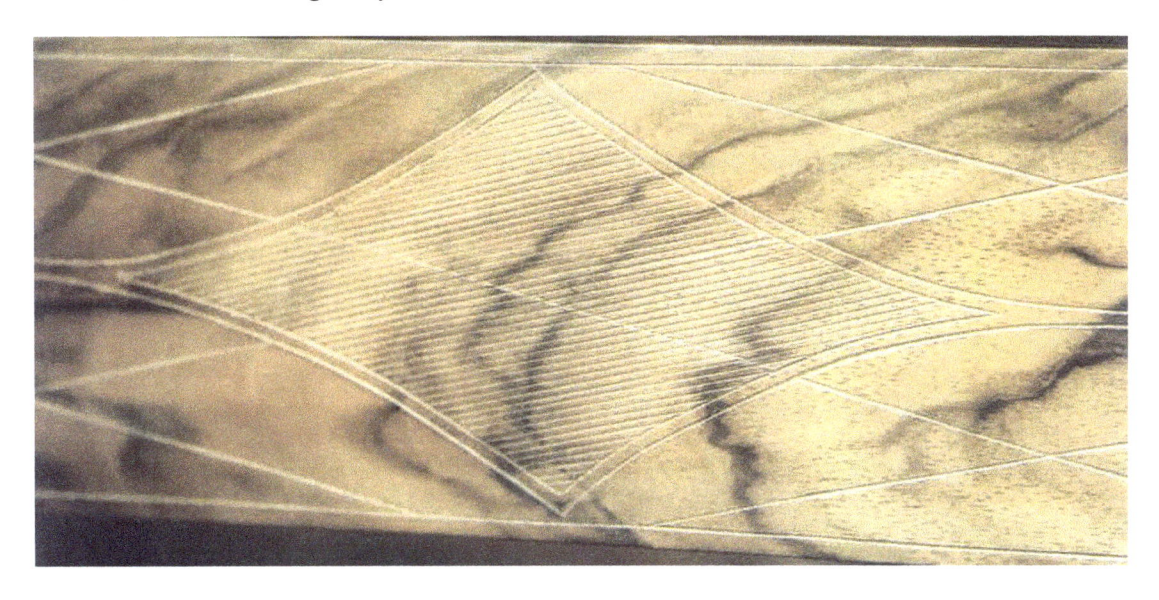

With all of the lines inside the diamond tracked in, all in one angle, track the checkering lines for the other angle. Just a note here, unless the wood you are checkering is absolutely straight grain, expect one angle to cut harder / softer than the other. You may also find that the cut on one angle is not as "clean" as in showing the grain of the wood as the other. When this happens, after deepening the checkering lines to full depth, use a fine grade of pointer and cut in the direction which provided the cleanest cut.

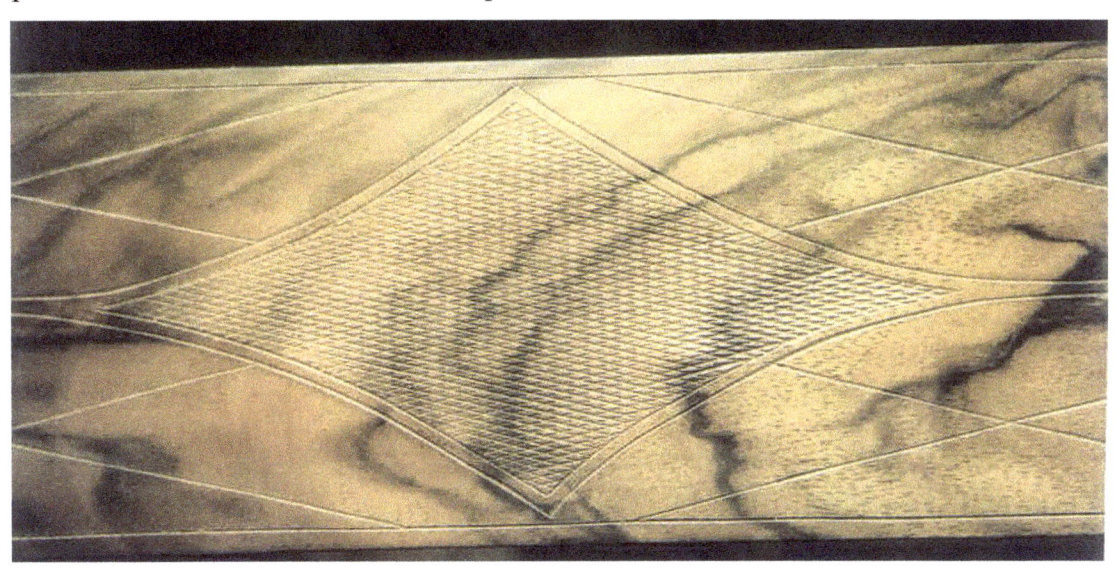

With all of the lines tracked in on one of the panels, select another panel and repeat the process one line at a time, being careful to stop before the ribbon.

The picture below is an excellent lesson in planning for an error. At the arrow, notice the line is not as clear or narrow as the other lines.

Right, I messed up and cut the line too wide. To correct it I cut the side of the line and also deepened the cut more than the other parts of the line. Notice that the area with the "corrections" is also the area to be checkered. Right, the checkering will cover my error. I have repeatedly stated that not all checkering is perfect - it is only made to look so.

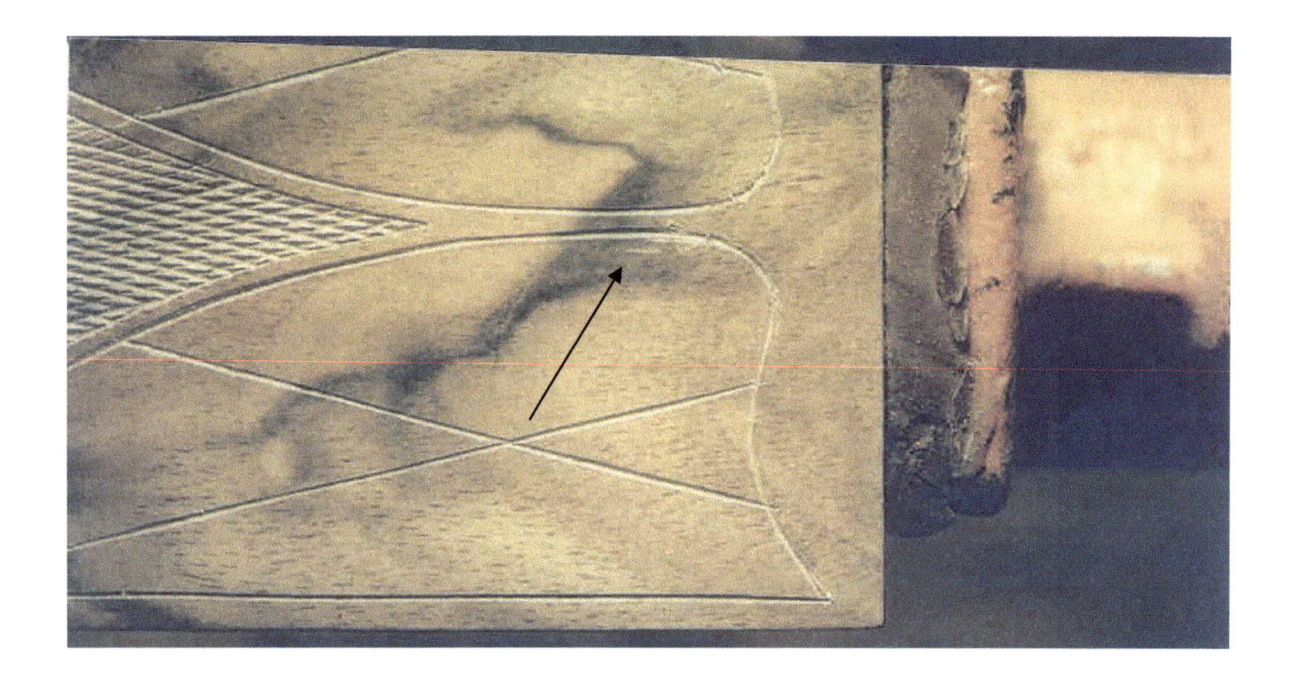

The tenth step is to take all checkering lines to full depth. I do this in two steps. I take the lines to full depth with a Medium grade pointer, and then change over to a fine grade of pointer and go over each line lightly in the direction which allows the grain of the wood to come up through the checkering. Yes, it takes a little extra time, but when someone compliments your work by saying that the checkering is so good, that the grain of the wood comes through, it will have all been worth it.

The eleventh step is to clean up all of the borders to include the ribbons. I generally use a ninety degree edger to clean up the borders - one whose cutting area is reduced to about half the length of the cutting tool. With this short cutter I can maneuver around all of the angles and joints without increasing the width of the border.

The final step is to seal the checkering. I use a thinned down solution of whatever the stock or forearm is finished with. In this manner, I am assured with compatibility.

Stocks and Buttstocks

Before I cut a single bit, I draw out the pattern with a white pencil. On some finishes, I run a damp cloth over the pattern area before beginning to drawing the pattern. I have found that the "semi-moist" surface holds the white line of the pencil better than a dry surface. Please notice two things about the pattern: first, the master lines establishing the ratio of the diamonds to be cut are "whited in." Second, one of the two lines of the ribbon is EXACTLY where I want one line of the ribbon to be, and the other line is free handed in to give perspective of the width of the ribbon.

Once I am satisfied with the layout of the pattern, I will sometimes leave the piece sit for several minutes or several days until I am comfortable with the pattern and have determined how I will cut it.

Some people like to do one side or the other first. I prefer to do the side I envision being the hardest or requiring the most time. There is probably some great observation relating back to my childhood based on my choice, but I am just more comfortable doing it this way.

With the buttstock in the checkering vise, I use a 60 degree pointer with the rear half of the teeth removed to cut the border lines, and the ONE line comprising the ribbon. Remember? I had previously said that one of the two lines was EXACTLY where I wanted it to be, and the other line was only there to add perspective?

A common mistake is to "close" the ribbon with the borderline. That is to run the lines of the ribbon directly into the border line.

The opposite is to leave the ribbon lines open by flowing them into the border in a natural arc, making the panels separate from one another. For that reason, the first area I cut is the area at which the ribbon line meets the borderline.

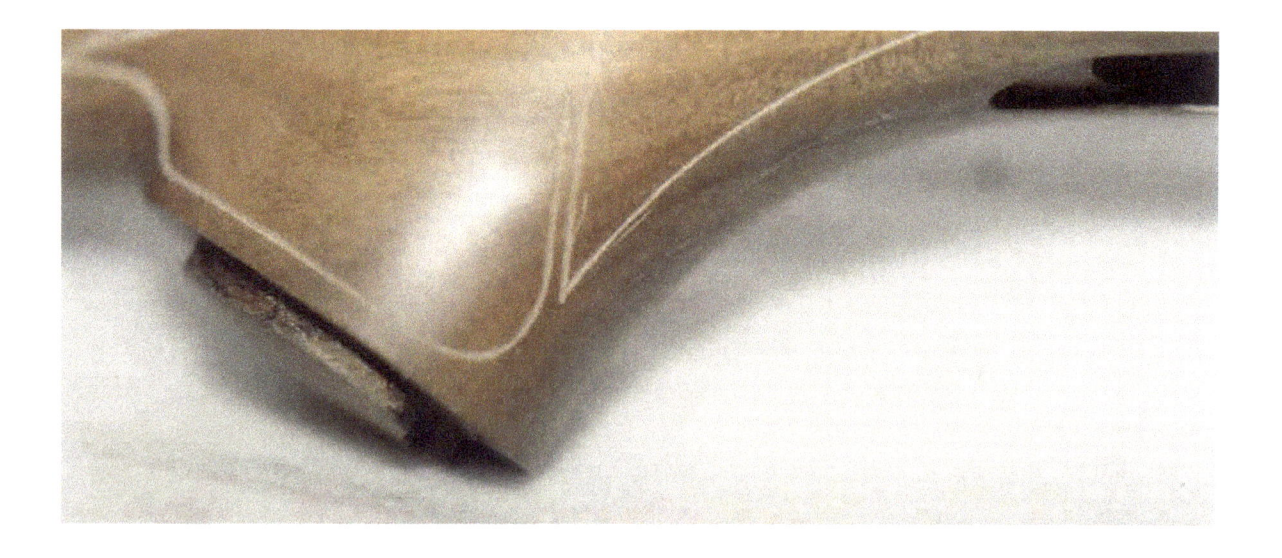

With the one line of the ribbon cut, I then use the spacer - in this case the medium spacer with the rear half of the teeth removed - to cut in the second line. By tilting the tool head slightly and letting the one edge track the line I have made, the opposing edge just barely trails a line into the finish. In this way, I can insure I am following the track of the first line. Do not try to take the lines to full depth; that will come later. Just cut them deep enough to be recognizable as lines and be able to follow them with a pointer – to deepen them slightly – and serve as a stop for checkering lines terminating at them. When you are cutting, look just ahead of the cut line you are tracking. In doing this, you will better follow the cut line than if you were watching the cutter head or the line being cut.

Don't believe me? OK. Look directly down at your feet and try to walk a straight line, your line will not be straight. Now focus on an object in the distance and walk towards it, your line will be straight. It works for me, and hopefully for you.

With the borders and master lines cut into the butt stock, it is time to get serious about checkering this piece of wood. Please make note that the master lines – other than skipping over the ribbon or the pattern, continue on the line. While it is very difficult to maintain these lines, it is the sign of fine checkering.

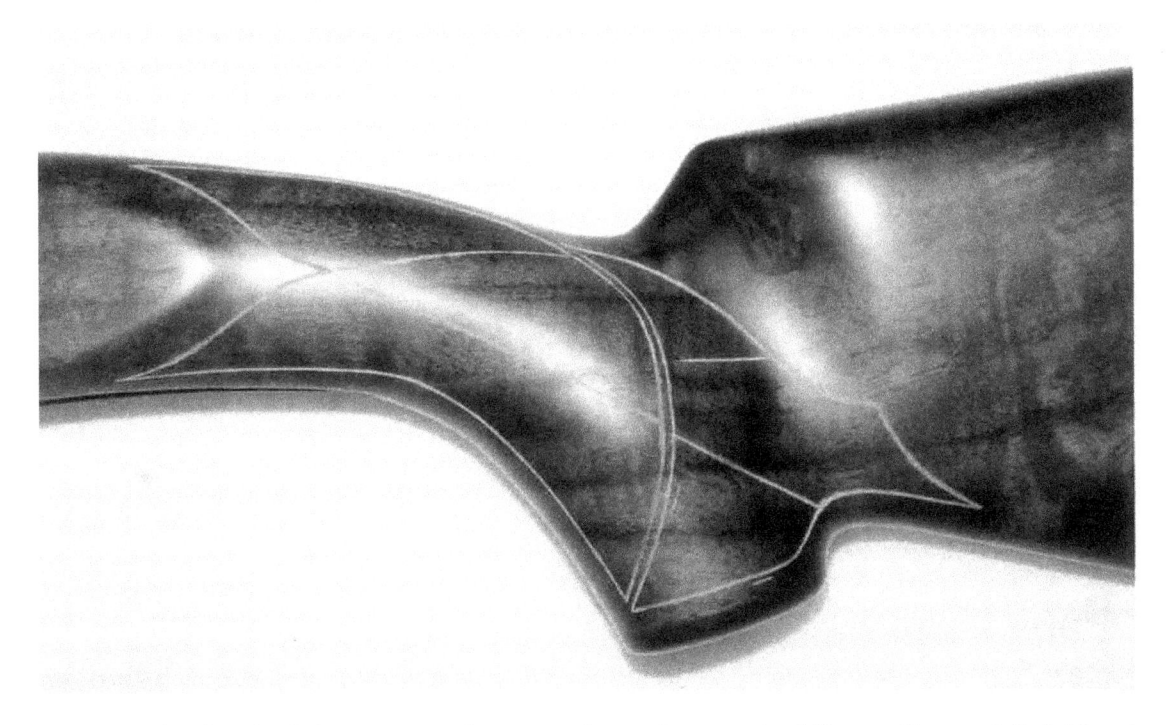

Not having had the opportunity to evaluate the wood while sanding and finishing it – it was received finished, just needed checkering – I had to make a determination on what line spacing the wood would accept based on the apparent figure of the wood. Twenty-eight lines per inch would really be pushing it, and twenty-six would be alright for most of it with only a few small areas presenting some problems, but I felt the wood would accept twenty-four lines per inch checkering.

With the buttstock secured in the pipe checkering vise – I really like the wood to be secured even when I am working with no more than a white Marks All pencil – I made sure the three line spacer in the checkering handle was sharp. As it turned out, I could see small flat spots on the bottoms of the first two teeth of the spacer and I replaced it with a new three line spacer.

Yes, there have been times when I used a fine stone to "tone up" the first few teeth, but those times are long since past. I have learned many a lesson the hard way, but seldom the same lesson twice!

I start by trailing one line of the teeth of the spacer in the master line, making no more than a light scratch. If it looks good, I go over it making it a little deeper. Three or four passes creates the depth I am comfortable with. I then use two rows of teeth on the spacer to track in the already cut lines, and ***cut only one new line at a time***.

Why use a three line spacer if I am only cutting one new line at a time? Because by tracking two established lines, I am able to obtain more stability than by tracking only one line and cutting two new lines. Bottom line – I have fewer "non-straight" lines to deal with.

My first positioning of the spacer is near the closest border. I take the line to the opposing border and then come back with my next line being started closer to the opposing border as I want to make maximum utilization of the just established line.

Thus, each line will be shorter than the preceding line. To reduce the opportunity of "line deviation" – another work for "non-straight" lines – I only cut a half dozen or so lines before either working off of the other master line, or just reversing the buttstock and completing the lines I have just started. Using the pipe clamp checkering vise makes switching ends on the work very quick and very secure.

The following photograph illustrates the lines I have cut before switching the work around and completing the lines.

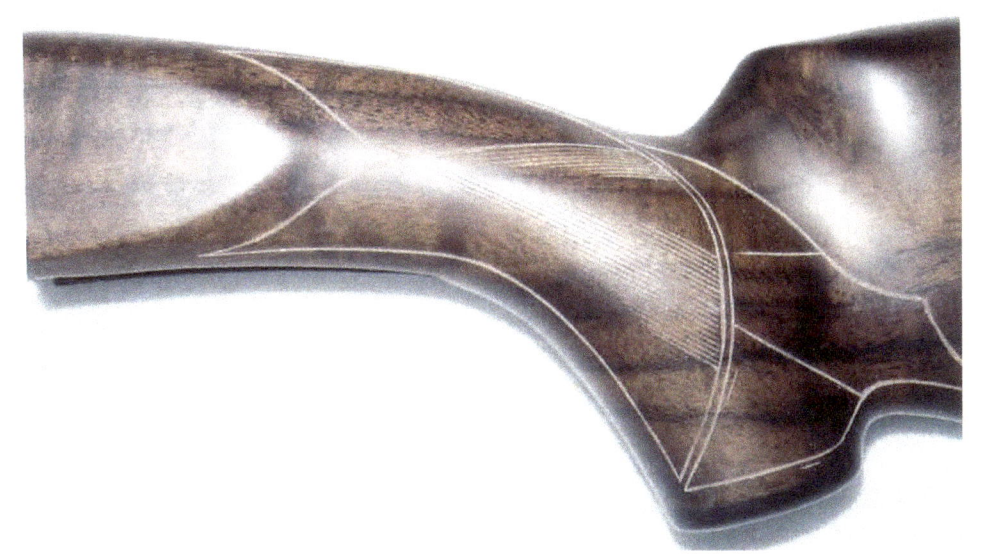

Once the lines have been completed, I begin making new lines in the same manner. Each line becoming shorter than the one preceding it, but carrying the line to the border. Depending on the pattern and the line spacing, I will repeat this process dozens of times before the job is complete.

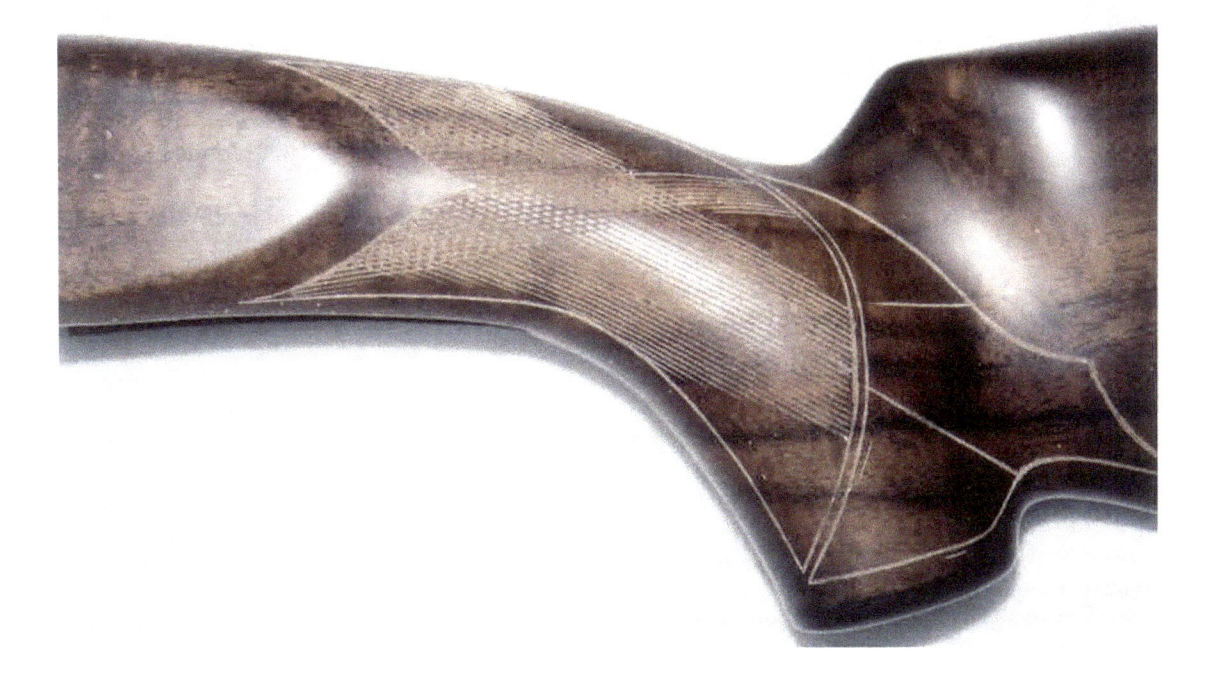

While I like to checker six to ten lines before switching ends with the butt stock, I often cut fewer lines if I am going over a palm swell, around the top of the grip, creating very short lines in a confined area, or …. Basically, I change ends when I feel the need. If there are lines too wide or not wide enough, I switch ends and make corrections.

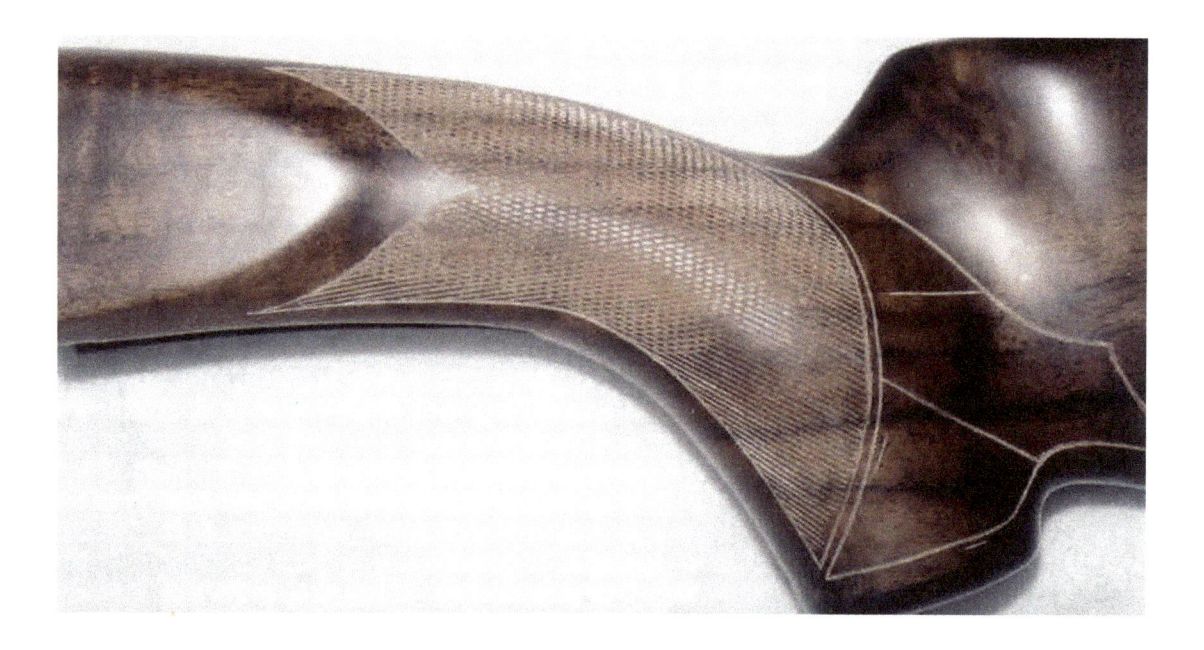

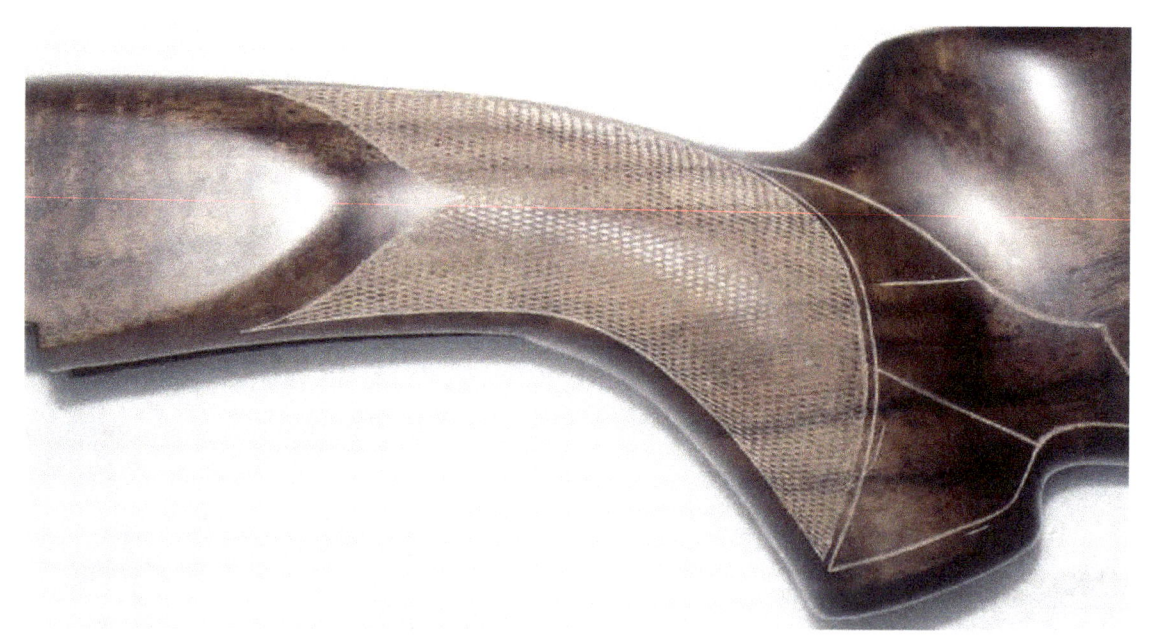

The rear half of the ribbon pattern is more difficult as the lines are much shorter, especially near the top of the grip area. Having "drug" the tail of a three line spacer beyond the border into the checkering pattern on checkering jobs such as this, I "shorten" a three line spacer by grinding off a little over half of the length, just as I did the 60 degree pointer used to cut the border lines. This modified tool makes cutting short lines much less hazardous to my health.

Before we go any further, yes, I have a lot of "special" tools for certain patterns and cuts. After cleaning up borders over runs and other errors for a number of years, I realized a three or four dollar cutter was a cheap tool. I would really like to see Gunline make a series of cutters with half the length of their standard cutter. I know I would certainly buy and use a bunch of them. Don't hesitate to stop cutting after only an inch or so and re-adjust the piece being worked on to a different more accessible position. This self imposed requirement is why I like using the pipe vise in my bench vise as a checkering cradle.

And why I especially like having a forearm mounted on a piece of pipe and the pipe held by the bench vise.... The important thing is to be comfortable cutting the line and not be in a bind. How many times have you looked back on something you have done and chastised yourself for not taking a little more time to make an adjustment or explore an alternate method?

If there are areas of the pattern at which the ribbon narrows or blends into a border or even splits into two ribbons, do not try to track in the two ribbon lines with the spacer right up to the point of narrowing, widening, or splitting! Allow yourself space to gracefully blend the lines in, whether narrowing or widening the ribbon. About an inch most times is necessary to blend the lines into the new requirement, but sometimes more. Once again, it is easy to cut a line, but very difficult to "uncut" one!

For this reason, indicate the line to be cut with a white line from a sharpened white pencil. It is much easier to follow/cut a line with an edger than it is to determine the path of the line as you are cutting it. Been there, done that. Please learn from my mistakes.

The picture below is of a pattern on a Winchester Model 42 buttstock. Wanting to bring the center of the checkering point to a point directly behind the receiver tang, I allowed myself over an inch to widen the ribbon and bring the two lines to a point.

With the short 60 degree pointer, blend the lines into the narrowing, widening or splitting as required by the pattern. Don't worry about taking these lines to full depth, as this is the last thing done when completing the pattern. I call it cleaning up the borders.

I prefer to lay out all of the checkering lines for one section at a time. In this manner I can more accurately judge my progress.

Now some people like to checker in absolute silence, but for others not even the noise of customers or other workers in the shop bother them. I fall somewhere in the middle. I do not like to work in silence, but working alone as I do, I find the CD player perched on top of one of the gun safes to be an acceptable, if not controllable, noise. Having grown up in the late 50's and early 60's, I like music of that era to work by. To each his own, and I have a stack of CD's including the Beach boys and Duane Eddy as well as some Merle Haggard, Hank Williams, Jr,.

Forearms

The very first thing I do when beginning to lay out a pattern on a forearm area of a rifle stock, or on a forearm from a two piece set it to determine the centerline of the area to be checkered. Regardless of how you do it, and there are many ways, an accurate line indicating the centerline of the forearm must be present.

One of the easiest ribbon patterns to cut for the beginner is one using the checkering lines as border lines of the ribbon. I did a forearm several years ago on a trap forearm for a Winchester Model 12, and then broke up the set – the customer did not like the figure in the forearm - and ended up selling the forearm as a single piece.

In laying out a pattern such as this, determining the centerline of the area to be checkered is critical. Of special note is the white pencil lines are guide lines. To be changed if needed. The next question to be solved is the size of the diamond. I chose one half the length of the area to be checkered; then drew it in using the white pencil and the three and one-half plastic template. In this case, the ribbon was the width of two checkering lines. Experiencing something between a brain fart, and a total eclipse of the conscious, I decided to add "supports" to the center diamond. The initial plan had been to have it without any connections to the sides or the end of the pattern.

For the person cutting a pattern such as this for the first time, I would suggest an unsupported diamond.

I do not recommend starting out with a pattern as shown below. Not only are they very difficult, but they are very time consuming. The Model 12 Winchester Trap gun that this forearm went on was a very special project. It was to be my gun. The one I would shoot in singles Trap.

I haven't had a lot of time to shoot it, but when I place it in the rack…..

Section 09
Glossary of Terms

Adjustable Buttplates

Adjustable butt plates are butt plates, usually made of aluminum, which mount to the sole of the buttstock, and to which a recoil pad or buttplate is attached, and which allow adjustment of the plate holding the recoil pad up, down, sideways, or canted. There are a variety of adjustable butt plates available, three of which are shown. The center one is a product of the Stock Shop and features movement up, down, left, right, and unlimited canting; then being locked in place with an allen wrench inserted through a hole into the recoil pad. In this manner, once the pad is mounted on the gun, and the recoil pad mounted to the adjustable buttplate, adjustment of the recoil pad's position requires an allen wrench inserted into a hole in the recoil pad, no removal of the recoil pad to expose the adjustment.

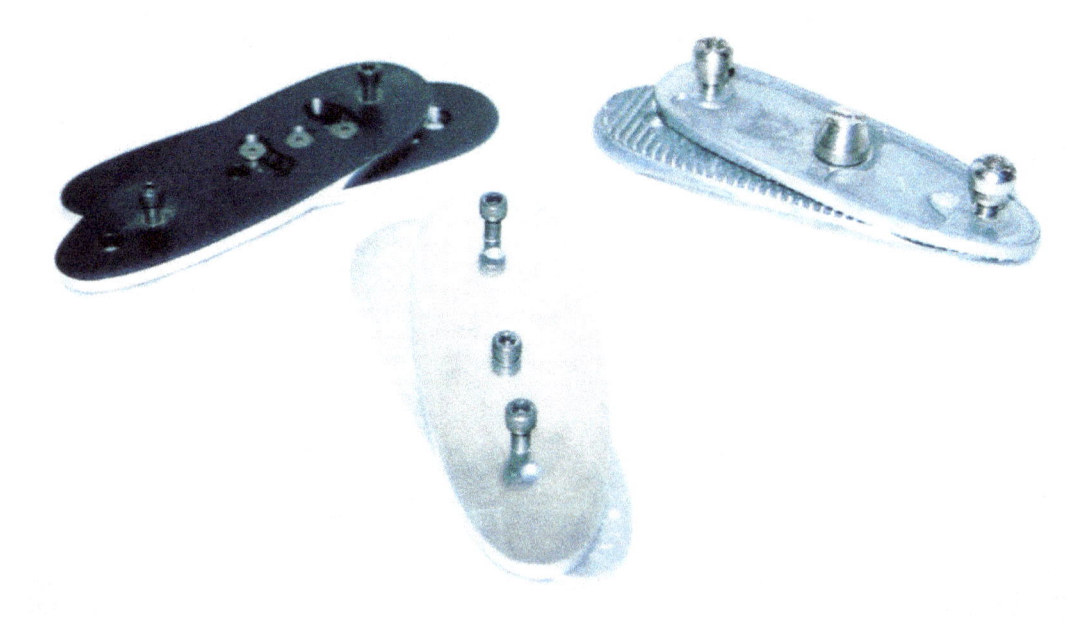

Anticipated Border

The anticipated border is the temporary line, usually a white line, to which opposing lines are cut. It is the anticipated border which will become the actual point pattern border when all lines are extended out from the master lines to a distance desired. Because cutting checkering lines is not an exact science – rather an art form – the checkered lines may not run exactly true because of the skill of the person checkering, the curvature of the wood, or the need to make a "correction" of previous lines.

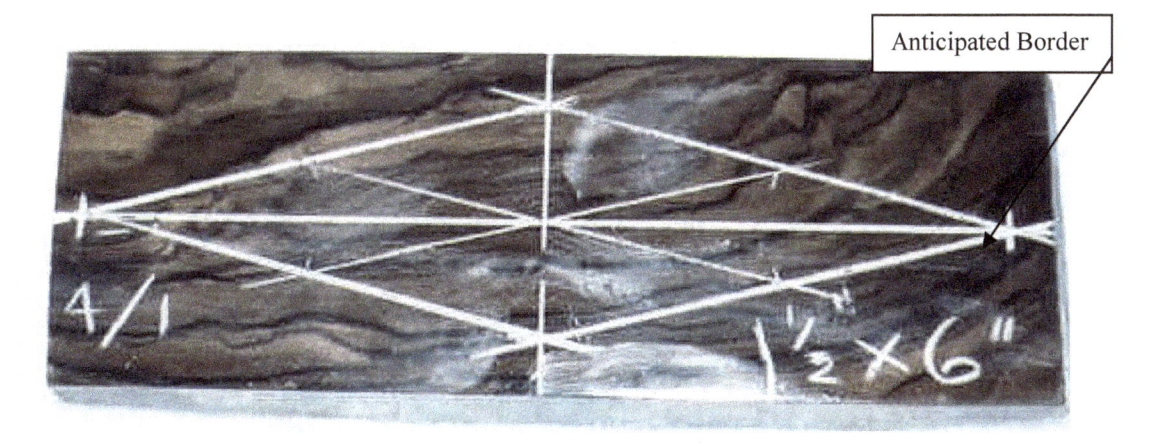

Barrel Channel

The barrel channel is the groove or inletting in the wood into which the barrel rests and is partially surrounded by wood from the forearm. On semi-finished rifle stocks, the wood between the forearm tip and the receiver will often have only a narrow groove – often a half inch – cut into the wood. Other stocks will have a barrel channel inletted to accommodate a barrel contour, such as military step contour, light sporter weight barrel, etc.

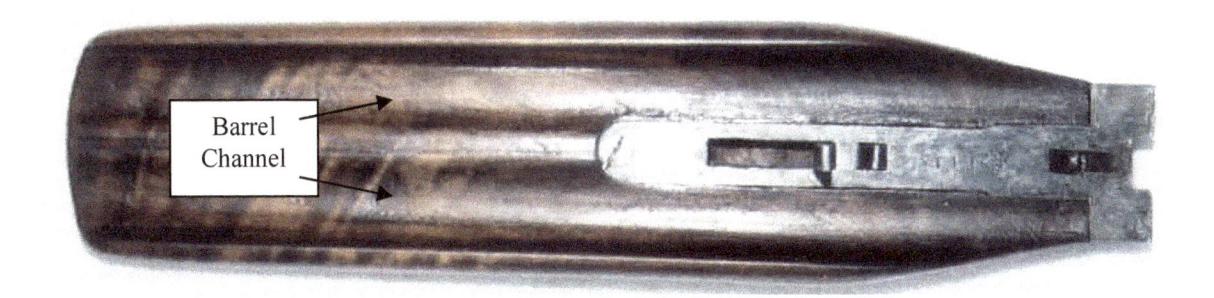

Bead

A checkering bead is the rounded border surrounding the checkering pattern. The difference between the border and the bead is the border is flat, and the bead is cut with a convex cutter and is rounded.

Border

A checkering pattern with a border is one with parallel lines to the outside of the checkering lines. Borders can be used to emphasize the detail of the checkering, or they can be used to hide a run-over made when cutting the edge of the pattern.

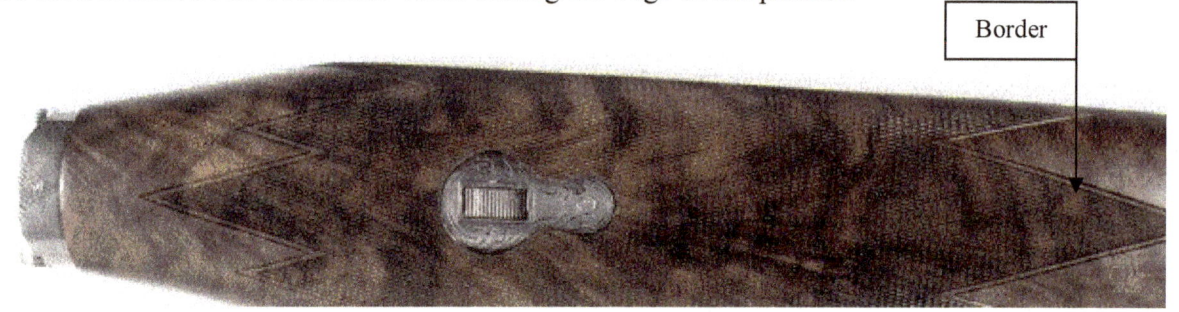

Borderless

A checkering pattern considered borderless is a pattern in which the edges are a single cut line into which checkering lines terminate.

Butt

The butt of the buttstock or stock is the "end of the stock" which is placed against the shoulder for aiming and/or firing. It is to the butt of the stock that the recoil pad is attached.

This is sometimes referred to as the "sole" of the stock.

Butt Plate

A butt plate is usually made of steel, plastic, or hardened rubber and is affixed to the butt of the stock or butt stock with screws or other fastening devices. The buttplate is not intended to reduce recoil, but is intended to protect the butt of the stock or buttstock from abuse and the elements. Many arms makers used the butt plate to identify their company by having their name, logo or other recognizable feature molded into the butt plate.

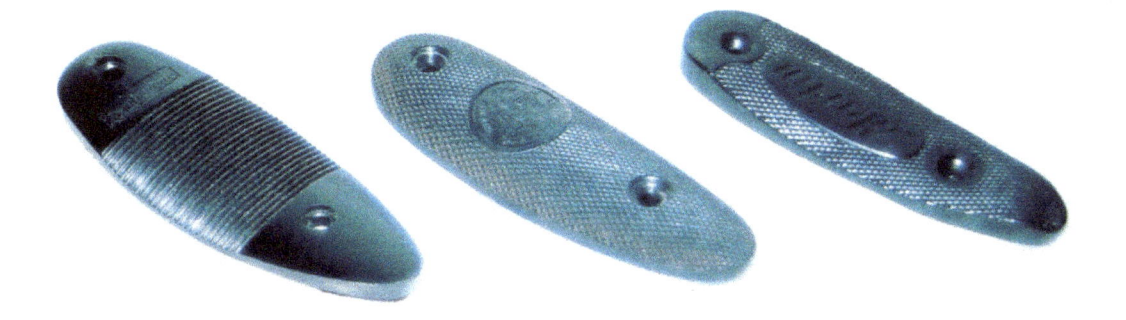

Cartridge Trap

A cartridge trap is a device, usually made of metal, inletted into the belly of a stock - especially European hunting rifles and drillings – used to store additional ammunition for emergency use. While not common in today's hunting rifles, the requirement to install one is a challenge and should be approached with caution. A correctly inletted cartridge trap is a beautiful item, one that is not correctly inletted is a mess.

Cast

The cast of a stock is determined as being the distance between the centerline of the stock, and the imaginary centerline extending from the top center of the barrel(s) back to the butt. A simple way of measuring the cast of a stock is top lay a straight edge – a metal yard stick will work well – down the center of the barrel rib and extending to the butt of the stock and determining cast as the difference between the two lines.

Centerline

The top centerline of a stock is a straight line from the top center of the receiver, and to the top center of the butt end of the buttstock. The bottom centerline is a straight line from the bottom center of the receiver to the bottom center – toe – of the buttstock. The location of these lines is necessary in determining toe in or toe out of the stock.

Crotch Figure

This is the term used to describe the grain or figure in a piece of wood coming from the crotch or "Y" of a tree. The crotch grain is very dense, and if not properly dried, subject to checking-cracking.

Edger, checkering

An edger is a checking tool with teeth much like a hand saw and is used for cutting/deepening the edges of a pattern. Edgers come in sixty degree or ninety degree angles. I favor the sixty degree edger when one is needed. When using an edger on highly figured wood, one must be extremely careful or the edger will pull wood, leaving unsightly and hard to repair gaps.

Fiddleback Figure

Fill-in Pattern
　　A fill-in pattern is a pattern on which all of the borders have been pre-determined. The pattern can be a point pattern or one with flowing borders such as is shown in the borderless pattern illustration.

Fleur dis Lei
　　Fleur dis Lei is the term used to describe the figure in the checkering pattern. There are many variations of the fleur, with most developed to suit the checkering style of the person performing the work.

Flat Top Checkering

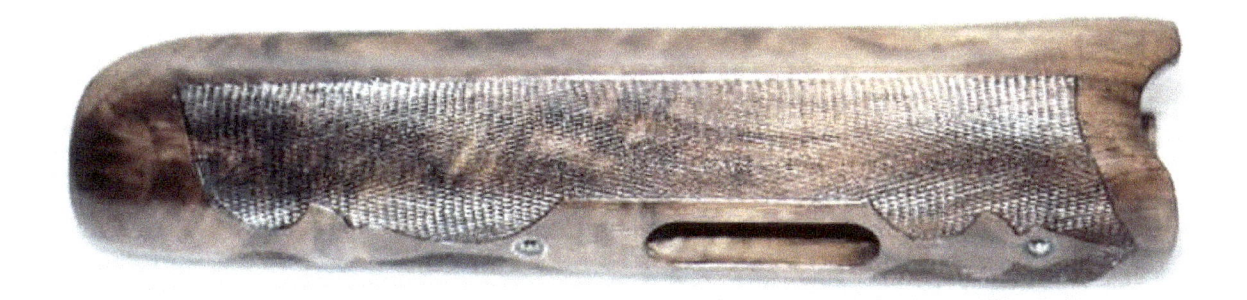

Flat top Checkering is the term used to describe – very simply – checkering whose tops are not brought to a point, but left flat on top. Many of the older guns have this type of checkering.

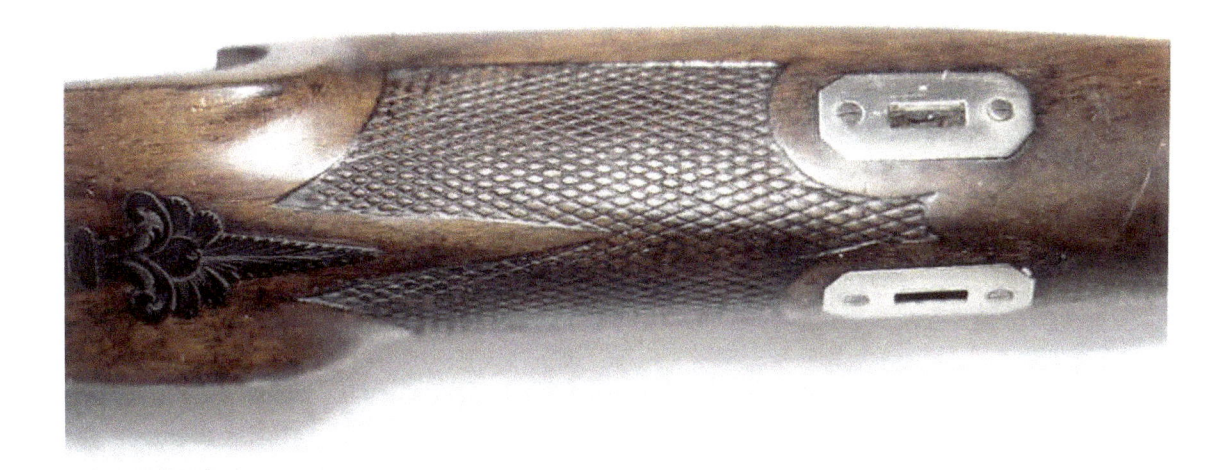

Forearm bushing

The fore arm bushing is a metal bushing, visible on the bottom of the forearm into which the forearm screws are affixed. The bushing serving as a "nut" to the forearm screw. The accurate location of the forearm bushing can be difficult.

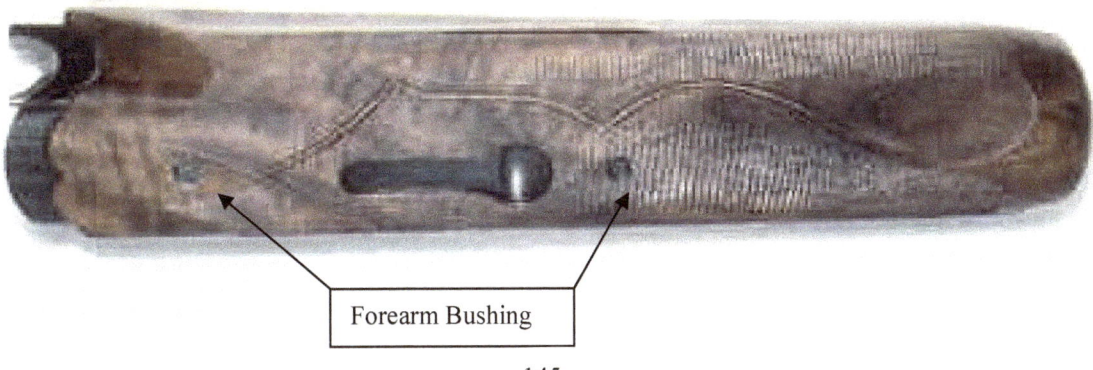

Forearm Iron

The forearm iron is that piece of hardware to which the wood forearm attaches. The forearm iron is fastened to the barrels/receiver in a variety of ways, to include a simple arched spring. In the photo above – of a Krieghoff K-80 forearm with forearm iron - the forearm is attached to the barrels with a latch controlled by the lever as shown.

Forearm Latch

The forearm latch is the means by which the forearm is "Latched" to the barrel and receiver. Some forearms may not have a visible forearm latch, using spring tension alone, others, such as the Krieghoff, Perazzi and Beretta forearm latches are evident in their appearance and functionality.

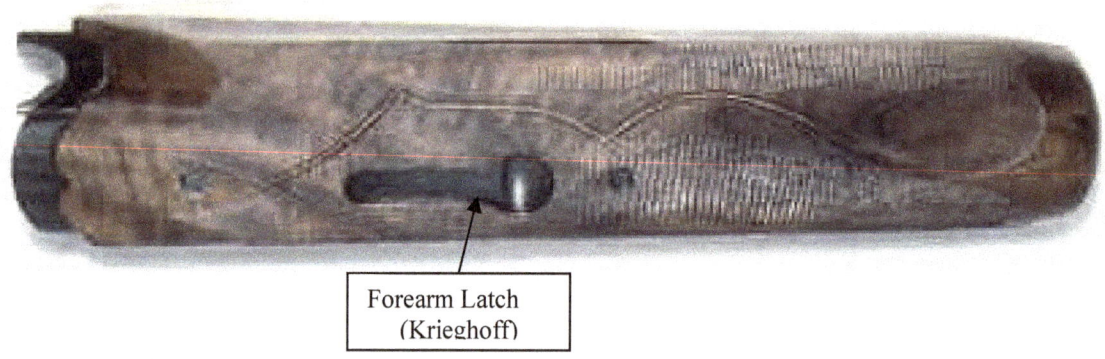

Forearm Latch (Krieghoff)

Forearm Tip

The forearm tip is not only decorative, but functional. It is often make of a contracting wood, such as ebony, but for many years buffalo horn was used. It serves a functional role in that it seals the end grain of the forearm from moisture. There are many methods of attaching the forearm tip to the stock.

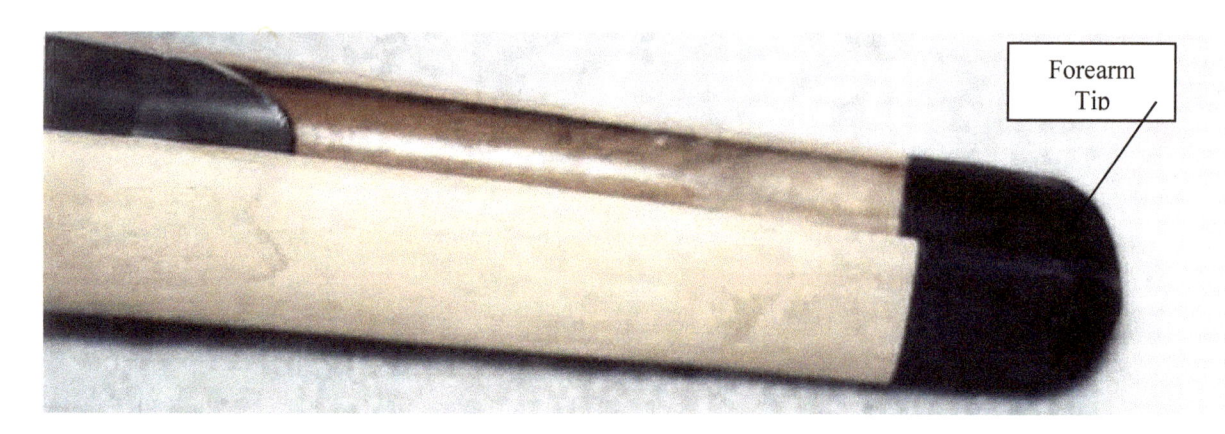

Forearm Tip

Heel

The heel of the stock is the top of the butt of the stock.

Impressed Checkering

Impressed checkering is just as the term implies: checkering that is pressed into the wood. This is also referred to as reverse checkering. This is a quick and inexpensive way in which manufacturers can provide a form of checkering on guns. Perhaps the best known illustration of impressed checkering was on the Remington Model 1100 and 870 shotguns. Other manufacturers also used impressed checkering, to include Winchester and Ithaca.

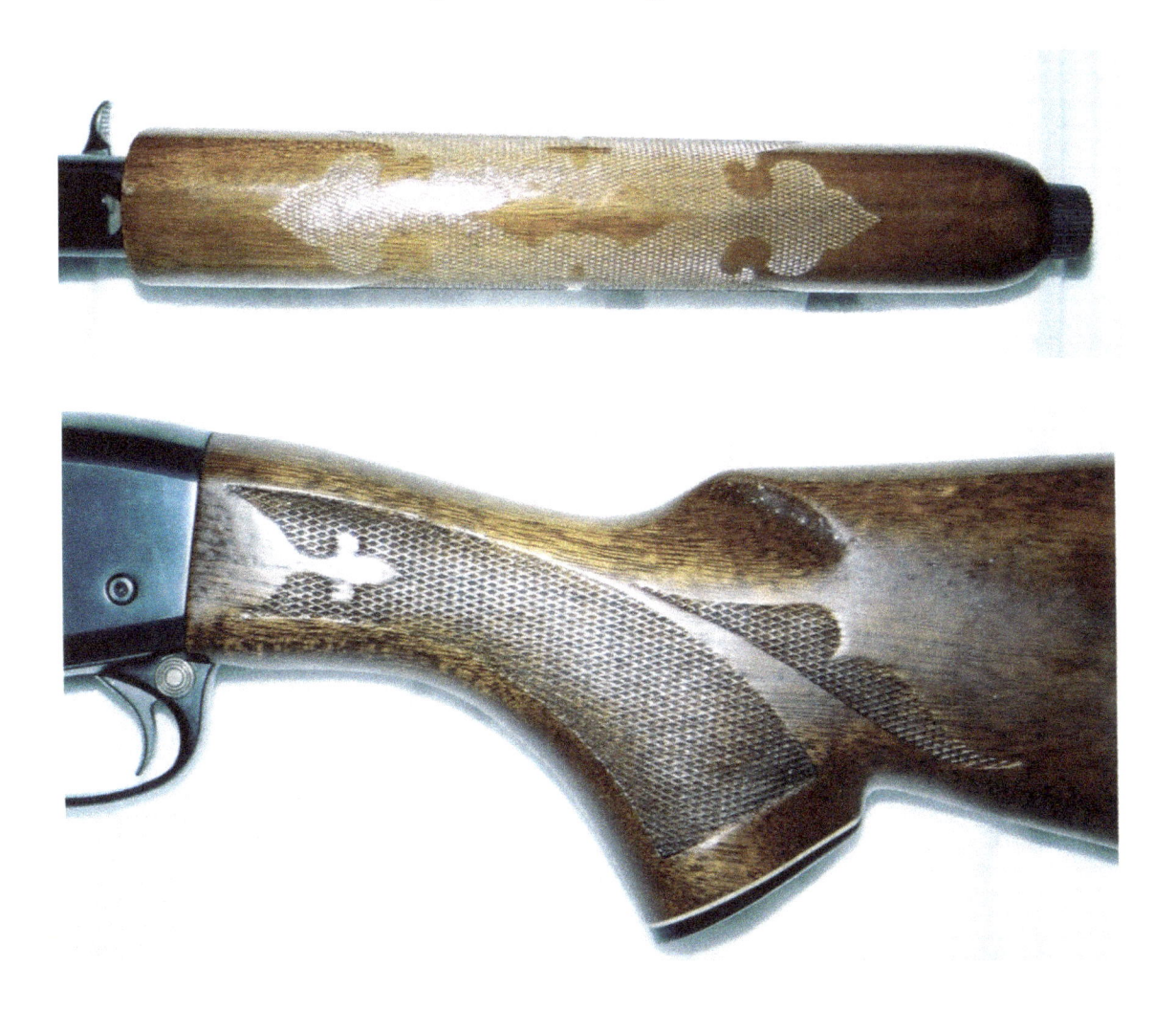

Length of Pull

The length of pull is the distance between the center of the trigger to the center of the curvature of the butt, or lacking a curvature, to the center of the butt.

Lines per Inch

The term, lines per inch, is a term used to identify and describe the number of lines of checkering per inch width, as well as the spacing between lines of checkering. Spacers, such as those produced by Gunline, used to layout the checkering lines, are identified and can be ordered as one cutting X lines per inch. Most suppliers offer spacers ranging from sixteen to twenty-eight lines per inch. Naturally, the more lines per inch, the finer the checkering.

White Pencil

I use a white compound pencil, marketed as the "Marks Everything Pencil" for all of my draft lines when creating or copying checkering patterns or making master lines. I purchase mine from Brownell's Inc, and consider them one of my primary checkering tools. I have used different colored grease pencils, but the white pencil is far superior for my uses.

Master Lines

The master lines are the two lines initially established and from which all other lines emanate. The master lines establish the ratio of the diamonds to be checkered.

Pitch

Pitch is the angle of the butt to the axis of the bore. Pitch can be measured quickly by placing the butt of the weapon on the floor and keeping the butt flat, move the weapon until the receiver comes in contact with the wall. If the muzzle of the barrels do not contact the wall, the weapon has negative pitch. The amount of negative pitch is the distance from the wall to the top of the barrel(s) at the muzzle. This measurement can be noted as 1 inch for a 28 inch barrel length. The second way of measuring pitch is to secure a straight edge down the center of the barrel(s) of the weapon, extending it back over the butt of the stock, and determining the angle of the butt to the plane of the rib in degrees.

Pointer

A pointer is a checkering tool used to deepen checkering lines. It has teeth very much like a file. It comes in a sixty degree and a ninety degree angle, in both a fine and medium cut, and in both short and long configuration. I use the pointer for the vast majority of my work.

Point Pattern

A point pattern is a pattern in which the ends - on a forearm and forward area on a grip pattern – in points established by the border, or in the case of "true" checkering, the checkering lines themselves. Point patterns can also be a form of fill-in pattern as the outline of the checkering pattern is cut and the interior lines fill in the void. This most often happens in production guns, some quite expensive.

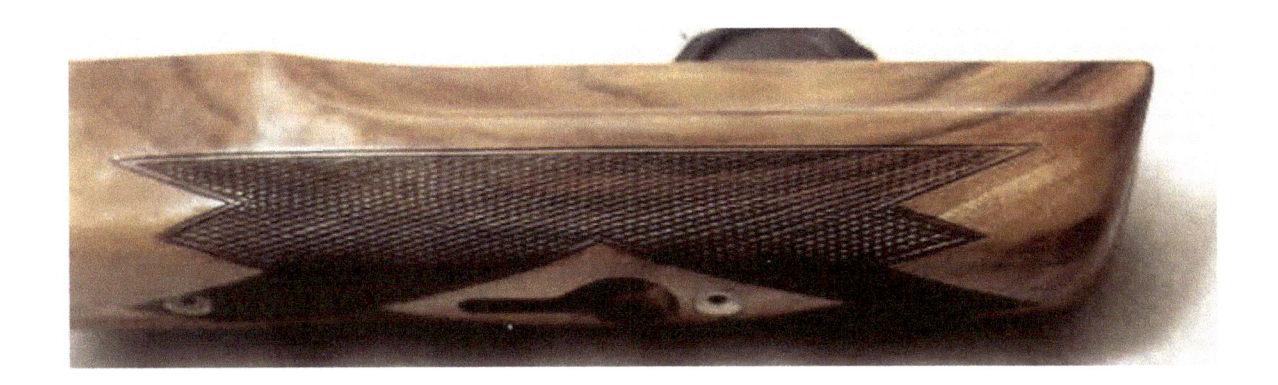

Ratio

The ratio is the term used to describe the length and width of the diamond formed when checkering. A four to one ratio would be a diamond four times as long as it is wide. When laying out master lines and establishing point patterns, a plastic template of the desired ratio – 3 to 1, 4 to 1, etc – is used. I make these templates by drawing out the diamonds of the desired ratio, and then copying them onto transparency stock. By cutting the diamonds from the transparency stock, I have a very handy tool in laying out master miles and establishing parallel lines

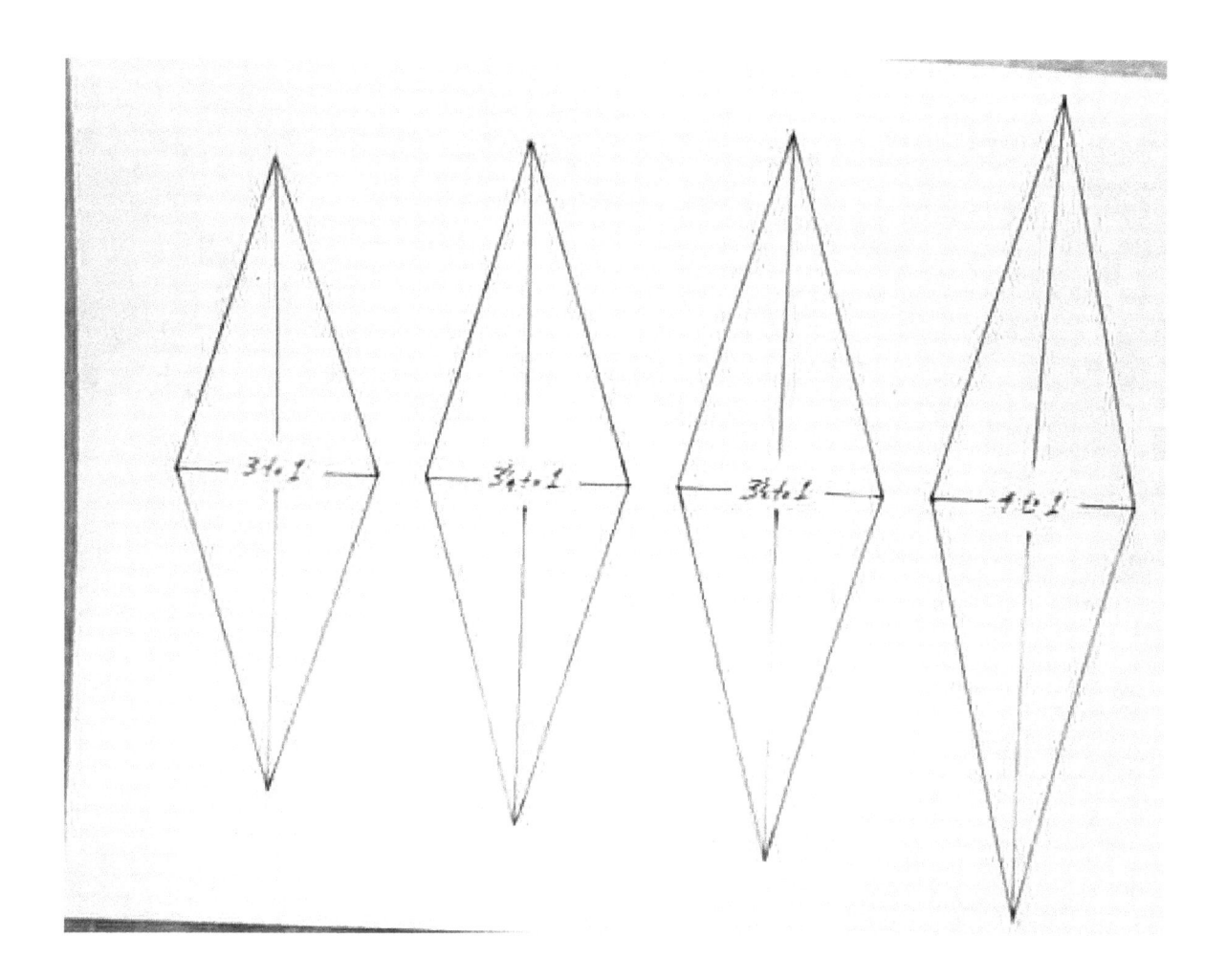

Receiver

The receiver of the firearm is that portion to which the barrels and stock are affixed. The receiver usually carries the manufacturer's identity and the serial number of the weapon. Receivers may be secured to the stock or buttstock through the use of a stock bolt passing through the butt and strewing into the receiver. The receiver may also he held in place through the use of tang screws passing through the butt between tangs.

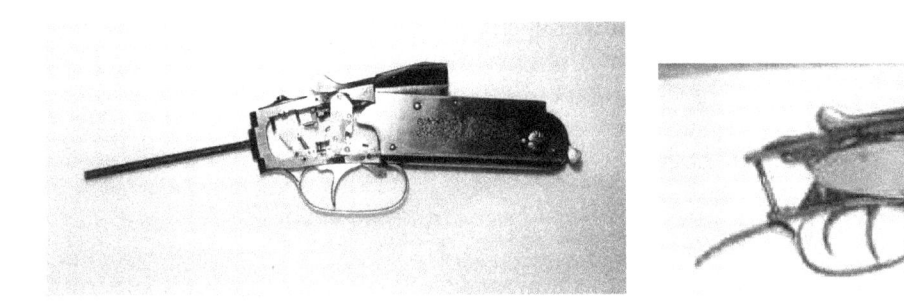

Receiver Face

The receiver face is that metal of the receiver coming into vertical contact with the stock. Contact between the receiver face and the stock is essential if the recoil is to be transferred evenly to the stock. If contact between the two surfaces is not equal to the contact at other points – upper and lower tangs – the area having the greatest contact will compress over time, often resulting in stock failure. Where there is little contact surface between the receiver and stock, the inletting is crucial if the stock is to endure the recoil of continual shooting.

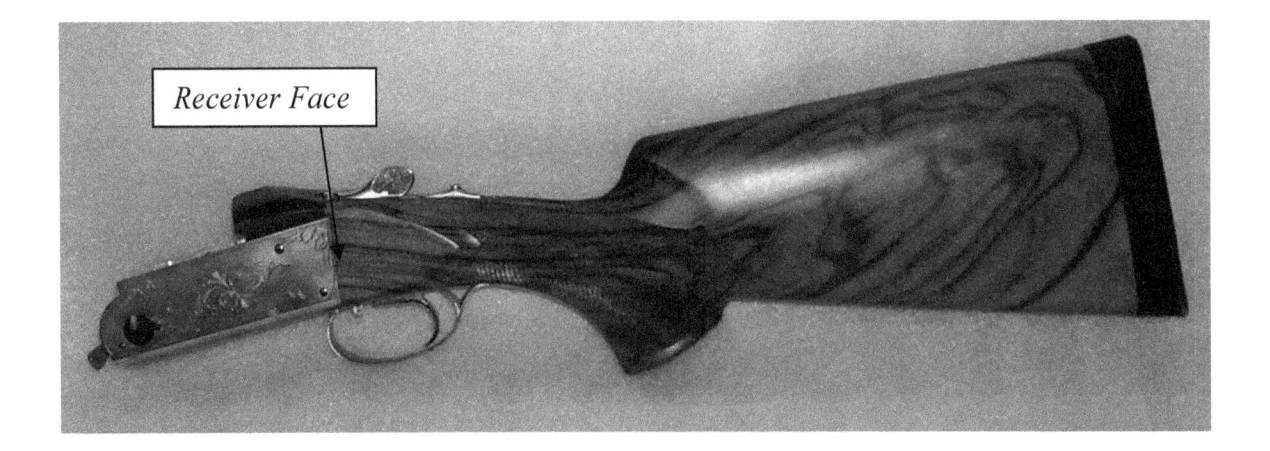

Recoil Pad

The recoil pad, usually made of rubber, is installed on the butt of the stock to absorb some of the recoil. With few exceptions, recoil pads must be ground to fit the stock upon which they are being placed. Pachmayr and Sims Vibration Laboratories (Limb Saver) manufacture a fine line of rifle and shotgun recoil pads, as does KickEez, and Terminator. The pad should be selected for to fulfill the purpose intended. A Trap pad on a gun to be used for Sporting Clays is an unnecessary handicap.

Ribbon Pattern

A ribbon pattern is one in which ribbons of uncheckered wood separate checkered areas within the checkering pattern. The width of the ribbons will vary, some are even tapered, and ribbons unmarred by over runs attest to the skill of the person doing the checkering. The ribbon can follow the path of the checkering lines, such as in this Model 12 Winchester Extended Trap forearm,

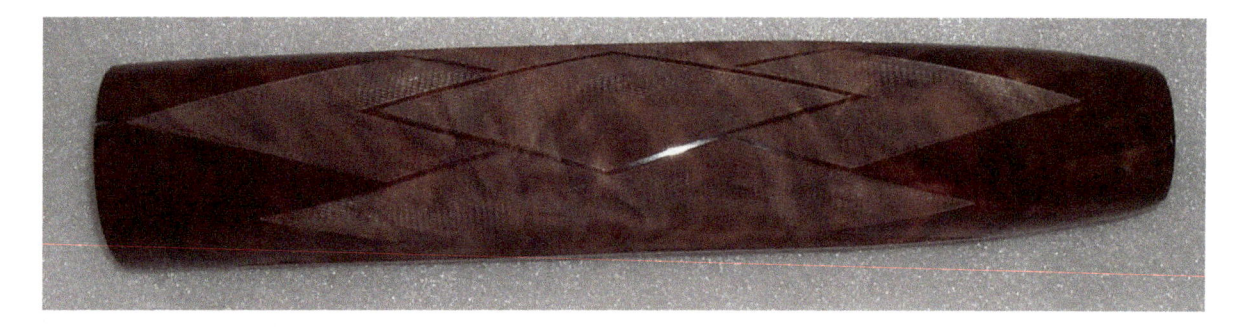

or the ribbon can create a pattern of its own as it separates the panels of checkering.

Scallop

Many European receivers have scalloped receiver faces. Scalloped outlines in checkering are more scarce in today's checkering than prior to World War II. A prime example of the use of scallops in the checkering outline can be found on this Ithaca 4E Trap gun. Please note the scallops are not only found on the face of the stock, but also at the rear of the checkering pattern.

Scallops

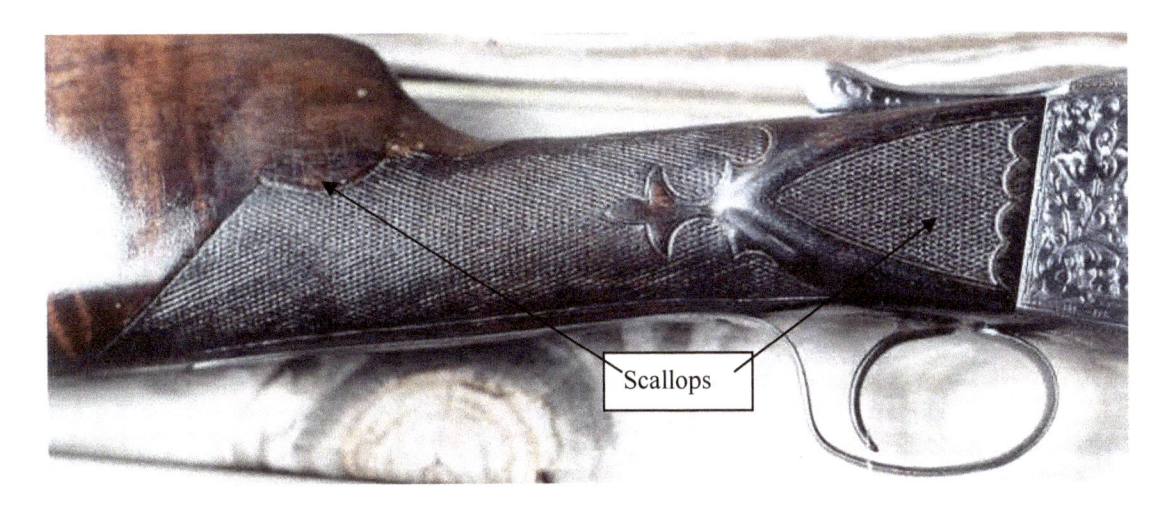

Sidelock

Sidelocks are of two distinct types. The first type id the functioning sidelock on which the hammer and sear are positioned. Such as shown below. A good example of the second type is the Beretta 687 EELL. The Beretta sidelock has no other function besides being decorative – it contains no functioning parts. Regardless of the type of sidelock, they are difficult to stock, and demand a checkering pattern to compliment the lines of the action.

Skeleton Buttplate

A skeleton butt plate is an outer metal frame inlet into the wood of the butt. The wood coming up through the center of the skeleton butt plate is then contoured into the lines of the buttplate, creating an attractive and protected butt for either rifle or shotgun. The wood surrounded by the skeleton buttplate is most often checkered. Parker Shotguns often were equipped with skeleton grip caps and skeleton butt plates. The metal of the skeleton buttplate is often engraved.

Skeleton Grip Cap

A skeleton grip cap is usually made or steel with a hollow center section through which wood from the grip area is exposed. Most often, this exposed wood is checkered. The rim of the skeleton grip cap is often used to engrave the name of the customer for which the stock was built, as well as the name or shop which build the stock.

Sling Swivel Stud

A sling swivel stud is the means by which detachable sling swivels are installed onto the rifle. The sling swivel stud is a headless screw with wood screw threads and a hole in its upper shank through which the pivot pin of a detachable sling swivel attached. It can also be a machine threaded screw attaching to an inletted threaded nut in the barrel channel. There are other means of establishing the sling swivel stud, to include many varieties of snap in and quick detachable units, but the screw in and machine thread screw are the most common.

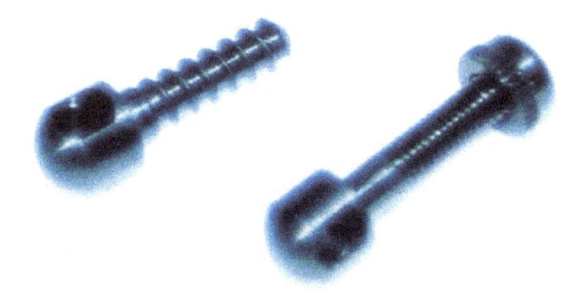

Sling Swivel Base

A sling swivel base serves the same purpose as does the sling swivel stud. That purpose of providing a means of attaching the detachable sling swivels. The difference being while the sling swivel stud screws directly into the wood, the sling swivel base is a formed piece of metal, held in position in the stock by screws.

Spacer, Checkering

A spacer is a checkering tool which has two or more rows of "teeth" cut into it at a specified distance. The spacing between the rows of teeth determine the lines per inch (lpi) of the checkering. For example, a spacer of 28 lpi has a row spacing of 1/28th of an inch.

Toe

The toe of the stock or buttstock is the bottom point of the butt of the stock. It is in this area that the wood is the weakest and most likely to chip off. A properly fitted buttplate or recoil pad can reduce the chance of the toe of the stock chipping off.

Wrap Around Pattern

A wrap around pattern is one which covers the entire area – or wraps around – such as over the top of the pistol grip on a rifle or shotgun, and around the forearm. The opposite of this is a panel pattern which encompasses only the sides – a specific area – of the buttstock, stock or forearm.

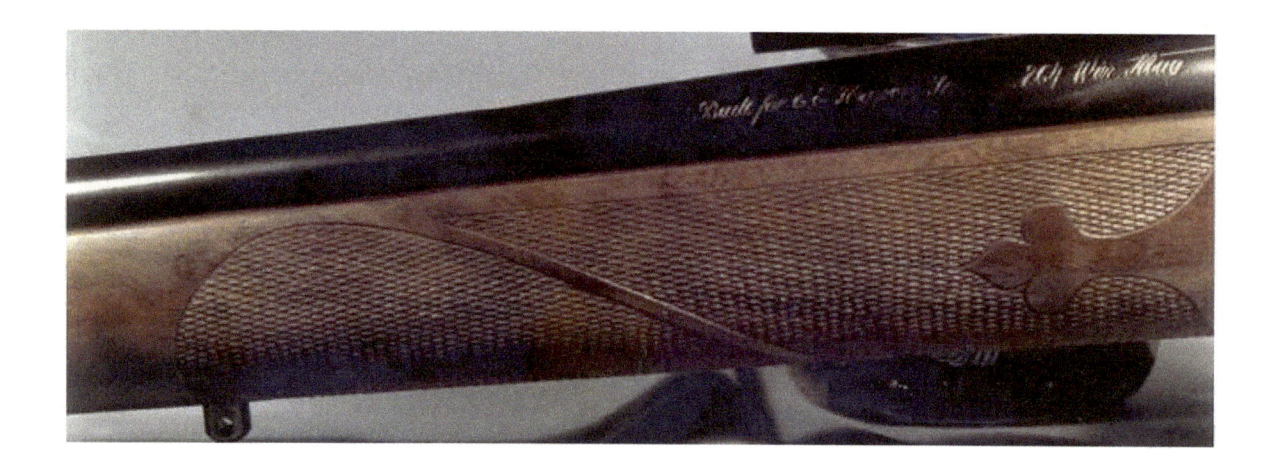

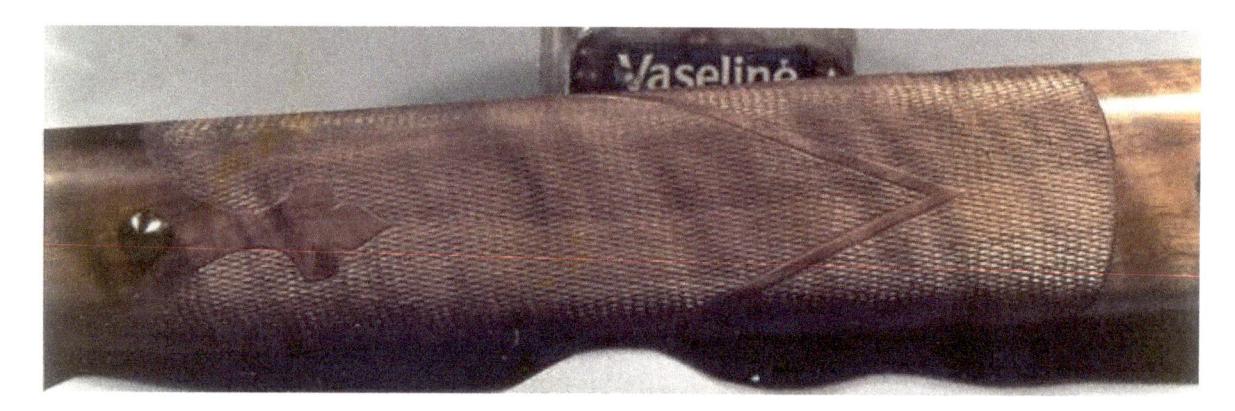

The term "wrap around" is meant to include running the pattern over the top of the pistil grip area. Much more difficult than it appears.

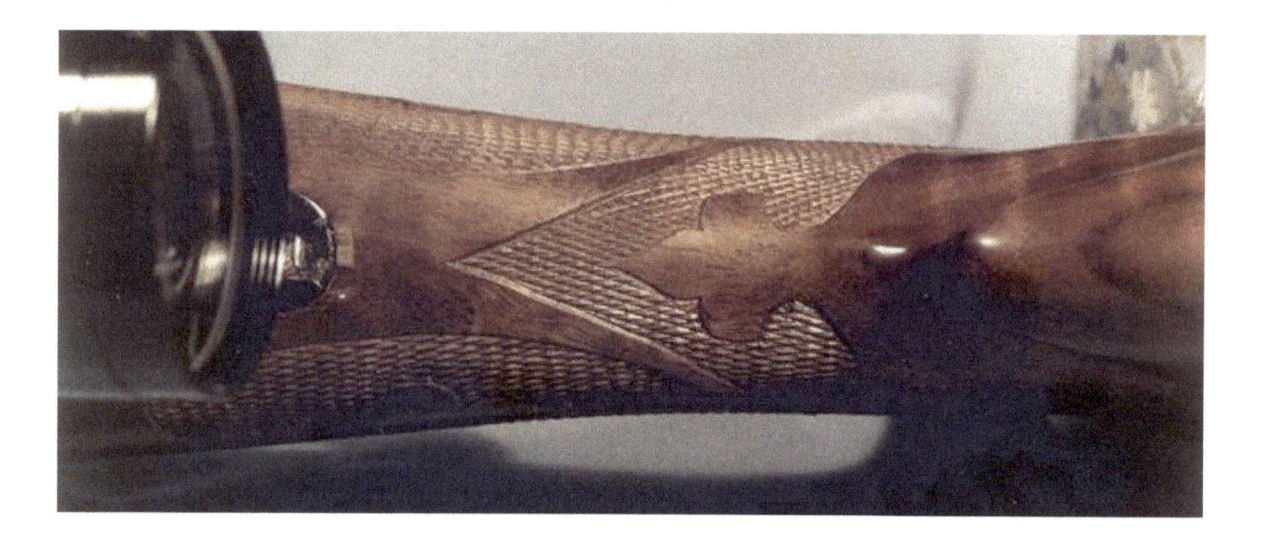

SECTION 10

Jobs Completed

Krieghoff Model 32

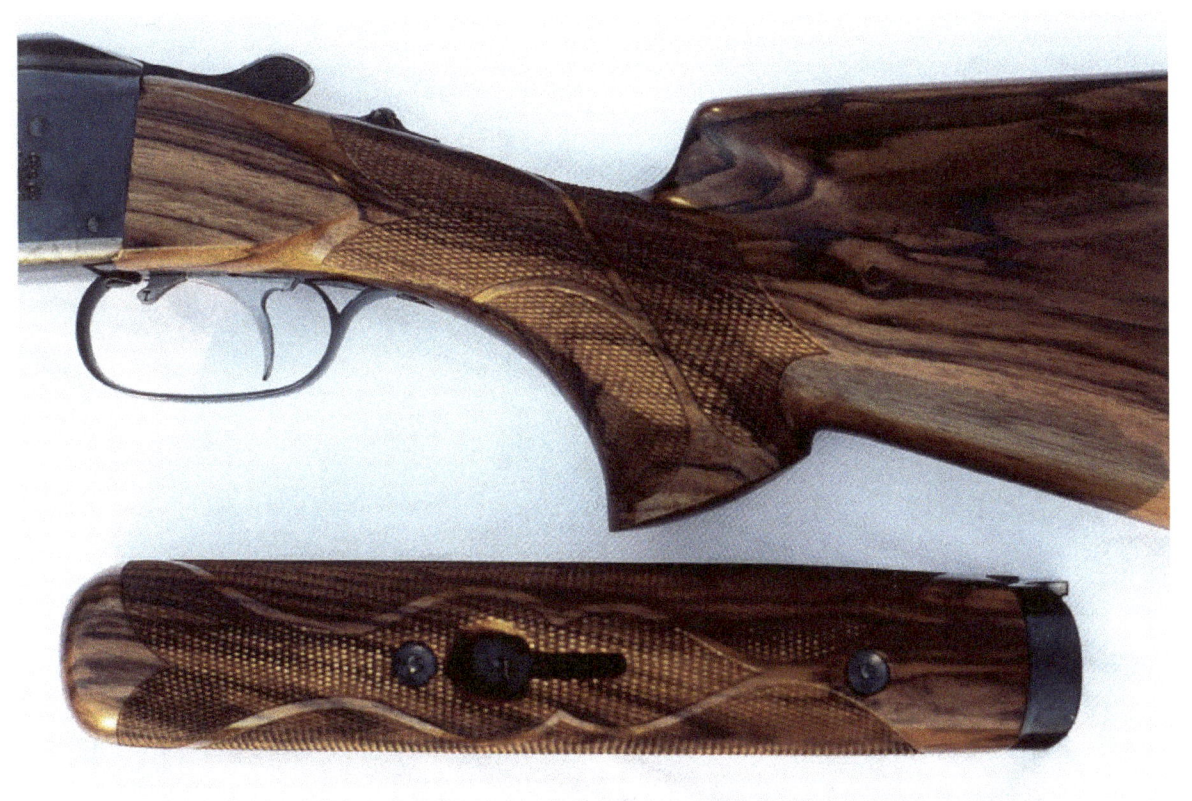

Krieghoff Model 32

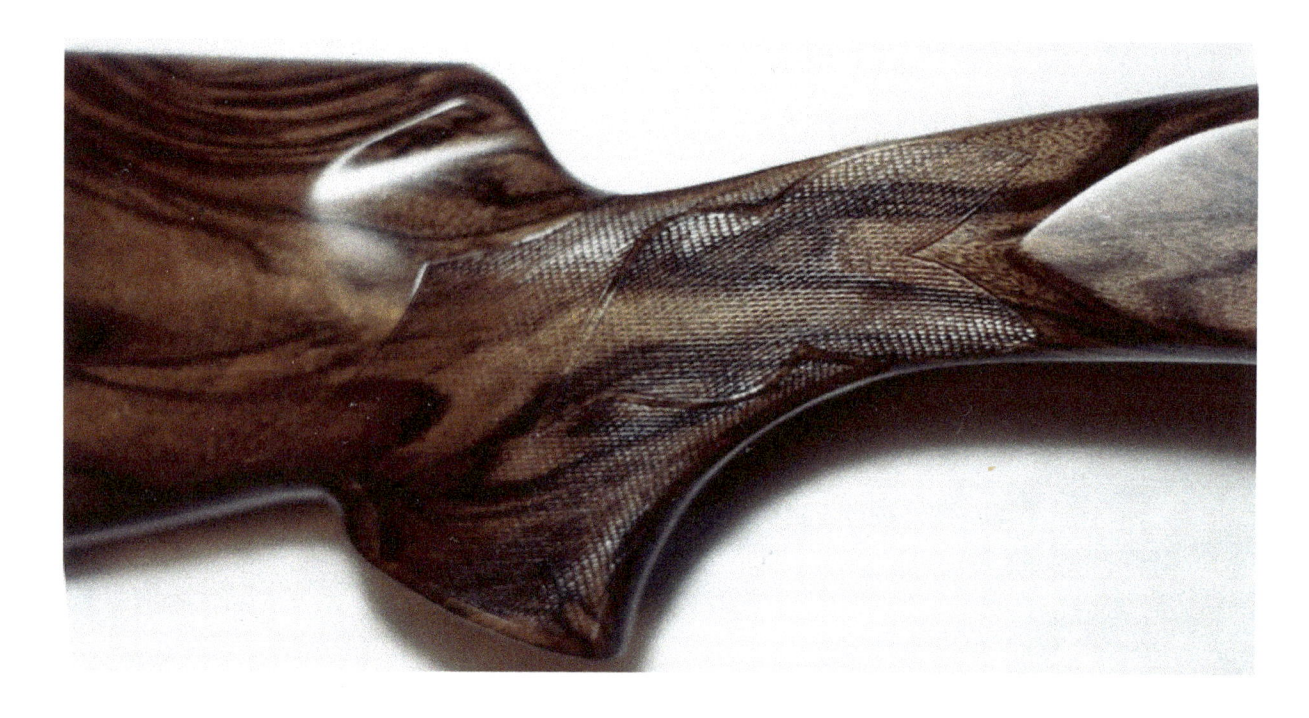

Remington Model 1100

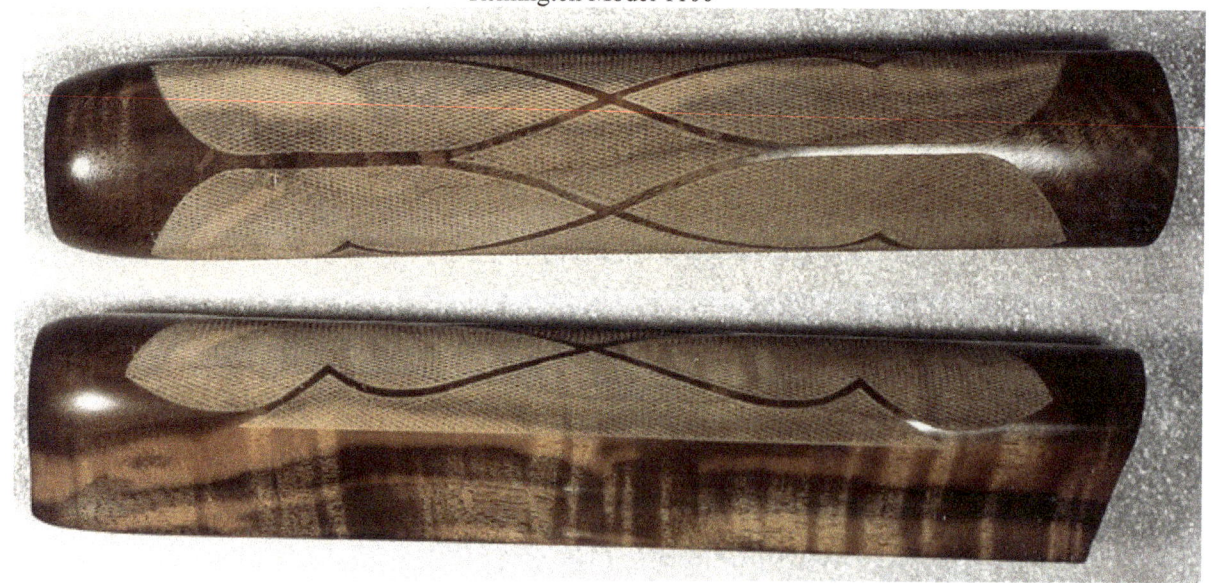

Remington Model 1100 Ducks Unlimited

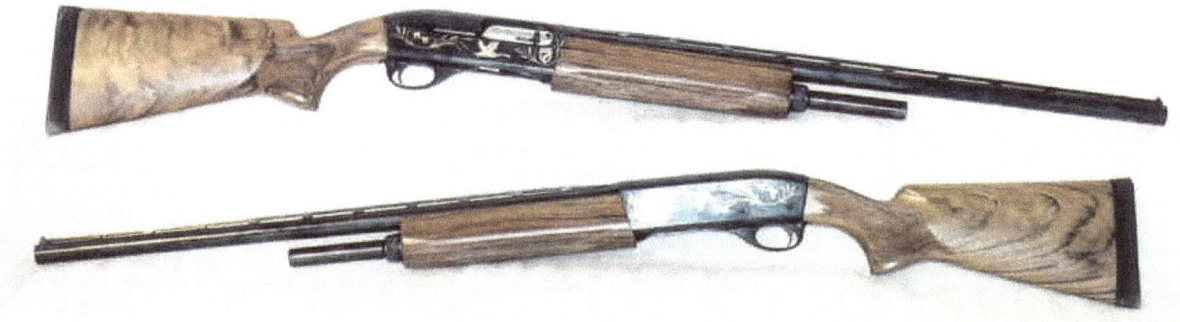

Krieghoff Model K-80

Krieghoff Model 32

Remington Model 1100

Krieghoff Model K-80

Krieghoff Model K-20

Krieghoff Model K-80

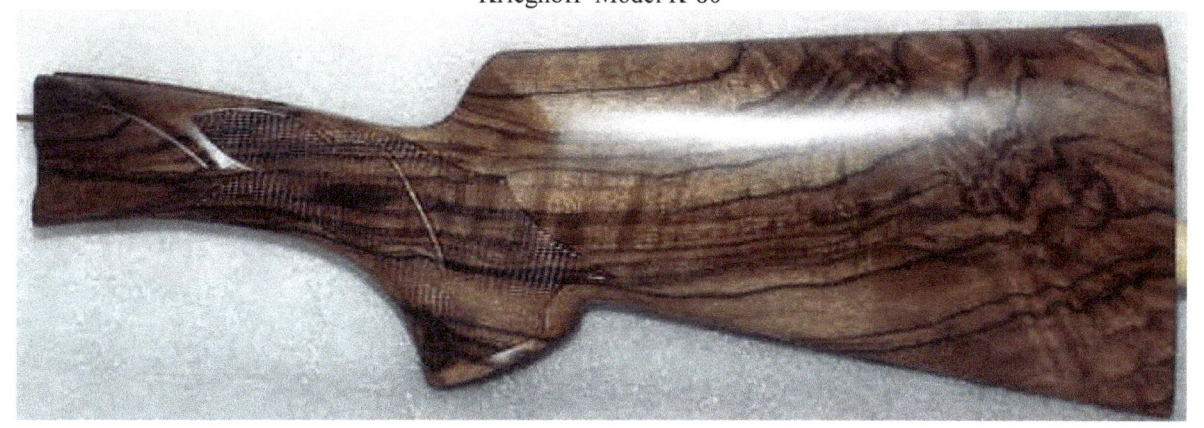

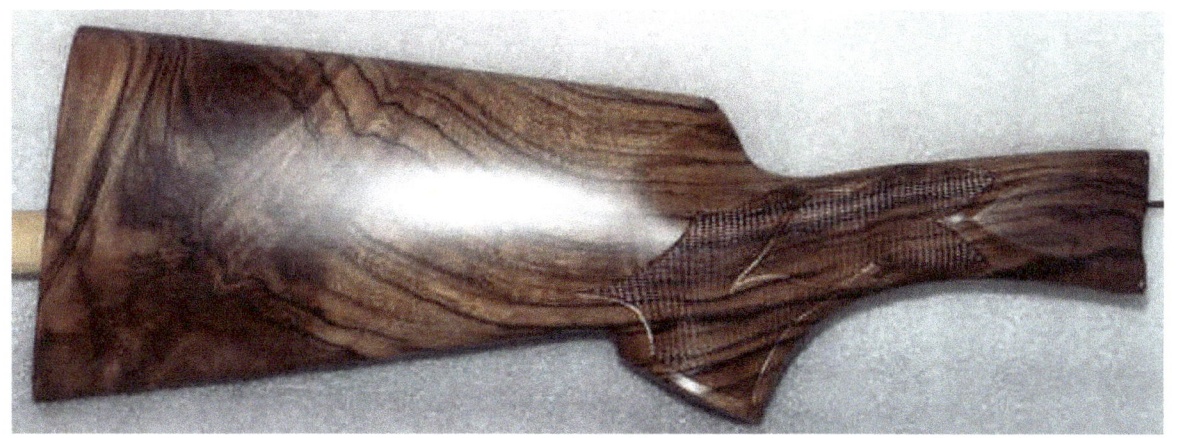

L. C. Smith

Winchester Model 101, 20 Gauge

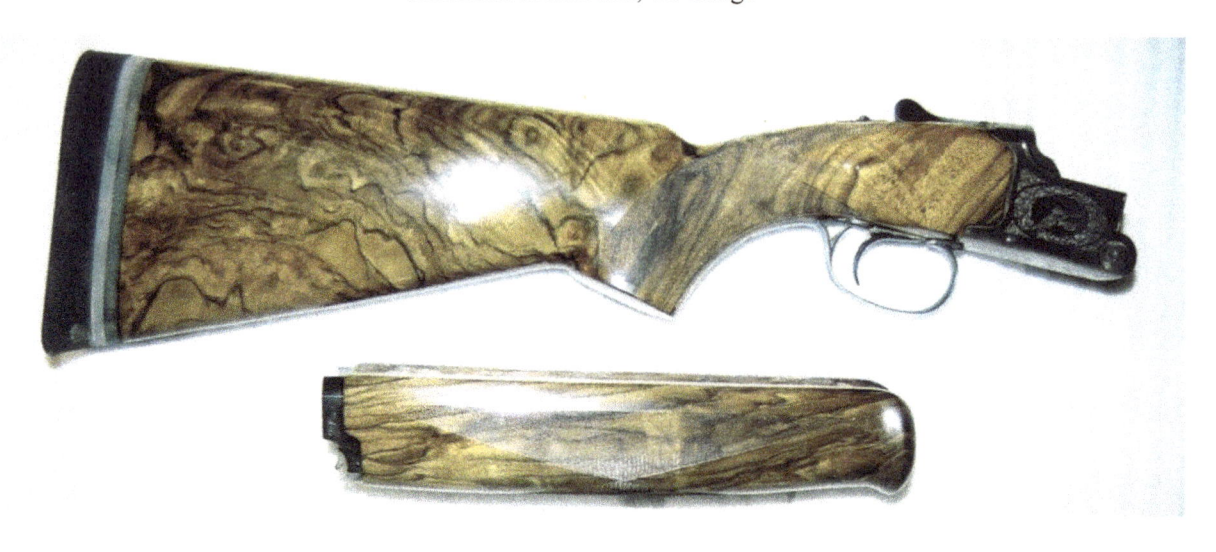

Beretta ASE 90

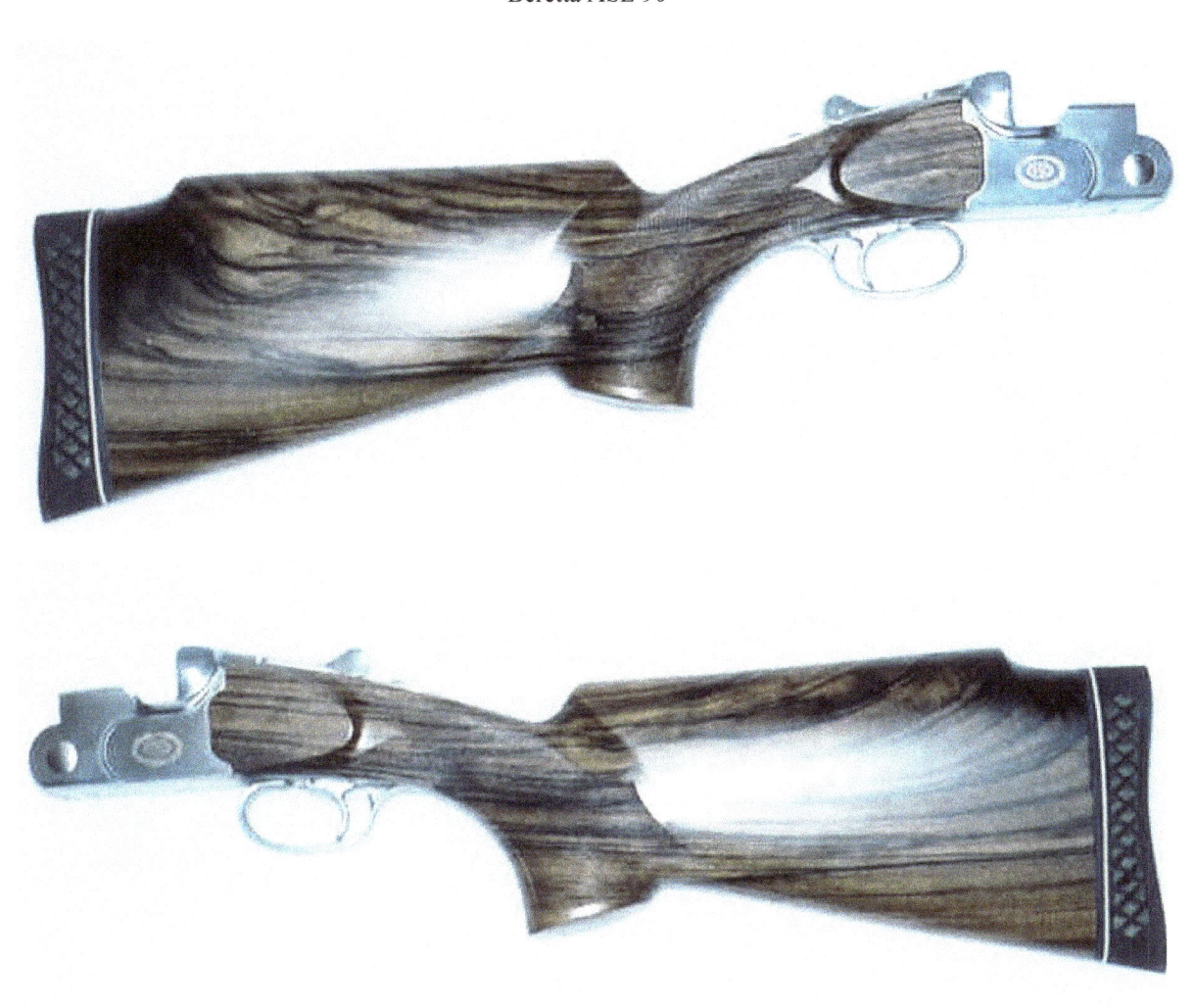

Krieghoff Model K-80

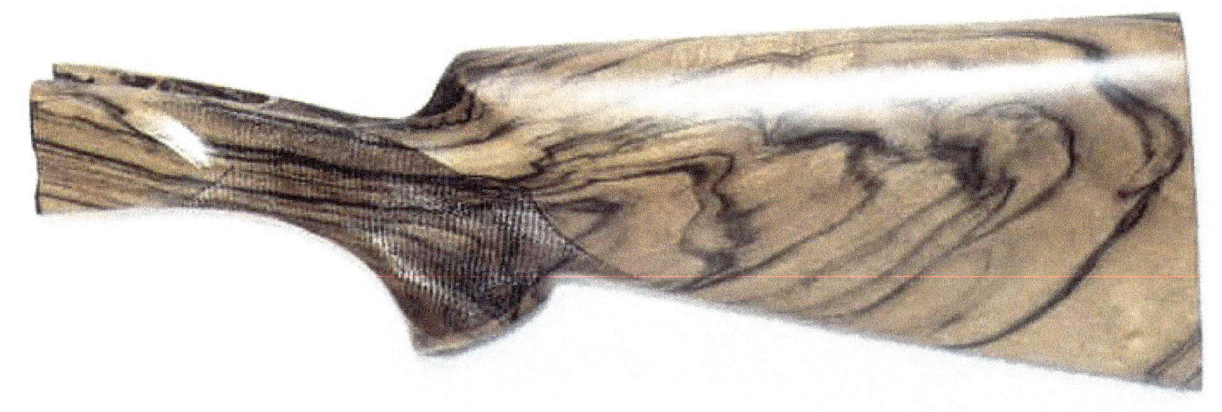

Beretta ASE 90

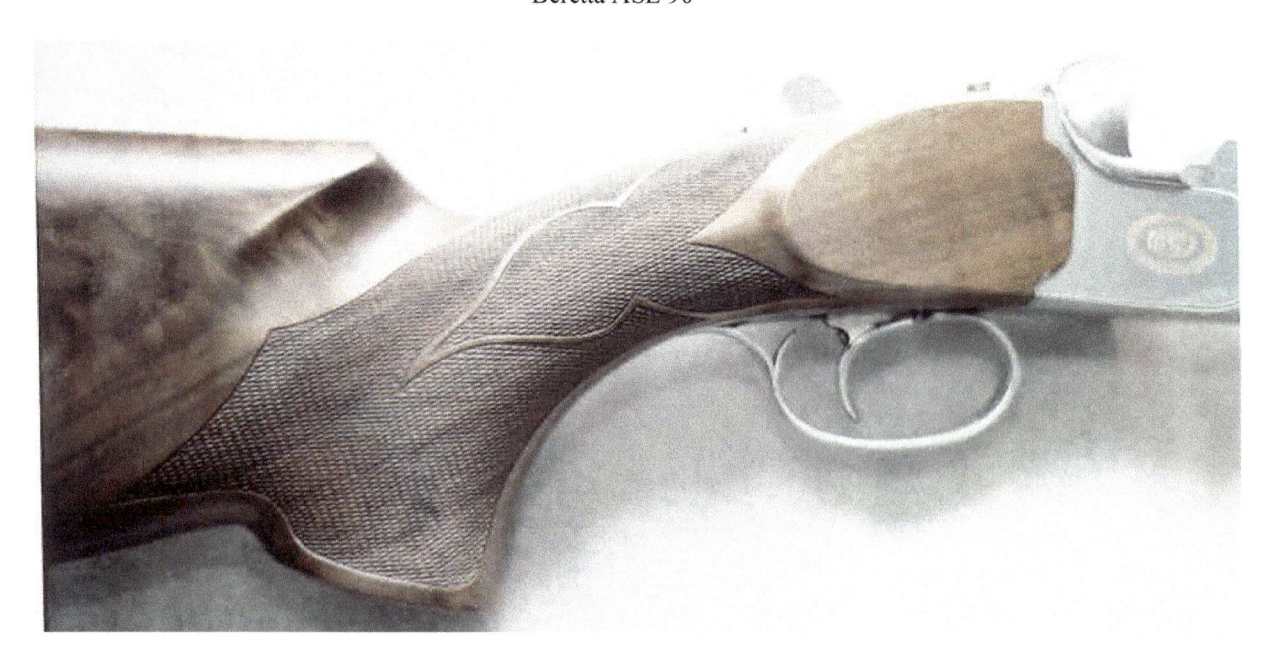

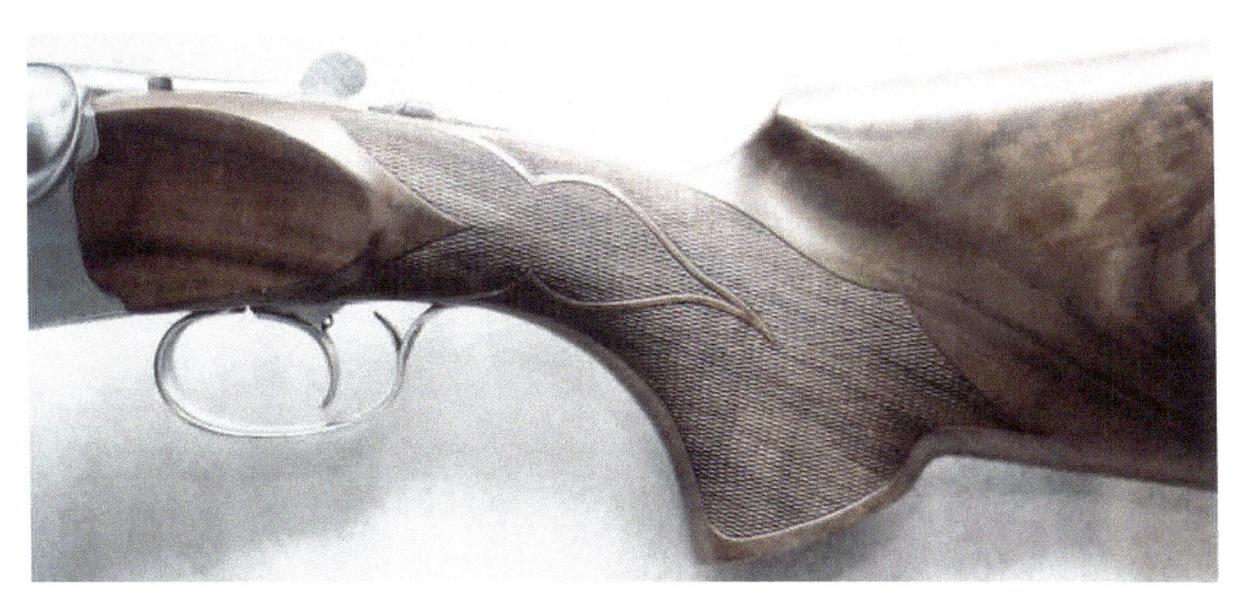

Beretta Model 682

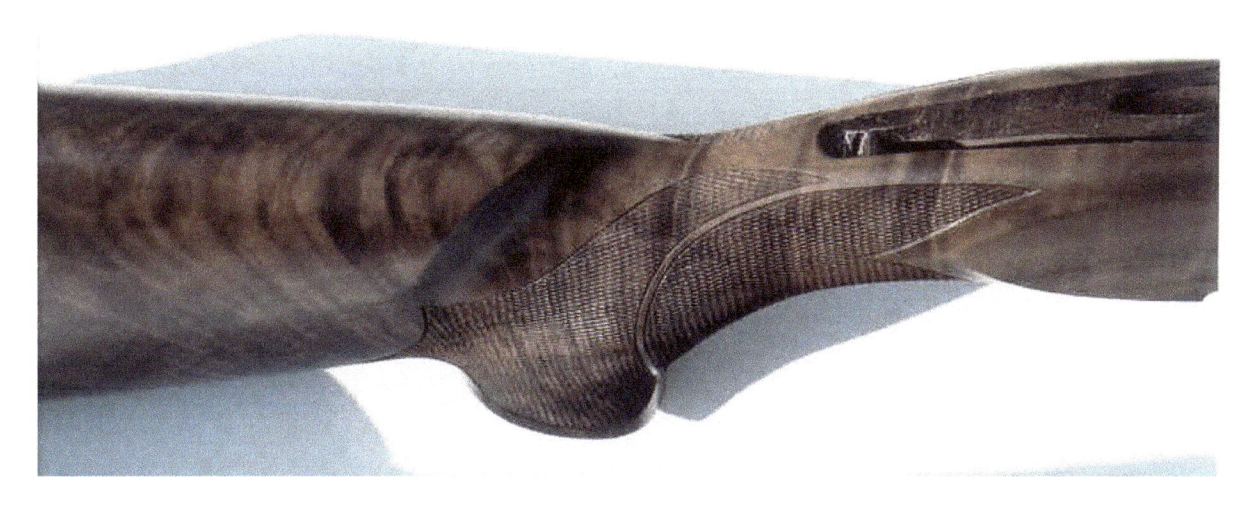

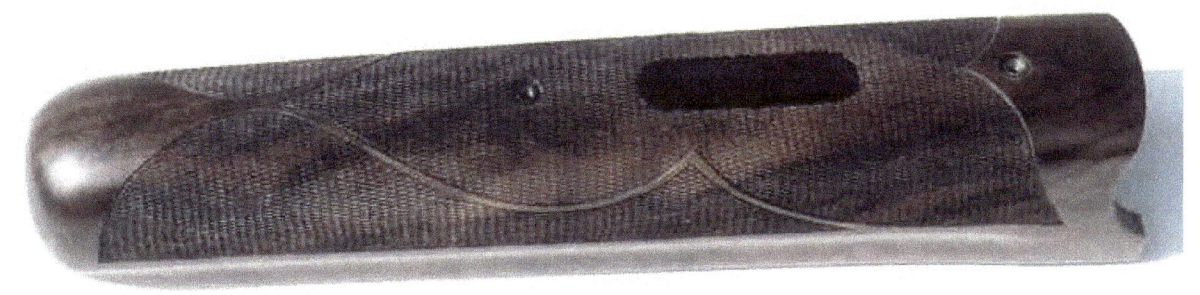

Commercial Mauser, 375 H&H Magnum (with Canjar Trigger and Thumb Safety)

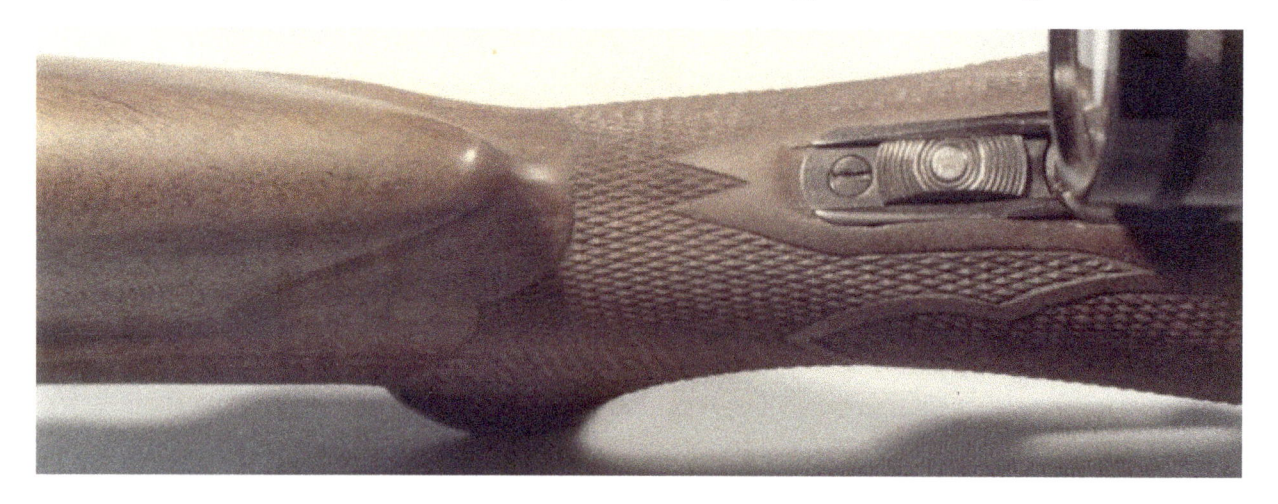

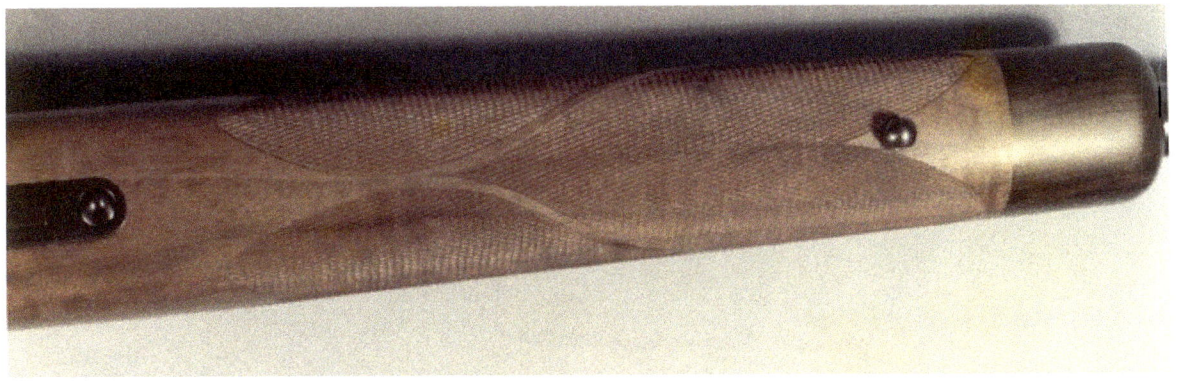

KOLAR

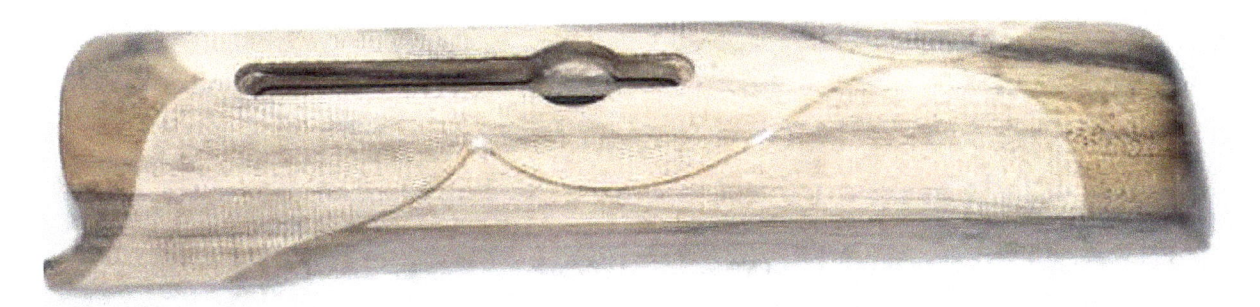

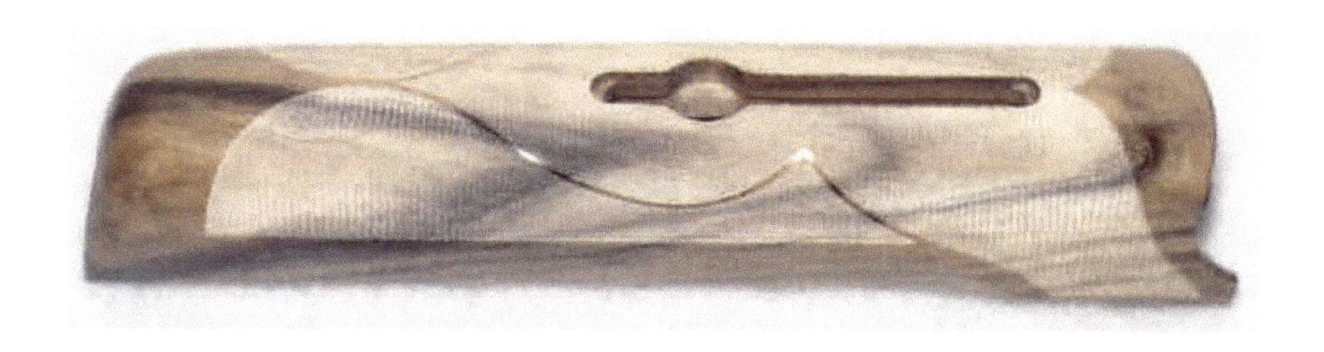

Krieghoff Model K80

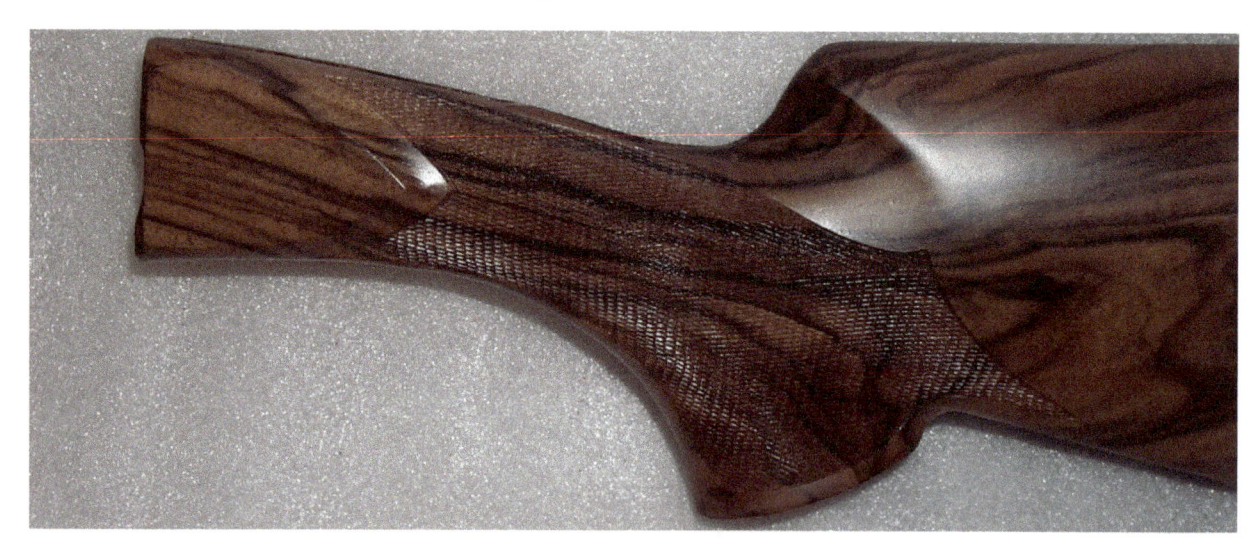

Krieghoff Model 32

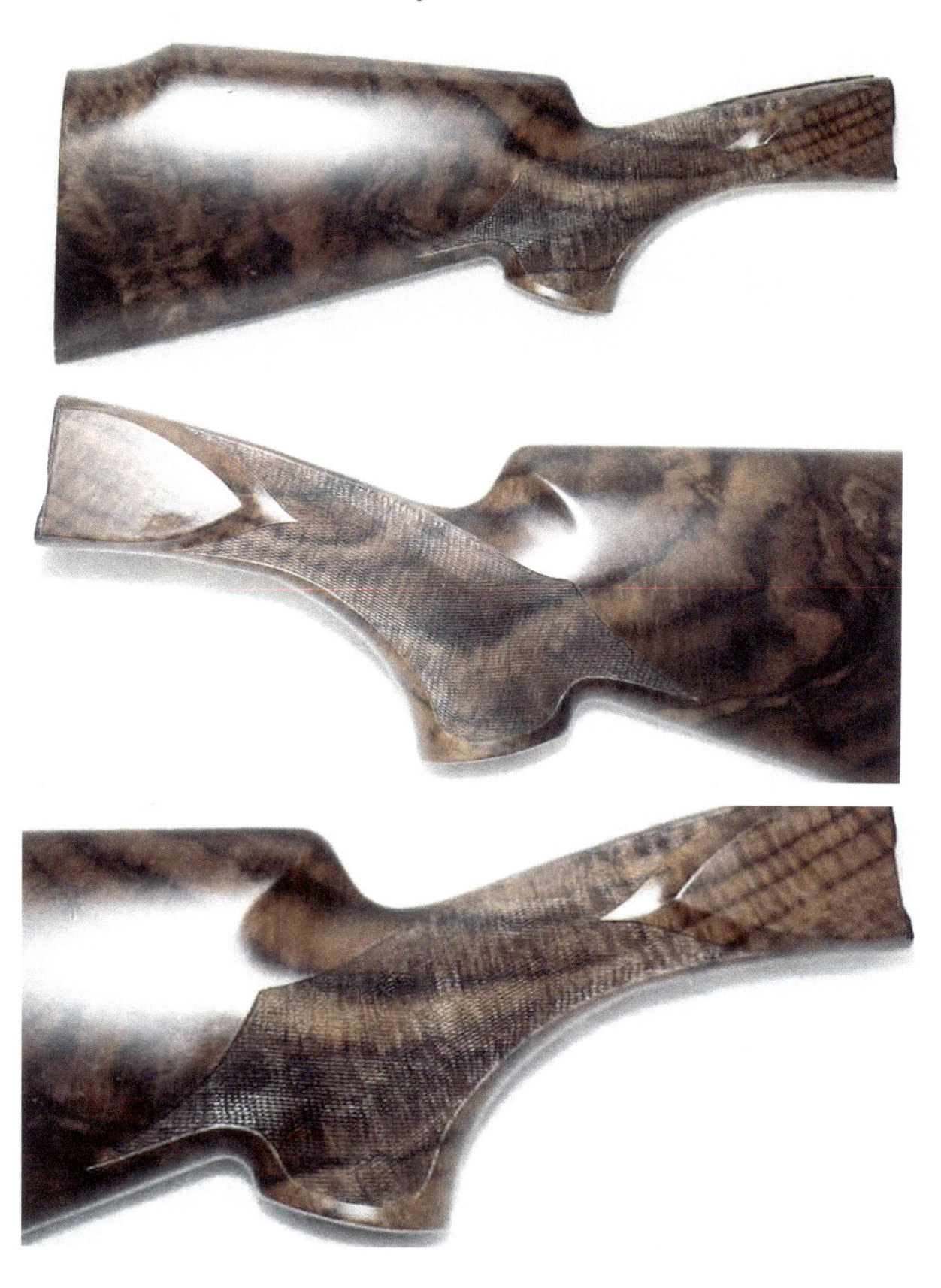

Krieghoff Model 32

Krieghoff Model 32

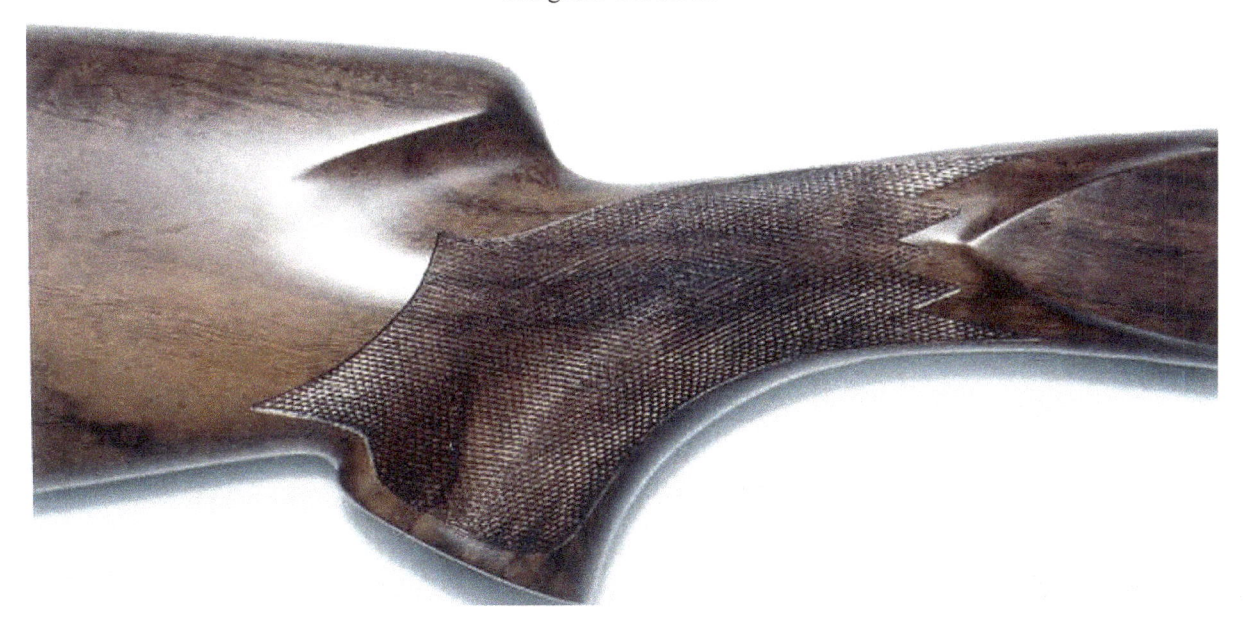

Krieghoff Model 32

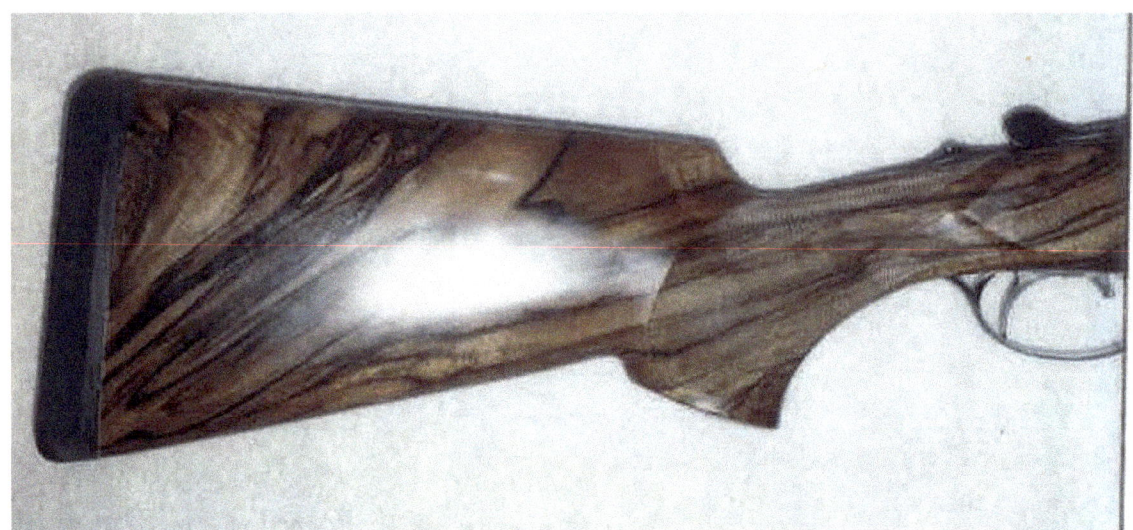

Krieghoff Model K80

Krieghoff Model K80

Krieghoff Model K80

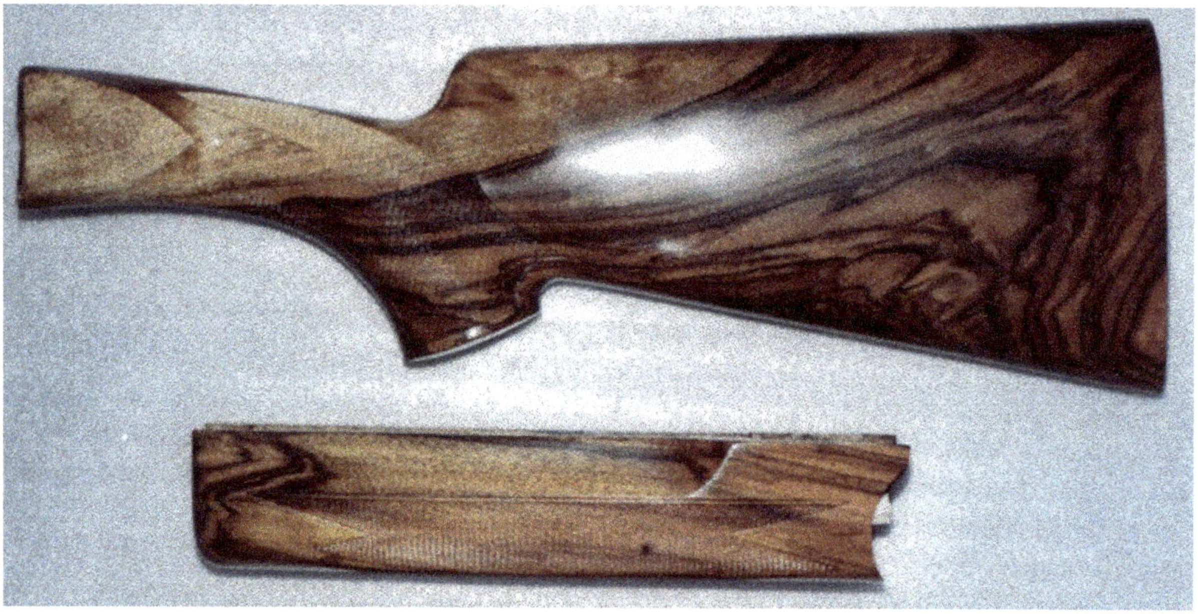

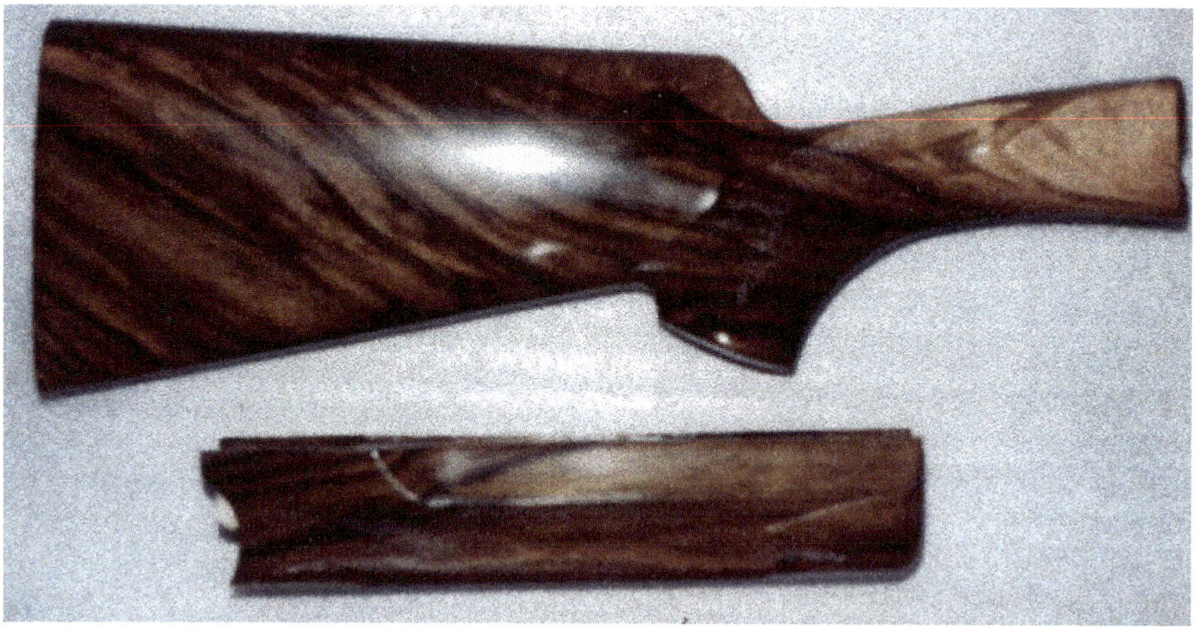

About the Author

Sherman was born in Southern California and raised in the agricultural area of the Northern Sacramento Valley where hunting the canals and rice fields with a single shot Winchester bolt action rifle brought about the love of guns and hunting. But it wasn't until he was in the Army that he sought to explore stock work and checkering and began learning his chosen craft. Now, some forty years later, he is identifying the problems he had in learning, and with his writing and illustrations, hopes to assist others in not having to make the same mistakes.

Working in his small shop in Manchester, TN, he explains his cluttered work space as organized chaos, but knows where most everything is. His three ring binders full of tracings of checkering on shotguns and rifles reflect a long history of his interest, and ability to duplicate factory checkering on many makes, models and grades of firearms he has come across.

An active supporter of new shooters, he is a constant fixture at SCTP, NSSA and ATA AIM competitions, offering assistance on stock fitting and modifications.

CPSIA information can be obtained
at www.ICGtesting.com
Printed in the USA
JSHW020719200220
4334JS00001B/1